THE
RISES & FALLS
OF THE
ROYAL STEWARTS

THE
RISES & FALLS
OF THE
ROYAL STEWARTS

OLIVER THOMSON

'Aren't any more than a steward?'
William Shakespeare

First published 2009

The History Press
The Mill, Brimscombe Port
Stroud, Gloucestershire, GL5 2QG
www.thehistorypress.co.uk

British Library Cataloguing in Publication Data.
A catalogue record for this book is available from the British Library.

ISBN 978 0 7509 4964 4

Printed in Great Britain

Contents

* dates refer to approximate period of office or on the throne

Preface

This is very far from being the first book about the Stewarts but it is different from the others in at least four ways. Firstly it focuses not just on the better-known royals but on many of the other ambitious, sometimes devious men and women in this family who helped to boost or sometimes hinder the progress of the dynasty. Secondly, it is more a collage of biographies than a history, looking at the psychology rather than just the politics. Thirdly it relates the ups and downs of the family to the huge portfolio of properties that they owned, the castles, mansions and palaces that they lived in and which still survive. Finally, it gives more space to before and after the royal period, looking at the extraordinary manoeuvres, personalities and coincidences and the many fascinating drop-outs who tried to keep pace. Nor does it just end with the anti-climax that was Bonnie Prince Charlie but follows through to Bute, Castlereagh and other later Stewarts like Jeb, the dashing general of the American Civil War, or Don Jacobo Stuart, the Spanish naval captain who earned the respect of Nelson.

Note on Spelling of Names
I have tried to match the use of the three variant spellings 'Stewart', 'Stuart' and 'Steuart' as closely as possible to the common usage by specific branches of the family. In certain periods, however, some of them used at least two versions at the same time and particularly in the early period it would be wrong to suggest that some members of the family exclusively used one version or another. Similarly, for the 'Mac' families mentioned I have in the earlier periods simply standardised to lower case Mac with capitalised letter to follow.

We have an additional problem in that the number of Christian names was relatively restricted, so we have a very large number of Johns, Jameses and Roberts; sometimes parents even had two children of the same name in case one of them died. To distinguish themselves they usually added the name of an estate or castle, but even this can be confusing as later in life they might have been given a better estate or title.

Acknowledgements
Thanks and love to my wife Jean and the family in Blanefield, Kirklee and Torbreck

Introduction

This is the story of the remarkable family of stewards who became Stewarts, then Royal Stewarts, then Stuarts. The interest in this thousand-year family saga lies not just in the fascination of the individual lives, remarkable as so many of them were, but in the cumulative thrust of successive generations, the genetics of ambition as year after year they schemed to achieve power, then sometimes carelessly threw it away. The family was remarkable in the first instance for its sheer power of survival: in twenty-four generations there was only one break in the direct male line. That came after six hundred years when they produced Mary Queen of Scots, although as she married a Stuart who fathered her heir, there was no break anyway.

The Stewarts were also remarkable for the length of time that they held on to sovereign power – some 340 years, still nearly fifty years longer than the dynasty of Hanover-Windsor which came afterwards (due for its tercentenary in 2014), longer than the Bourbons in France (259 years), the Hohenzollerns in Prussia and Germany (217 years) or the Romanovs in Russia (304 years). Only one major dynasty in modern European history has exceeded their total: the Habsburgs in Austria (645 years with gaps.)

Yet compared to their longevity as a dynasty, the lives of the individuals were frequently violent and short. Of the fourteen Stewarts who wore a crown, eight failed to reach the age of fifty and only three (Robert II and Robert III of Scotland, James II of Great Britain) passed their sixtieth birthdays, bringing the average age at death to forty-seven. Six out of the fourteen died violent deaths: two were murdered (James I and James III), two were executed (Mary Queen of Scots and Charles I) and two were killed in battle (James II and James IV). The premature deaths were inevitably followed by premature accessions; while their average age for inheriting the crown was twenty-three, six came to the throne before their tenth birthdays and by a miracle survived the machinations of those who sought to take advantage of their youth.

Of the eleven Stewart kings, at least eight had frequent extramarital affairs, one was homosexual, and their queens not only had to suffer that indignity, but also in most cases early widowhood, followed by further misfortune when they remarried. All three of the regnant Stuart queens in Britain led largely miserable lives and produced only one surviving child between the three of them. Apart from Mary Queen of Scots' brief episode as queen of France the only other Stewart to become a queen outside Britain, Elizabeth, Queen of Bohemia, had a normal family life but was driven out of Prague with her husband after only one year on the throne. Eleanor Stewart, the only Scottish princess to marry a Habsburg, also missed out on a crown as did her sister Margaret who married the future Louis XI of France but died before he became king.

Of the uncrowned members of the main family at least another hundred were murdered and about the same number (plus one king – James II) were murderers themselves. At least double that number were executed and three times as many killed in battle. Many of them were highly talented and led exciting lives. There were fine generals like John Stewart Earl of Buchan, Marshal Bernard Stuart of France, Prince Rupert of the Rhine and James Fitzjames Duke of Berwick. There was one British prime minister, John Stuart, Earl of Bute and two foreign secretaries; Robert Stewart, Viscount Castlereagh who committed suicide and Michael Stewart, a former schoolmaster from London who became a Labour politician. In addition there were priests, explorers, artists, pirates, robbers, other assorted malefactors and ordinary working people. As well as their legitimate children most of the Royal Stewarts produced bastards whose careers are often even more exciting, like Janet Stewart who became mistress of Henri II of France.

Above all, this was a family whose huge ambition thrived on mobility. Having migrated from the Baltic to Brittany, they then after a few generations transferred to the Anglo-Welsh border, then to western Scotland, then to Edinburgh as kings of Scotland, then to London as kings of Britain, to France and Italy as exiles, finally throughout the English-speaking world, still prolific.

Part One

THE BRETON
APPRENTICESHIP

The Royal Stewarts
(dates refer to period of office or on the throne)

Walter the Steward (*c.*1137–77)

Alan the Steward (1177–1204)

Walter the Steward (1204–34)

Alexander the Steward (1234–83)

Robert the Bruce

James the Steward (1283–1309)

David II

Marjorie Bruce=Walter the Steward (1309–28)

Robert II (Steward 1328–71, King 1371–90)

Robert III (1390–1406)

James I (1406–37)

James II (1437–60)

James III (1460–88)

James IV (1488–1513)

James V (1513–42)

Mary Queen of Scots (1542–67) = Henry Stuart, Lord Darnley

James VI and I (1567–1625)

Charles I (1625–49)

Elizabeth Queen of Bohemia = Frederick

Charles II (1660 85)

James II = Anne (1) = Mary (2) (1685–8)

Sophia = Ernst August of Hanover

Queen Mary (1688–94) = William III (1688–1702)

Queen Anne (1702–14)

James The Old Pretender (d.1766)

George I (1714–27)

Bonnie Prince Charlie (d.1788)

George II (1727–60)

Charlotte Duchess of Albany

George III (1760–1820)

George IV (1820–30)

William IV (1830–7)

Edward Duke of Kent

Queen Victoria (1837–1901)

Edward VII (1901–10)

George V (1910–36)

Edward VIII (1936)

George VI (1936–52)

Queen Elizabeth II (1952–)

Chapter One

Flaald, Steward of Dol

The slow painful rise of the family later known as Stewart began in the Breton town of Dol, more than three and a half centuries before they won their first crown. This small town lies in the north east corner of Brittany, some five miles from the sea, and in those times was much more important than it is now, for it had a cathedral with its own archbishop. It stood on the crossroads between two very different regions of France: one was Brittany which had acquired its name because of the number of British refugees who had settled there during the Saxon and Viking invasions of their homeland. They included two Cornish holy men, St Samson who founded Dol and St Malo who settled on the nearby coast. The other region was Normandy, which had acquired its name because of the large numbers of Northmen or Vikings who had displaced the original population. Brittany too had been conquered by the Northmen but in smaller numbers, so the existing population, more Celtic than French, had survived. The cultural differences between the Viking settlers of Brittany and those of Normandy were almost as great as those between them and the rest of France. This meant that Dol, in its position close to the frontier was a dangerous place, where a young fighting man might make his mark.

Thus in about the year 1020 Junkeneus the Archbishop of Dol (d.1032) appointed a man called Flaald to be his steward. Traditionally the post had been that of a senior butler as the Latin title *dapifer* or 'feast-bearer' implies, but by this time such duties were largely ceremonial. What it really meant was that the archbishop needed a skilled bodyguard to protect him against his enemies. His brother was the lord of nearby Combourg, and Flaald, the ancestor of the Stewarts, was probably attached to that household too.

We do not know much detail about Flaald except that he must have been a competent fighter with access to the new fashion of chain mail, used to fighting on horseback with sword and axe, and able to justify his upkeep as an armed retainer.

We can also, with near certainty, say that he was a third or fourth generation Viking settler whose forebears had come to Brittany about a hundred years earlier. They may have come directly from Scandinavia, or possibly, as later legends suggested, previously been settled in Scotland. Such a story was told about that other Breton-Viking family, later called Bruce, which was also destined to play a major role in Scottish history. When William Shakespeare in his *Macbeth* included a little piece of propaganda for the first Stuart king of Britain, he borrowed his version of the story from the chronicler Holinshed who in turn took it from a poem written by John Barbour around 1370 and paid for by Stewarts. It portrayed the dynasty as descended from a Scots general, known as Banquo, whose son Fleance supposedly went into exile in France; it is far-fetched, but conceivably there might be a grain of truth in it. At least Flaald and Fleance begin with the same two letters and there was later a Flancus referred to as owning property near Sporle in Norfolk, a place where Walter, the first of the Scottish stewards many years later, had an estate.

In 1027, a few years after Flaald's appointment, a tanner's daughter in Falaise, some ninety miles from Dol, gave birth to the illegitimate son of Robert the Magnificent, Duke of Normandy. The child was William, who against all the odds was to make himself the Duke of Normandy and set in motion a train of events which not only brought the knights of Brittany into the Norman ambit, but involved many of them in his invasion of England.

Meanwhile, in about 1031 Duke Robert, whose mother Judith came from the ruling Breton family, began a war with his first cousin, Count Alan of Brittany. Count Alan was trying to take over control of Mont St Michel. In retaliation Robert attacked Dol and burned it to the ground. Alan counter-attacked at Avranches but was defeated and the career of Flaald the Dapifer must have reached a very low ebb. Many Breton knights had begun to look elsewhere to find their fortunes in areas such as Italy and Sicily where their military skills were appreciated, but Flaald stayed in Dol as it was rebuilt and came under increasingly Norman influence.

The precise role of Flaald in this fighting is unknown but the fact that from then on he was a Norman rather than just a Breton perhaps benefited his career. It was the Duchy of Normandy that was perfecting new skills in armour, castle-building and man management backed by brutally enforced oaths of loyalty and the literate infrastructure of the Catholic Church. The Bretons on the other hand, despite their infusion of Scandinavian blood or perhaps because of it, and their lesser skill in imitating Frankish culture, were seen as primitive. They were an odd mixture of Viking and Celtic races, some Welsh, Cornish and even Scottish asylum seekers over the years had intermixed much less with the French and continued in greater isolation than their Norman cousins round Rouen, who rapidly copied almost everything from their French neighbours.

For the long term career of Flaald and his family, the destruction of their home in Dol was a small price to pay for the possibilities of service in the aggressive new duchy of Normandy.

Chapter Two

Alan, Steward of Dol and Earl Harold

The fact that Flaald's son and successor as Dapifer of Dol was called Alan (fl 1040–80) reflects the fact that he was born when Alan, Count of Brittany was still his undisputed overlord. But the troubles of Dol were destined to return. Within thirty years of the town being rebuilt after its destruction by Duke Robert it was besieged once again. The new bishop, Juhellus (d. 1078) was referred to in papal propaganda as lascivious and corrupt, a reasonable excuse for attacking him. The turmoil of the Dapifer family was to continue.

Significantly, the late Duke Robert had chosen Alan, Count of Brittany as one of the guardians for his young son, William the Bastard, so for a while there was no need for conflict in the frontier area round Dol. Remarkably Count Alan and his colleagues supported the child duke through his minority, perhaps preferring a youngster whom for the time being they could control, to an adult who might interfere with their freedoms.

A few years later the stigma of bastardy would have negated young William's claim to inherit and provided a good excuse for rebellion, but in the 1030s this was still not the case, even though he had several cousins who had a better technical claim to be Duke of Normandy. William, however, survived to come of age and around 1044 began to make his own decisions. He also began to show that he was an extremely competent soldier and leader of men. His skills were honed by a series of rebellions, the most significant in 1047, when King Henri of France came to his aid. As William's strength increased, the French began to perceive him as a threat and launched an invasion of Normandy which he repelled without too much difficulty. Then in 1053 he conquered Maine and married Matilda of Flanders, thus greatly adding to his prestige.

Meanwhile, it was becoming increasingly obvious that the saintly Edward the Confessor, King of England was never going to produce an heir, so the Duke of

Normandy, as Edward's cousin, saw himself as a credible successor to his throne. William was not, however, in a position to canvas any local support, until by a strange coincidence one of England's most powerful earls fell into his clutches. Harold son of Godwin had just succeeded as Earl of East Anglia and though he had no royal blood in his veins was sufficiently respected as a soldier and leader to be another possible candidate for the throne. In 1063 – as is graphically illustrated in the Bayeux Tapestry – after a good dinner at Bosham, Harold sailed for France on a mission to negotiate the release of his brother who had been captured by the Normans. Unluckily for him his ship was blown off course and went aground on the shores of Ponthieu, part of Normandy, near the mouth of the Somme. He was arrested by the local count and taken to Duke William who treated him to a mixture of lavish hospitality and emotional blackmail. After entertainment at the palace in Rouen he was given a valuable suit of armour. Then with elaborate ceremony, to which the English were not yet accustomed, Earl Harold was dubbed a knight by William, thus cunningly emphasising the position of moral superiority which the Duke was trying to establish over him.

Soon afterwards, William decided to conduct a new campaign against the Bretons, who as usual were endeavouring to claim independence from Normandy. The Norman army headed towards the frontier town of Dol which was held by the rebellious Conan, Count of Rennes, aided we must assume by the Steward of Dol, Alan son of Flaald. On the way some Norman knights were trapped in a marshy quicksand by the River Couesnon and Harold took a major part in the rescue. Then they began the siege of Dol which Duke William referred to as 'une orgueilleuse bicoque' – an upstart shanty town – and the defenders can be seen on the Bayeux tapestry pouring water on the leather shields nailed to the castle walls to stop it catching fire. In the end, the Breton Lord of Dol, Rhiwallon chose to surrender rather than see his town destroyed, so Alan, who had married a lady called Tittensor, called the youngest of his three sons Rhiwallon and once more came within the orbit of the Normans.

Earl Harold meanwhile rashly swore an oath to Duke William that he would support him in his claim to be the next king of England. It is hard to believe that he did so with the intention of breaking it as soon as he went home, but Edward the Confessor died eighteen months later and the temptation to seize the English throne proved too much for him.

In faraway Scotland, the usurper Macbeth had been defeated in battle and killed in 1057. He was succeeded after a short gap by Malcolm III Canmore (1031–93), father of the man who was later to persuade the family from Dol to come to Scotland. When William of Normandy, angered by Harold's failure to keep his promise, began to cast covetous eyes across the Channel and when Malcolm of Scotland picked the English princess Margaret as his second wife we see the start of the extraordinary chain of events that was to take the family of Dapiferi from Dol to the throne of Great Britain.

Chapter Three

Alan II, the Crusader

As Alan II succeeded his father Alan I as Steward of Dol (*Alanus Dapifer Dolensis-Senescalus Dolensis*) the destiny of the Normans was about to take an entirely new course. So far as we know he was not in the first wave of troops which Duke William led across the English Channel and with which he won control of England at the Battle of Hastings. Perhaps he was too young and his father, if he was still alive in 1066, was too old. But there were certainly two Breton counts who played a significant part: Alan IV, Count of Brittany was a favourite of Duke William who now styled himself King William I of England, and rewarded him with lands in North Yorkshire, around Richmond, from which he took the title of his new English earldom. The other was Ralph the Gael known as the Staller who was made Earl of East Anglia but was not satisfied, rebelled and ended up as an exile back in Dol.

King William was far from pleased and decided to teach the Bretons another lesson. The chroniclers referred to them as 'Breton filth' and 'polygamous barbarians addicted to wars, feuds and brigandage' (William de Poitiers). But for once King William did not prove invincible. The new count of Brittany, Hoel, came to Ralph's rescue and summoned additional help from the impetuous King Philip of France (1052–1108). This combination was sufficient to drive off William the Conqueror and save the city of Dol. It also perhaps began to see a rise in the fortunes of the Dapifer family, for a few years later Alan was wealthy enough to be a major benefactor of the abbey of St Florent-de-Saumur which soon had a daughter house at Mezuoit near Dol where his brother Rhiwallon became a monk.

At about this time King William began to fall out seriously with his own three sons, particularly his favourite, the eldest, Robert of Curthose (1054–1134) who at the age of twenty-three already wanted a dukedom for himself. He also wanted the punishment of his two younger brothers William and Henry who, amongst other provocations, had held noisy dice parties in the room above the one where he was conducting a council of war and even urinated on it from above. His father refused to discipline the boys so Robert petulantly appealed to King Philip of France for help, an act of treachery which was to become almost commonplace for the eldest sons of Norman kings and bedevilled their years in power.

King William by this time in his fifties and becoming obese, besieged his son Robert in Gerberoy, east of Rouen, but suffered a humiliating defeat. Robert had to be bribed with vast treasure by his mother before he backed down and accepted the offer of the Norman dukedom to be conferred as soon as his father died.

Quite what was Alan the Dapifer's role in these civil wars we do not know, but after William I's death in 1087 it is clear that the family's primary allegiance was to his youngest son Henry, who in the division of spoils became Count of Cotentin, the great peninsula of Brittany. Robert was given the promised Dukedom of Normandy and the middle brother, William Rufus, the crown of England as William II. Soon afterwards the three brothers began to fall out again. William attacked his younger brother Count Henry in 1090 and Duke Robert came to Henry's aid. A year later when Henry was besieged by William in Mont St Michel just a few miles from Dol it was Duke Robert who sent food and drink across to the starving garrison. On that occasion Henry had to surrender and went into a brief period of exile in Paris but ten years later he was to make a spectacular comeback.

In this constant squabbling between the three brothers, Alan the Dapifer transferred his allegiance to Duke Robert, for he joined him in the contingent which left to take part in the First Crusade in 1096. Robert himself was to come back from it covered in glory and ready to pick further fights with his two younger brothers. William Rufus was, so far as he knew, still the King of England and the fractious young Henry still Count of Cotentin. Alan the Dapifer, so far as we know a bachelor and a fervent Christian did not come back from the Holy Land, for he had won himself a guaranteed place in heaven by dying soon after the siege of Antioch in 1098 along with his master Roland the Archbishop of Dol. What Duke Robert did not realise was that during his long absence the situation had altered radically.

Part Two

THE ENGLISH INTERLUDE

Chapter One

Flaald the Fighter

Alan the crusader had left no son and it was his younger brother Flaald who became the new Dapifer of Dol in 1098. But within two years he had left the little city to find fortune elsewhere. The catalyst for this move was without doubt the ambition of William the Conqueror's youngest son, Count Henry of Cotentin (1068–1135), who was discontented with his share of his dead father's empire and had gathered around himself a coterie of faithful Breton knights. On a Thursday in April 1100 Henry was in an adjoining glade of the New Forest when his brother the bachelor King William II died from an allegedly accidental arrow ricochet. With a few followers, Henry made sure his brother's body was taken care of and then headed off to nearby Winchester to seize the royal treasury. So rapid were his actions that by Sunday he had himself crowned King of England while his elder brother, Duke Robert of Curthose, who had at least as good a claim, was still wending his way back from the Middle East. It was remarkably efficient: almost as if it had been planned.

It is highly probable that Flaald was not far from Henry's side during that eventful week. Certainly we know that he was in England quite soon afterwards, for in 1101 he was present in Monmouth when a priory was dedicated by his immediate master Rhiwallon Count of Dinan, now also Lord of Monmouth. Unless he was by that time too old Flaald was almost certainly at the final battle between King Henry and his brother Duke Robert at Tinchebray in 1106, when Robert was captured and then held a prisoner for the rest of his very long life – he died in Cardiff Castle at the age of eighty having spent his remaining twenty-eight years in various dungeons.

We certainly know there was a group of Breton knights fighting at Tinchebray under Count Elias of Maine. And these reliable Breton knights were a key part of the new breed of immigrants encouraged by Henry I to settle in England. So too were some of the reliable Breton clergy-men, for it is believed that Flaald's brother Rhiwallon, the monk of Mezuoit, also came across to settle in an English monastery. Certainly the monastery which the family founded at Sporle in Norfolk was staffed from the family's favourite French monastery at Saumur, to which Rhivallon (b. 1058) had been attached.

Chapter Two

Alan Fitzflaald, Sheriff of Shropshire

A few years after the accession of Henry I in 1100, Flaald died and his son Alan, the new Dapifer of Dol was given a much more prestigious post. He had been in England since at least 1101 and had earned his spurs in the new king's service. He was appointed Sheriff of Shropshire and given land at Oswestry where he refurbished the castle built there earlier by Rainald Bailleul (part of another family which was to make its mark in Scottish history). This town of St Oswald's Tree had until recently been in the hands of the Welsh and was still very close to the Welsh border; therefore it was a key location in the defence of the march. Possibly Alan's appointment owed something to the fact that he married his predecessor's daughter, Avelina de Hesdin, but it was all part of Henry's plan to place reliable knights on the Welsh border with Roger Montgomery, his new Earl of Shrewsbury as the senior baron in the area.

Meanwhile, King Henry had married Princess Edith (d. 1118) half-sister of King Edgar of Scotland (1097–1107). She was the daughter of Malcolm Canmore and his saintly wife Margaret who was herself a member of the old English royal dynasty. The pious Edith renamed herself Matilda, tolerated her husband's numerous affairs and made a habit of washing the feet of lepers, sometimes of kissing them. But most significantly she brought with her from Edinburgh to London her young brother Prince David (c. 1082–1153) as a kind of minder or perhaps to finish off his education. It was this opportunity for the teenage David to mingle with Norman knights that was to make possible the next major leap forward for the family from Dol.

Prince David still had two elder brothers (both of whom might produce sons) who stood between himself and any expectation of the Scottish throne, so he actively pursued a career in England. A year after his first move south he accompanied King Henry's feudal host to Cherbourg where he witnessed a charter by Robert de Brus (Bruis or Brix on the Cotentin peninsula), another supporter of the new king, who had won extensive lands in Yorkshire. His family too was to play a major role in Scotland in the not too distant future. The Brus charter was for transferring a church at Querqueville near Cherbourg to the control of St Mary's of York, but its real significance lies in this first known contact between the Bruce family and their future patron, David of Scotland.

A dozen years later in 1114 David added to his Anglo-Norman connections by marrying Maud of Huntingdon, a rich widow. So Prince David of Scotland also became Earl of Huntingdon in England with lands as far afield as Northampton, an area where yet more Norman knights were ready to take an interest in the young Scottish prince: Hugh de Morville, Robert Avenel, David Olifard, Geoffrey de Melville, Randolph de Soules, the Giffords, Grahams, Lindsays, many names of Norman French families later to feature prominently in Scottish history. Among them in particular were the de Biduns (later Beatons) who came from Dol and were also neighbours of David's near Huntingdon. It was perhaps they who introduced Prince David to Alan the Sheriff of Shropshire.

Meanwhile, Prince David's eldest brother King Edgar of Scotland had died childless in 1107 after a mere ten years on the throne. His next brother Alexander I (1077–1124, king from 1107) had taken over and David was now unexpectedly only one life away from the Scottish crown.

In 1114 the two brothers King Alexander I and Prince David of Scotland joined their brother-in-law Henry (also Alexander's father-in-law, for he had married Henry's illegitimate daughter Sibylla) on a campaign along the Welsh border. This gave the opportunity to meet March lords such as Alan, Sheriff of Shropshire and perhaps also his four young sons. David had by this time begun to collect ambitious Norman knights as potential retainers to back any power moves that he might contemplate in Scotland. He had actually used the threat of calling on their services to browbeat his brother Alexander into making him Prince of Cumbria, so he now had extensive estates both north and south of the border.

Sometime soon afterwards Alan Fitzflaald died at Oswestry, but the contacts made in his lifetime were to prove crucial for the future of his family. He had become quite rich, for in addition to the old family seat at Dol and the newer one at Oswestry he had acquired lands in Sussex, Norfolk and Yorkshire. In Norfolk he had founded the new priory at Sporle as a daughter house of the family's favourite abbey of St Florent-de-Saumur as well as patronising his local abbey at Wenlock. But with four sons to receive an inheritance it was questionable whether even after these acquisitions he could satisfy all their ambitions. As it happened hard times were just around the corner.

Chapter Three

William Fitzalan and the Wars of Matilda

When Alan Fitzflaald died in about 1120, his eldest son Jordan went back to Dol to carry on the family tradition as Dapifer to the count or archbishop, but kept several English estates at Tuxford in Nottingham and near Lincoln. In the years that followed, however, Dol proved no more comfortable an inheritance than that of his three siblings. While little is known of Jordan and his successors we do know that there was another violent rebellion in that part of Brittany in 1148. It was reconquered by Henry II for the Plantagenets in 1166 and the cathedral was destroyed in 1203 by his son King John, who felt so guilty afterwards that he paid for the construction of a beautiful new building which still stands today. Jordan had married a lady called Joan but they seem to have had no surviving children and he was succeeded as Dapifer by his brother, another Alan. After that the male line of the Dapiferi of Dol seems to have run out.

William Fitzalan (c. 1105–60), the second son of Alan, meanwhile inherited the family estates in Oswestry, Fotheringhay and Arundel, as well as in due course the sheriffdom of Shropshire, but within fifteen years he was to lose nearly everything in the civil war that followed the death of Henry I. He had added to his wealth by a good marriage to Isabel de Ingram, which gave him the additional lordship of Clun with its 12,000 acres of forest, and had also founded Haughmond Priory. Some years later when the family had recouped its losses after the civil war, their grandson was destined to marry the last of the d'Albini of Arundel so that the later Fitzalans took over the earldom of Arundel and held it for some three hundred years until their male line died out in 1580. But though distinguished, William's descendants were to be much less famous than those of his younger brother Walter.

Alan's third son Walter received a much smaller portion of the family inheritance, with a couple of minor Shropshire estates in return for which he had to bring himself and two other knights to join his brother's contingent in the feudal host.

He also received a small manor at North Stoke near Arundel. Of the inheritance of Alan's fourth son Simon we know even less, but the fact that like his brother he was later to emigrate to Scotland suggests that his prospects were not great in England.

Events elsewhere were due to have a considerable impact on the future lives of the three Fitzalan brothers who for the time being had stayed behind in Shropshire. In 1124 David of Cumbria, the young Scots Prince who had met the family while campaigning nearby ten years earlier, had against all the odds inherited the crown of Scotland, for both his brothers had died childless before him. By this time David had become a great admirer of Norman fighting techniques and the administrative efficiency of Henry I, so it was not surprising that he should recruit some of his friends from Huntingdon, Northampton and the Welsh border to help him in his task of modernising the kingdom of Scotland. William Comyn who had worked for Henry I in his chancellery was brought north as chancellor for David and the Durham monk Ailred to be tutor for his sons. Two other connected events were to add momentum to King David's recruitment campaign. The first was the drowning in 1120 of King Henry I's only son on the famous *White Ship* as it attempted in bad weather to sail back across the Channel from Barfleur. Since he had no other legitimate sons, this meant that Henry's heir was his daughter Matilda (1102–67). Formerly married to the Emperor of Germany, another Henry, but left a widow and by this time wife of Geoffrey Count of Anjou, she was available to take over as queen of England, although female heads of state were a medieval rarity. The second event was the death of King Henry in 1135 followed by a quick *coup d'état*, in which the throne meant for Matilda was instead snatched by her cousin, Henry's nephew, Stephen of Blois. This resulted in a civil war, some of the bloodiest events of which took place in Shropshire.

It was natural for the three Fitzalan knights to side with the Empress Matilda, as her father had been their chief benefactor. It was also unsurprising that David of Scotland should exploit the situation in England to support the weaker side (Queen Matilda) against the stronger (King Stephen). In 1138 David invaded England and though he lost the Battle of the Standard near Northallerton he continued to make life difficult for Stephen. Soon afterwards the Fitzalan boys' uncle Ernulf de Hesdin was forced to surrender Oswestry to King Stephen after a long siege and was hanged as a traitor. By this time several of David's Anglo-Norman friends had been given Scottish baronies and were fighting by his side, one of them Walter Fitzalan. Another was certainly Robert de Brus, ancestor of the future Scottish king of the same name in its anglicised form and holder since 1124 of the Scots barony of Annan.

Two years after the Battle of the Standard and the sack of Oswestry by King Stephen further disaster struck the Fitzalans when the Welsh Prince Madoc ap Meredith of Powys took advantage of the English civil war to invade Shropshire and capture Oswestry for the Welsh. It was to be nearly two decades before the town and castle were restored to William Fitzalan. Meanwhile his two younger brothers had lost patience and set off to seek new careers in Scotland where their friend King David had challenges to lay before them.

Part Three

HIGH STEWARDS OF SCOTLAND

Map of Scotland showing Stewart Properties up to 1370

1. Renfrew
2. Blackhall
3. Crookston
4. Dundonald
5. Innerwick
6. Drep
7. Auchinleck
8. Inchtalla
9. Loch Rusky
10. Preston
11. Bathgate
12. Bunkle

13. Rothesay
14. Eilean Dearg
15. Durisdeer
16. Dreghorn
17. Cambusnethan
18. Tippermuir
19. Innermeath
20. Garlies
21. Dalswinton
22. Corsewall
23. Stenton
24. Legerwood

25. Hassendean
26. Dunoon
27. Lochranza
28. Brodick
29. Kildonan
30. Skipness
31. Castle Sween
32. Red Castle
33. Mains Dundee
34. Longformacus

Chapter One

Walter Fitzalan, Lord of Renfrew and the Battle of Knock Hill

Walter Fizalan seems to have entered the service of David of Scotland in about 1136, two years before the Battle of the Standard; his signature was on David's charter that year for the new abbey at Melrose. Soon after that he was given a significant group of manors in the Paisley area, on the south side of Glasgow and Innerwick near Dunbar on the Scottish east coast. Like his colleague Robert de Brus, who had lands in Yorkshire, he still at this time held on to some of his English properties, including Manwede in Sussex.

By this time King David was nearly sixty and Walter perhaps about half that age, but the young man seems to have been marked for rapid promotion along with two other Anglo-Norman knights. One was Hugh de Morville, a friend of the king's from his Huntingdon estates, who was now given large tracts in the Borders and Ayrshire. The other was Robert de Brus, like Walter a knight of Norman extraction who had been given Annan and other lands in Dumfries. De Brus married a local heiress, Agnes. All three knights were with David at the disastrous battle against King Stephen at Winchester in 1141, when another Norman knight, David Olifard, saved the Scots king's life and was rewarded with land on the Clyde at Drumsargad and later Bothwell. Walter himself attended Matilda's court in Oxford soon afterwards. Not long before this Walter himself had been favoured with the title of King's Steward or Dapifer – perhaps he had told King David that his family held such a position back in Brittany; otherwise it seems an amazing coincidence. The previous incumbent had been the Englishman, Aelred, acting as tutor to the king's two sons, who resigned in 1134 to become a monk at Rievaulx. In about 1160, Walter's title was to be confirmed as hereditary to the Fitzalan family, so that later they came to be known as Stewarts, a corruption of their job title. Just as in Dol, the feast-bearing part of the job had become purely ceremonial. Perhaps the duties included running the royal household and fixing the wages of the servants, but mainly the appointment simply distinguished Walter as a senior, trusted baron who took precedence over anyone but a belted earl or a royal prince. The blue and white squared pattern (*fesse chequey*) on his coat of arms was not so much a steward's napkin as a portable base for counting coins. Certainly we know that the job involved Walter in attending the king as he moved from one royal palace to another in the rotational style favoured by medieval monarchs, in fact the only way they kept their homes remotely hygienic and their kingdoms intact.

The placing of Walter Fitzalan by the strategically important Clyde estuary was significant. While on the north side of the river the western approaches to Glasgow were protected by the royal fortress of Dumbarton perched securely on its all but impregnable rock, the south shore of the Clyde was much more vulnerable. In addition the protection of Glasgow now mattered more to King David as his fine new cathedral there had just been dedicated in 1136. This vulnerability was a concern because of the threat that still existed from the Vikings, as they and their descendants dominated the west coast. More specific was the threat from the half-Viking Somerled (d.1164) who had carved out a sea-based empire from the Outer Hebrides down to the Isle of Bute and who played off his vague allegiance to the kings of Norway against his even vaguer allegiance to Scotland. We know that soon after the dedication of Glasgow Cathedral both Walter the Steward and Robert de Brus were with King David at Cadzow Castle in Lanarkshire for a council of war. For the time being Somerled was busy consolidating his conquests and had even served in David's army in 1138 but he was not expected to stay loyal forever.

In addition to his strategically vital Clydeside properties Walter had also been given a key location near Dunbar on the east coast where he built a formidable castle at Innerwick looking down on the main coastal route from Newcastle to Edinburgh. Here he had a small nucleus of knights at his disposal to help protect this vital route. This too demonstrates the trust placed in Walter by King David.

Apart from the unpredictable Somerled, other independent-minded, non-Norman magnates also threatened the integrity of David's kingdom at this time: Fergus Lord of Galloway was similarly of Norse extraction, and like Somerled relied on a fleet of fast-moving galleys with which he could commute from Northern Ireland where he also had vassals. To counteract this David installed a number of Norman knights along the Solway coast. The Brus family threw up their first motte at Annan, the Berkeleys at Urr, the de Soules at Hermitage, the Balliols at Buittle, and the Sommervilles at Carnwath. All were skilled, tough Norman knights and most had probably sided with the Empress Matilda against King Stephen in the civil war, so they had little to lose by accepting new posts in Scotland, however dangerous. They wore the state-of-the-art Norman armour of chain mail and helmet, and were used to harassing the peasantry into raising vast mounds of earth on which they at first built wooden castles, later stone ones. Inevitably many native landowners found themselves dispossessed, but in many cases the newcomers married their daughters, so all was not lost. Besides, the process was so gradual there was little opportunity for concerted rebellion.

Another threat came from the mysterious Aed, Earl of Moray and his ally Malcolm MacHeth, reputedly an illegitimate son of the previous king, Alexander I, who thus perhaps fancied himself as a candidate for the throne. He had married Somerled's sister in 1130 and rebelled in 1134, perhaps the first occasion when King David used his new Norman recruits in battle in Scotland. MacHeth was imprisoned at Roxburgh for the next two decades and a group of Flemish knights, the Freskins were given his lands in Moray to help bring it under royal control.

Meanwhile, Walter the Steward was settling in to his new estates. He was given the castle built recently by King David on an island in the Clyde just above Renfrew which was later known as Kings Inch, now smothered by industrial dereliction and realignment of the river. His other first home was Blackhall a few miles away by the River Black Cart at Paisley where he built himself a new hunting lodge. The area was reasonably prosperous, the land mainly flat and fertile while Renfrew itself functioned as a tidal port with customs exemption granted by the king for one merchant ship. Its stretches of salmon fishing were productive and there were rich shoals of herring in the firth beyond. For hunting there were the Fereneze Woods as well as the forest around Paisley. A few years later Walter also refurbished the old castle at Dundonald as his base for controlling North Ayrshire and completed construction of Innerwick Castle on its rocky promontory near Dunbar as his east coast power centre.

In addition to his own estates, Walter was responsible for at least five or six knights in Renfrew, Ayrshire and on the east coast who through him owed military service to the crown and in return had manors of their own in the surrounding area. Of these the name later most famous was that of Richard le Walleis, a man like Walter himself from the Welsh border of Shropshire who was given Elderslie near Paisley and probably Riccarton in Ayrshire. His precise relationship to the later guardian William Wallace is not clear, as William's father is known to have been an Alan Wallace, perhaps not of Elderslie as was often thought. A second knight was Robert le Croc, another friend from Walter's Shropshire days, who was given the area now named after him at Crookston in Glasgow, where he too built a castle. It is possible that Walter's wife Eschina de Mow (Molle or Morebattle in the Cheviots near the English border) was actually Croc's widow and already had four children (three sons, flatteringly called Walter, Alan and Simon) before bearing another four to Walter. She also perhaps brought him some Border properties, like Jedburgh, as her dowry, while Mow itself was given to Kelso Abbey for pasture. Walter's vassals around Innerwick also supplemented their income by renting pastures to the monks of Kelso. The Fitzfulbert brothers Peter and Robert took Pollok on the White Cart and Stenton in East Lothian while a third brother became canon at Glasgow's new cathedral. Robert of Pollok married Croc's daughter, known as Isabella de Molle. Another knight, Reginald or Ranulf, was given Cathcart and built the huge earthwork at Camphill. Other neighbours included the two brothers of Kent (also in Shropshire), Adam and Ralph who had Ingleston near Hillington and Ralston (Ralph's Town) while Robert de L'Isle (later Lyle – the original island was probably on the Severn in Shropshire) received Duchall near Kilmacolm. Ralph of Ness who also came from Shropshire and Nicholas de Cotentin both held land near the Steward's at Innerwick. Simon Loccard was another Norman newcomer who gave his name to two Symingtons, one in Ayrshire, the other in Lanark while Hugh of Pettinain gave his first name to Houston in Renfrew and his second to Pettinain in Lanark. Also an important follower of Walter's was Robert Montgomery, a relation of his old overlord the Montgomery Earl of Shrewsbury, who was given Eaglesham. Just to the west of Renfrew was the Templar base at Inchinnan – the Grand Master had visited Scotland in 1128 and been given Balantrodoch (now Temple near Rosslyn in Midlothian) as another base while the Knights of St John were given Torpichen in 1153. The one non-Breton vassal of the Steward's seems to have been a Viking called Arknell who held the area named after him – Arkleston – east of Paisley.

In addition to David's policy of encouraging the immigration of Norman and Breton knights to spearhead his defences he had also attracted Norman clergymen from England or sometimes direct from France to help reform his administration and the Scots church. He had already founded a succession of major new abbeys: Selkirk in 1113, Dunfermline in 1128, Melrose 1136, Kelso Abbey and Lesmahagow Priory in 1144. At the same time he encouraged his new barons to do the same thing, the Morvilles for example founding Dryburgh Abbey, just as Walter the Steward was later to found one at Paisley.

In 1153 David I died at the age of about sixty-five having outlived his own son Earl Henry (–1152). Walter, who had served him for some seventeen years, now became the Steward for his grandson Malcolm IV (1153–65) who was only eleven, while by this time Walter was approaching fifty. Meanwhile in England the troubled reign of King Stephen came to an end with his death in 1154 and his rival Matilda's son Henry II took over. Almost immediately trouble broke out in Scotland. Fergus of Galloway objected strongly when the impressionable young King Malcolm responded to the call of Henry II to join his army in Toulouse in 1159, when he was probably accompanied by Walter the Steward. This was the occasion when Malcolm, aged eighteen, was knighted by King Henry, for only a king could knight a king. The disgruntled Fergus joined up with some other earls to attack Malcolm in Perth but was defeated and retired to a monastery. Walter, despite his age, was almost certainly again in the thick of it.

Walter must have earned considerable admiration from young King Malcolm for in 1160 he received a royal charter* making the stewardship hereditary to his family and also endowing him with more land. This confirmed his holding of areas like Carthcart, Le Muerne (Mearns), Le Drep (near Carmunnock), Strathgryffe, Loch Winnoch and Talahret (The Hurlet) but added western Partick and Inchinnan by the Clyde together with Stenton, Hassendean, Legerwood and Birkenside near his existing holding at Innerwick on the eastern Borders.

---

* *'hac mea carta confirmavi haereditariae Waltero filio Alani meo Dapifero senescalliam meam tenendam sibi et heredibus suis'*

Three years later came another more serious rebellion, this time the long-expected attack by Somerled. This was the more shocking in that for some time the self-styled King (Ri) of the Isles had seemed to fawn on the young King Malcolm and even had the nickname 'Sit-by-the-king'. Somerled had just conquered the Isle of Man from his new father-in-law after a major naval battle off Islay, so that now he controlled all the islands and some of the mainland coast all the way from Ayrshire to Lewis. In 1164 Somerled decided to strike at the heart of Scotland and came up the Clyde with a fleet of a hundred longships, manned by as many as 4,000 men. Significantly it was near Renfrew that they came ashore and the battle took place at Knock Hill halfway between Walter's two castles of Inch and Blackhall. He himself had been on a mission to England at Fotheringhay Castle, one of his brother William's properties, just a dozen miles from his king's estates in Huntingdon and a mere thirty from his family's other lands round Sporle in Norfolk. Here he signed the deed also for his new priory at Paisley, so he may not have returned in time for the battle, but it has to be assumed that if he was not present himself, and after all he was at least fifty, then his son and retainers certainly were. However the chroniclers gave him no particular credit. Some gave it to the king, others to the bishop and monks of Glasgow Cathedral who had prayed to St Mungo for a miracle, some (*Chronicle of Melrose*) to the 'local' inhabitants of the area. Yet it was remarkable that such a large army as Somerled's was so rapidly and heavily defeated when its attack had been so unexpected – there was not enough time for a feudal host to have been summoned. On that basis and bearing in mind the further honours heaped by the king onto the Steward it is hard to believe that the 'locals' were any other than the Steward's retinue. Both Somerled and his eldest son were killed in the battle or executed shortly afterwards. The body of the self-styled King of the Isles was taken away to be buried in his own newly founded abbey at Saddell in Kintyre.

The Battle of Knock Hill was a major turning point for the west coast and for the Fitzalans. There was no couterattack against Somerled's surviving troops because King Malcolm had no fleet with which to chase them, but there was a move to take over the islands in the Firth of Clyde for the crown, the Cumbraes, Bute and Arran, and in this project the Stewards were to play a prominent role. It was probably at this time that they first took over Rothesay, and the forest of Cumbrae became a favourite place for hunting deer. In gratitude soon after the battle Walter began to build his new priory (later abbey) at Paisley. He had already, with the help of Prior Humbald of Wenlock, imported a group of Cluniac monks from Shropshire for his Church of St Mary and St James at Renfrew, so some of these were now transferred to the new building at Paisley dedicated to St Mirren (the local saint), St James (patron of the Dapiferi of Dol) and St Milburg of Wenlock. It was to become the largest Cluniac foundation in Scotland although it was to be eighty years before it was allowed by its mother house in France to be called an abbey.

Now well past the average age for this period, Walter outlived Malcolm IV who died at the age of twenty-four in 1165 having refused to marry, hence his nickname – The Maiden. There was only one possible illegitimate child to counteract his reputation for virginity, so it was his younger brother William who took over (William the Lion c.1143–1214). This impetuous, self-indulgent young man was thus the third king under whom Walter served and he did so for another dozen years. It is unlikely however that he accompanied the new king on his expedition to help Henry II of England in France the next year. Remarkably this was based at Mont St Michel and saw the restoration of Dol to Norman rule. By this time Walter's elder brother Jordan was probably dead so the new Dapifer – and the last we know of – was his brother Alan.

King William the Lion of Scotland was totally absorbed in the general display of knightly chivalry in the English camp, where jousting at tournaments was the favourite sport of the aristocracy. However he did not follow Henry II the next year when he began the messy conquest of Ireland and in the years that followed he fell into the trap of underestimating his royal neighbour. Henry had a difficult patch after 1170 when he took the blame for the murder of Archbishop Thomas à Becket and soon after that began falling out with his own four teenage sons. As ever, the sons of Norman monarchs were impatient to take over and greedy for the biggest share. William the Lion perceived this as an opportunity to snatch the Earldom of Northumbria for Scotland and without proper preparations he rashly invaded England. He was surprised in fog near Alnwick, badly defeated and taken prisoner by the English. The price of his release was the Treaty of Falaise, by which as King of Scotland he had to make subservience to Henry of England. In addition the five largest castles in Scotland were to be garrisoned by English troops at Scottish expense. William also lost all of his father's estates in Huntingdonshire and Tynedale plus any hope of recovering Northumbria. Symbolically the king of Scotland was now just a sub-king not a sovereign, and all his barons indirectly subjects of the English. This ill-conceived attack on England had brought disastrous consequences.

At about the time of this debacle Walter the Steward seems to have decided to retire, and became a brother at Melrose Abbey to which he gave the lands of Mauchline to cover his expenses. For the good of his soul he had endowed Paisley Abbey, and founded another new church at Auchinleck. Two years later he died at Melrose and his body was brought back to his priory at Paisley for burial.

Walter's youngest brother Simon had also come to Scotland and settled in Kilmarnock where his fair hair led to him gaining the nickname *Buidhe* (yellow) which in due course became the surname of his descendants, Boyd. Apart from joining Walter in signing one or two documents, Simon does not seem to have achieved the prominence of his brother and as we shall see it was to be some three hundred years before the families were briefly linked again by marriage and in the power struggles of medieval Scotland. Meanwhile the slow but steady rise of the Stewards was set to continue. A Norman/Breton upper class had been foisted on the Scots almost by stealth.

Chapter Two

Alan the Steward and the Crusades

It is not certain whether Alan Fitzwalter (fl.1177–1204) the new Steward of Scotland was really a crusader or whether it just suited him and his descendants to imagine that he was one. Certainly Barbour said he was one, but he was on the Stewart payroll so his statement is short on credibility. After all it was good for the family image and if it was all a lie then it was made plausible by the fact that Alan's great-grand-uncle, also called Alan, was undoubtedly a crusader, who in fact had died during the First Crusade, and other members of the family were certainly crusaders. The story is also plausible because Alan must have been just into his early forties when the Third Crusade was called and if he did not go on it himself it is reasonably certain that some of his knights did for several of his tenants at Innerwick raised money for the purpose. In addition the new Hospital of St Thomas at Acre in the Holy Land was given the land at Spittalhill (i.e. Hospitalhill) near the Steward's castle at Dundonald, so that is a reasonably strong indication.

Though for a variety of reasons very few Scots heeded the summons for the Crusade there was at least a small contingent of Scottish knights who did set off to the Holy Land, amongst them David Rufus of Forfar, Osbert Olifard of Bothwell and Alan's neighbour in Tranent, Robert de Quincy. The most notable absentee was of course King William the Lion who chose not to join the group of kings from all over Europe who went to save Jerusalem, but by then he had suffered a spell of captivity in England with its rueful consequences and saw his priorities as closer to home. Besides he had still to produce an heir to his own throne (Alexander II was not born until 1198). It is conceivable therefore that as he was not going himself he may have sent his Steward instead.

Before examining this problem further let us consider the new generation of this ambitious family. Walter Fitzalan the first Steward had at least four children, three of them daughters. One seems to have married Donald the grandson of Somerled and progenitor of the clan Donald. Another married Walter's vassal Robert Montgomery of Eaglesham and the third died as a child. The only surviving son was Alan who became the new royal steward in 1177. He was probably then in his early thirties, a few years younger than King William the Lion, whose disastrous surrender to the English had led to Scotland's most important castles being taken over by English garrisons.

Relief for Scotland came from a most unlikely source – the capture of Jerusalem by Saladin, which triggered the Third Crusade, left Richard Coeur de Lion (1157–99: ruled from 1189) so desperate for money that he sold Edinburgh back to the Scots. This so-called 'quit claim' got rid of at least some of the unpleasant consequences of the treaty signed by William the Lion.

The recruitment campaign for the crusade undoubtedly penetrated Scotland, attempting to stir up the kind of anti-Islamic hatred which it had managed to induce elsewhere in Europe, but it met with a generally poor response compared with the estimated 100,000 men from other parts of Europe. Perhaps William and his court had still to come to terms with the disaster at Alnwick and the harsh treaty dictated by the English king at Falaise.

Those Scots who did want to join Richard had quite a long wait. For all his apparently manic enthusiasm to head for Jerusalem, Richard was very slow organising his crusade, and even slower about travelling to the Holy Land. It was July 1190 before he even crossed France, three years after the first plaintive call for help was heard from the East.

Alan the Steward meanwhile had, according to some sources, married Eva, daughter of Swain of Tranent, clearly a man of Norse extraction, living not far from the Steward's estates at Innerwick, and she brought him Tippermuir, near Perth, as her dowry.

At length the Anglo-Scottish contingent arrived at the siege of St Jean d'Acre which had already lasted for three years. The French and German crusaders were besieging this huge fortress by the sea but were themselves besieged by Saladin. What Richard provided immediately was energy and leadership. An apathetic siege was rapidly transformed into an enthusiastic, totally reckless storming of the walls. Saladin's forces were beaten off with horrendous losses and the city at last surrendered. But the victory soon turned sour. An exchange of prisoners had been arranged on the surrender of Acre, to be accompanied by a gold ransom from the Saracens. Saladin was unfortunately slow in producing the gold and Richard in a fury ordered the execution of 2,700 Saracen prisoners. He also quarrelled so violently with Philip of France that most of the French crusaders packed up and went home.

After further desultory campaigning Richard departed the Holy Land as suddenly as he had arrived, leaving Jerusalem uncaptured, though he did organise a truce for the safe passage of pilgrims. Saladin died soon afterwards and Richard himself was famously imprisoned in Austria as he tried to make his way home by land.

Of the role of Alan the Steward in these events we have no reliable evidence but we do know that with King William the Lion he did journey down to Richard's second magnificent coronation ceremony at Winchester Cathedral when at last he returned from Austria in 1194. Both William and his steward Alan had taken part in the effort to collect money for the English king's ransom. It would have been a serious breach of honour for William to take advantage of Richard's absence on a crusade to invade England, but it is still remarkable that he was so loyal to the son of his great enemy. After all, he had recently dedicated his new abbey at Arbroath to St Thomas à Becket, an arch enemy of the Plantagenets.

Five years later the impetuous King Richard was killed at the siege of Chalus in France and Alan the Steward did not accompany William when he went down to Lincoln Cathedral to do homage to the new king, John Lackland (1167–1216, ruled from 1199), the undignified requirement of the Scots king since he had signed the wretched Treaty of Falaise. By 1197 Alan was in his fifties and seems to have taken part in the campaign to put down the pro-Viking lord of Caithness. He may by this time have been feeling his age or had fallen out of favour. Certainly we know that soon afterwards he suffered a severe royal reprimand for letting his daughter Aveline marry Duncan of Galloway without royal permission, so he was perhaps suspected of too much ambition. The granddaughter of this couple as it turned out was to be the mother of Robert the Bruce.

Alan had been Steward for twenty-seven years when he died, all of that time for the one king, William the Lion, who at the time of Alan's death was sixty and still had another eleven years left to rule. Of Alan's contemporaries the fourth Robert Bruce had died ten years earlier, William Douglas and Ronald of the Isles a few years later. Alan himself had consolidated the Steward patrimony which now dominated the Firth of Clyde as well as the main approaches to Edinburgh from the south. The family and its knightly adherents therefore had a crucial role in the defence of Scotland both with regard to possible Viking attacks in the west and English in the east.

Chapter Three

Walter the Judge

During the Stewards' slow progress to their first throne, Walter (fl. 1204–41) played a solid rather than a dramatic role. It could be said that in his period as Steward the family took one step forward and one back. Although he gained the first additional government post by his own merit, he also presided over the loss of territorial gains in the Firth of Clyde. By this time too the title Dapifer had mostly been replaced by the slightly better sounding Senescallus (seneschal – old retainer) which had sometimes also been used in Dol.

Walter was the second son of Alan and his second wife Alesta, so there is a slight mystery about what happened to his eldest brother David who was referred to in one document as Senescallus, perhaps using it as his surname rather than his title. He must have died just before or just after his father, for he acted as one of the guarantors for the engagement of the king's son Alexander to Princess Joanna of England. Walter was probably still in his early twenties and did not marry himself for another eight or nine years, when he made a respectable alliance with Beatrice or Bethoc Gilchrist, a daughter of the Earl of Angus.

Those years were quite eventful, seeing feverish diplomatic activity between the aging King William the Lion and the twisted but ingenious King John of England. The Scots Queen Ermengarde used her feminine wiles to mediate between them at Norham in 1209 and three years later after further negotiation John agreed to knight the heir to the Scottish throne, the fourteen-year-old Alexander – all part of the subtle spin by which the English kings emphasised their feudal superiority over the Scots. Meanwhile the main leadership in Scotland was provided by William Comyn who took the real responsibility for suppressing the revolt by the MacWilliams in 1210.

1214 was an important year for a number of reasons. William the Lion died at last, aged seventy-one, to be succeeded by Alexander II (1198–1249), still only sixteen. Walter the Steward was to serve him for the rest of his life, and that same year he and Beatrice enjoyed the birth of their first child, tactfully named Alexander. Meanwhile King John in England suffered the acute humiliation of being forced to sign Magna Carta as a token of English kings' acceptance of the principles of feudal law.

The spectacle of an English king in trouble often enticed Scottish kings into an invasion of England and young Alexander was no exception. Walter the Steward and his colleagues were summoned to join the feudal host in an attack on Northumberland, but King John, who was nothing if not resilient, decided to 'make the fox cub enter his lair'. For ten days he crossed into Scotland, burning Roxburgh, Haddington and Dunbar. Alexander and his advisers decided to couterattack by capturing Carlisle and sought the willing help of King Philip-Augustus of France to create a second front in the south. John made things easier by dying at Worcester, still only in his early forties and leaving a nine-year-old successor, Henry III (1207–72, king from 1216). It looked as if Alexander would have the ideal opportunity to snatch back northern England for himself, but the Pope saved the English by threatening excommunication for both the Scots and French kings if they took advantage of the English minority. So in 1217 the red-haired Scots King Alexander II, aged nineteen, paid homage to the pallid King Henry III of England, aged ten, all part of the subtle web of priorities dictated to Scots kings by William the Lion's wretched Treaty of Falaise, and the relative pecking order of payments into the coffers of the Vatican.

Three years later Alexander married Henry's sister Joan as already agreed, a marriage which was to last seventeen years without producing an heir. Walter the Steward went to York to help officiate at the wedding. Throughout that period Alexander's main preoccupation was subduing the north, west and east coasts of Scotland. His chief advisers were members of the Comyn family (originally from Commines near Lille) who now dominated Scottish politics, but Walter the Steward added to his largely honorary office the more meaningful post of Justiciar of Scotia, chief law officer for the north of Scotland. This was without question a position awarded on ability and was no empty gesture.

Indirectly King Alexander's determination to suppress the overambitious sub-kings of the west coast was to lead to the main reverse in fortunes which hit the Steward's family at this time. A feud among the MacDougall descendants of Somerled saw a request for help from Norway, and a MacDougall called Uspak or Gillespic returned with a Norwegian fleet to help put his house in order. As a result, in 1230 the MacDougalls, with Norwegian help conquered Arran and Bute which had been held by the Stewarts almost since the death of Somerled at Renfrew in 1164.

The Norse sagas leave us a remarkable picture of the siege of the round Stewart castle at Rothesay where an unknown member of the family put up stout resistance. He had boiling oil poured over the besiegers but they somehow managed to dig into the soft stone of the base walls. The castle was captured and the Steward's garrison commander was killed. Uspak also was fatally wounded and his Norse fleet headed back to Norway, but the islands in the Firth of Clyde were for the foreseeable future back in the hands of the Islesmen.

The other main change in Scotland was in Galloway, where the last great independent earl, Alan, died leaving only an illegitimate son. The consequent break-up of his south-western territory heralded the arrival and promotion of several Norman families: the de Quincies, Balliols, more Comyns and others. It also saw a number of forlorn rebellions which led to the execution of groups of wandering Irish Galwegians as far afield as Glasgow, one group being torn limb from limb tied to horses for the entertainment of the Edinburgh crowds. Walter himself was involved in the brutal Galloway campaign of 1233–4.

Two Scottish queens died in quick succession: the dowager Queen Ermengarde of Bellemonte in 1233 and Queen Joan, Alexander's childless English wife four years later on her way as a pilgrim to Canterbury. At this point in 1239 Alexander showed special trust in Walter the Steward by asking him to undertake the delicate task of travelling to Coucy, near Soissons, in France to negotiate terms and bring back to Scotland, if suitable, his new wife-to-be Mari de Coucy, daughter of a Picardy nobleman. He succeeded and presided over the king's second wedding at Kelso.

For the three years between the death of Alexander II's uncle, John of Huntingdon, and the birth of Alexander and Mari's only son in 1241, the future Alexander III, the heir to the Scottish throne was in fact Robert Bruce V of Annandale (1210–95) whose mother had been Huntingdon's sister Isabel and a granddaughter of King David. The increasing vulnerability of the royal house of Appin-Canmore, its growing difficulties in producing male heirs to order, was beginning to show. It was to lead eventually to the terrible power struggle between the various Norman families whose members had married spare royal ladies in the generations before.

As he grew pious in his old age Walter paid for a priest to care for the soul of the fifth Robert Bruce and handed over his estate at Tippermuir to the new abbey at Balmerino in Fife which Queen Ermengarde had founded and where she was buried, some sixty miles from the tomb of her husband King William the Lion which was in his own foundation at Arbroath. Walter also founded a small new monastery of his own at Dalmellington. Sadly this did not flourish for after nine years the monks and nuns tired of the bleak surroundings and headed back southwards. Perhaps also the family's loss of income after the capture of Bute by the Norwegians was too much of a setback. Walter had also organised the rebuilding of St Blanes' monastery at Kingarth on Bute, only for it to fall into the hands of the Islesmen.

Walter died in 1241 – the same year that Alexander III was born – probably in his favourite castle at Blackhall near Paisley, from which he had dispensed justice as Justiciar of Scotia for sixteen years. It had also been the base for his favourite pastime, hunting. It was perhaps he who had built a new stone castle at

Renfrew slightly to the south west of King's Inch, now sadly also buried under modern buildings. Though he donated some land between the two rivers, Black and White Cart to Paisley Abbey where he was in due course buried, it was on the express basis that the gift did not include 'my wildfowl and beasts'. His only other gift was land for a leper colony at Morriston.

Walter's career had been somewhat overshadowed by the thrusting ambition of the Comyn family who now between them held three earldoms, Buchan, Angus and Menteith as well as the lordship of Badenoch, substantial new baronies in Galloway, and most of the senor executive positions under the crown. But they had come so far so rapidly that in due course they would push the other lords, particularly the Bruces and the Stewards into alliance against them. Neither the Bruces nor the Stewards yet had a single earldom, but the Bruces had acquired one great advantage: royal blood through the marriage in 1206 of the fourth Robert Bruce, to Isabel, one of the spare granddaughters of David I. There had thus been the three year period 1239–41 before Alexander's son was born during which the fifth Robert Bruce was the heir to the throne. At that time no one could have guessed that this blood connexion might in a few years' time become critically important to the future of Scotland and, indirectly, the future of the Stewards.

Chapter Four

Alexander of Dundonald and the Battle of Largs

Alexander (1214–84) was twenty-seven when he took over in 1241 as the fourth hereditary Royal Steward of Scotland. He had been married a few years earlier to Jean of Bute, an heiress of the Somerled dynasty whose branch of the family had probably lost out in the invasion of her island eleven years earlier, but her theoretical dowry still carried credibility for the Stewards should they be in a position to reclaim Bute. It was thus Alexander's ambition to confront the Islesmen and their Norwegian allies which was to shape his career and enhance the image of the Stewards for the generation to come.

Meanwhile, he settled in and rebuilt Dundonald Castle which had been given to him before his father's death and which guarded the Ayrshire or 'Kyle' section of the family estates. Alexander was now regularly referred to in documents as Senescallus rather than Dapifer, the marginally more prestigious version of the same job title, but still translated as Steward. He accompanied King Alexander II on two important campaigns, one to pacify Galloway, the other an initially successful attempt to subdue the Western Isles, still officially under Norwegian control. However it ended disastrously when the king, still only fifty-one, caught a fever and died on the island of Kerrara near Oban in 1249. The Steward Alexander had signed one of the king's acts that very morning.

The new king, Alexander III (1241–86) was a boy of eight. The Steward, now in his mid-thirties was thus involved in the typically murky politics of a royal minority. He shared some sort of ill-defined role in the regency, but for eleven years the real power ebbed and flowed between two more powerful cliques: the Comyn family on the one hand and the self-made Alan Durward on the other, with a group of supporters which usually included the Steward, the Morays and some others. The fifth Robert Bruce meanwhile was more interested in English politics, as he had been made governor of Carlisle by Henry III.

The Steward had a brief switch of loyalties to the Comyns in 1253 and in that year made a pilgrimage to Santiago de Campostella, shrine of the family patron St James, but apparently combined his religious duties with some negotiations with Spanish merchants who traded with Scotland. Certainly he was back with the Durward party by 1255 when young King Alexander was browbeaten by Henry III of England into a purge of his advisers under threat of an English invasion. He had married Henry's daughter Margaret (1240–75) four years earlier and Henry was outraged by the perceived ill-treatment of the homesick fifteen-year-old bride. Then, after another Comyn comeback, the Steward had a real taste of power from 1258–60 when he shared the regency with a smaller group that included the dowager Queen Mari de Coucy. He presided over some negotiations with the Welsh in 1258 that involved sending one of his men, Alan of Irvine, down south.

By this point, Steward Alexander seems to have been given other responsibilities. Perhaps based on his experience in the Western Isles campaign of 1248–9, perhaps also as the would-be lord of Bute and Arran he was expected to have ships of his own to conduct sea campaigns. In 1259 he led a naval expedition to conquer the Isle of Man, at that time used as a base for piracy, and was allowed by the English to victual in Ireland so long as he promised not to help the Welsh rebels. In 1261 he mounted another expedition against the Manx, this time with less success, but clearly his experience of amphibious warfare was increasing. From about 1260 he was involved in naval expeditions to subdue the various MacDougall and MacDonald leaders who resisted Scottish authority off the west coast.

In this task Alexander was aided by his younger brother Walter Ballach (or Bailloch) the Freckled (d.1292), who also turned into an accomplished sea-going commander, perhaps even more so then the Steward himself. The accoutrements of his tomb on Inchmahome in the Lake of Menteith suggest (though only faintly) that he might, like his younger brother, have been a crusader in Egypt with the French King Louis IX in 1249 and this could account for his all-round experience. There was another Walter Stewart who died on the same crusade at plague-ridden Damietta that same year. In 1261 Walter was fitting out a fleet in Ayr and repairing the castle there. About this time his services were sufficiently valuable for the king to let him use the title of Earl of Menteith which he had acquired along with its castle and priory on the Lake of Menteith, by marrying the last earl's niece, Mary, despite huge opposition from her family, the Comyns. Meanwhile his naval campaign resulted in the elderly Dugald MacSween, Lord of Knapdale and North Kintyre handing over to Walter his lordships and his two main castles, Skipness and Castle Sween (plus the lands of Killislate or Kedeslatt and Kilcalmone – Kilberry). The new earl and his family were to hold both for the next hundred years. Significantly Walter was the first member of the family to call himself Steward when he was not the steward, so he was responsible for the first use of the job title as a surname. He was also the first in the family to hold an earldom and brought about a huge accrual of new estates to the overall Stewart portfolio. At the same time he founded a new mini-dynasty of Stewarts who held Menteith, nearby Loch Rusky Castle and large areas of Kintyre.

News of the activities of the two nautical brothers must have reached the ears of King Haakon IV the Old of Norway (1204–63, king from 1217) who sent an ultimatum demanding acknowledgement of his authority in all the west coast islands as had been agreed in a treaty of 1098. This was acceptable neither to King Alexander III who had come to Ayr to be near the scene of action, nor to Alexander of Dundonald. The latter in particular wanted to hold on to Bute and Arran, while the king wanted guarantees against piracy by the Islesmen. Ewan, the MacDougall leader offered to act as mediator but without any result. Angus Mhor, the MacDonald chief was in an even more awkward position as his younger son Angus Og was held in Ayr by the Scots as a hostage for his good behaviour.

Haakon set off from Norway with a fleet of around a hundred ships which he expected to double with recruits from his Hebridean allies. After a short stay at Kirkwall he came southwards to Skye where he passed through the narrows, where the name of Kyleakin (Haakon's Narrows) recalls his passage. Joined by the Manx fleet he headed down to the Mull of Kintyre and attacked Bute. The Steward and his brother had newly fitted-out ships but presumably far too few to head off two hundred. We know that Walter actually ordered two hundred oars and four sentries to guard his ships, but never hired crews. Yet since ships at this time only had an aggressive, not a defensive function, this is not necessarily a sign of cowardice. The Norwegians would have to be tackled on dry land.

According to the sagas, the aged King Haakon offered to meet his opposite number Alexander III in single combat, but the young Scots king refused on the grounds of their age difference. Meanwhile the Stewart garrison in Rothesay surrendered much more easily than they had done thirty years earlier, giving Haakon the impression that resistance generally would be weak. Sixty of his ships were sent up Loch Long and rolled over the isthmus at Tarbet into Loch Lomond to pick up booty. The remainder of his fleet anchored ostentatiously between Cumbrae and the mainland on 29 September. The wind increased and veered round from north-east to north-west. Some of the Norse crews had to hack down their own masts to avoid capsizing – they carried spares. Walrus-hide cables parted. Around a thousand Norsemen found themselves driven ashore at Largs and at last the Scottish troops, which had been inactive up to this point, could achieve something. Some six hundred cavalry made up of local knights, many of whom we must assume came from the Steward or his brother's feudal retinues, attacked the stranded Norsemen and won a victory which was in itself no more than a minor skirmish, but hugely important for the morale of both sides. According to one suspect account by Bellenden, a writer and translator in the pay of James V, 'Incontinent Alexander Stewart of Paisley came with a bachment of fresche men' to save the day. The wind had done most of the work, for the tiny Scots navy had been quite incapable of standing up to the Norse. Piers Currie of Mauchline was the only known Scots casualty. The Norsemen retreated northwards to take stock and the elderly King Haakon died at Kirkwall on his way home.

Alexander the Steward had not long returned from a mission in London where he was sent to cajole Henry III into paying the balance of his sister Margaret's dowry. The remainder of his career after Largs was something of an anti-climax though he did receive Garlies Castle and its estates in Galloway which he passed on to his second son John of Jedworth or Bunkle, thus beginning what much later would become the Stewart earldom of Galloway. He himself lived on well beyond fighting age and was fifty years old even at the time of Largs. He is probably the Alexander who took charge of the force sent to capture the Isle of Man in 1267. The family regained Bute and Arran and may have helped in the subjugation of the MacDonalds of Islay, but it was Alan Durward who led the Scots army into Caithness to assert Scots authority there against the Norse. The Campbells were planted on Loch Awe to create a new frontier in Argyll. Alexander III had, with luck, achieved more than might have been expected.

His English opposite number, Henry III, was much less lucky. The year after Largs he suffered a rebellion by his own barons which led to his defeat in battle by Simon de Montfort, and his subsequent imprisonment. Eight years later he was murdered.

In 1281 Alexander the Steward, in one of his final known acts, was a witness to the marriage agreement between Alexander III's daughter Margaret and the new king of Norway. His brother Walter Ballach Stewart, Earl of Menteith was in charge of the flotilla which took the princess over to Norway for the wedding and lost some ships in a storm on the homeward journey. One of these wrecks is associated with the ancient and popular *Ballad of Sir Patrick Spens* whose grave was supposedly in the Orkneys, though the ballad has him sinking off Aberdeen:

They hoysed their sails on a Monenday morn
Wi a the speed they may
They hae landed in Noroway
Upon a Wodrensday.

By this time Walter had begun the rebuilding of Brodick Castle and Rothesay as well as improving his other castles at Sween, Skipness, Loch Ranza on Arran and Eilean Dearg on a tiny island in the Kyles of Bute, so that he controlled the area around the Firth of Clyde, still of vital importance to the defence of Scotland. Between them the two brothers Alexander and Walter had considerably enhanced the overall prestige of what we may now call the Stewart family.

Apart from Walter, the sailor earl, the Steward had four other interesting siblings. Of his three sisters one married the Earl of Dunbar, another married Duncan the Earl of Carrick and the third, it seems probable, married the MacDonald Lord of Islay, so the family's network of relationships and influence was expanding steadily. The death of the third brother fighting for the crusading King Louis IX of France in Egypt in 1249 added lustre to the family. On the same expedition his brother-in-law Patrick, Earl of Dunbar (husband of sister Euphemia) also died at Marseilles. In a similar crusade twenty years later the new Earl of Carrick was killed, an event which inadvertently thrust the Bruce family further up the aristocratic pecking order. The widow Marjorie trapped an apparently reluctant sixth Robert Bruce into marriage, thus giving him the earldom which was in her right and this he passed on to the seventh Robert Bruce whose career was to dominate the lives of the next three generations of the Stewarts.

Chapter Five

James and the Wars of Independence

James the Steward (1260–1309) took over his hereditary role at the age of twenty-two in 1282. While we know a fair bit about him, he is in many ways the hardest of the Stewards to understand. The twists and turns of his political career indicate a survivor who, if not totally devious, was certainly devoted very much to his own and his family's interests and whose nationalist credentials, if relevant, are more than somewhat suspect.

At this point in 1282 there were three generations of Robert Bruces alive: the fifth Lord Robert (1210–95), ex-governor of Carlisle and later known as the Competitor, the sixth Robert (1253–1304) the crusader who had married into the earldom of Carrick, and his son the seventh and most famous Robert Bruce (1274–1329) eventual king of Scotland. The Bruce was thus fourteen years younger than the Steward and at this point just eight years old. Of the other main players in the drama that was to follow William Wallace (c.1274–1305) was more or less a contemporary of the youngest Bruce. King Edward I of England was by now in his early forties. John Balliol (1250–1315) whose mother was a spare but soon to be significant great-granddaughter of King David's was in his early thirties. John the Red Comyn of Badenoch (c.1270–1306) who claimed a modicum of royal blood on account of descent from King Donald Bane III was a few years older than Bruce.

Finally there was one player who was soon to make his exit: Alexander III, still also in his early forties. His wife Margaret of England had died six years earlier. The younger of his two sons Prince David had just died, the elder Alexander died a couple of years later as did his daughter Margaret, the wife of King Eric of Norway, so his only direct heir by 1284 was his baby granddaughter Margaret, the Maid of Norway. There was the possibility that his new wife Yolande might be pregnant and it was while hurrying back to her side along the cliffs of Kinghorn that he fell from his horse and was killed in 1286. He was only forty-five, but the decimation of his nearest relations had left his dynasty in a precarious position.

The year after Alexander's death, James the Steward was appointed one of the six guardians in charge of Scotland: the others were two Comyns and two bishops. This was while there was still hope that the old king's young grand-daughter Margaret would return from Norway to succeed him and perhaps in due course marry Edward, the Prince of Wales (1284–1327) who was still only two years old. The three Robert Bruces all objected to this and showed signs of looking to England for help with their own claim.

James the Steward, who had served as a counsellor for Alexander III and was sheriff of Ayr was outnumbered by Comyn supporters in the council of Guardians. Together with his cousin, Alexander Stewart, Walter Ballach's son, the new Earl of Menteith and Lord of Kintyre he expressed support for the Bruce cause at a meeting with the two senior Bruces at Turnberry Castle, the main seat of the sixth Robert now that he was Earl of Carrick. The Bruces had just seized several castles in Dumfries to hem-in John Balliol in case he came forward as a candidate. The two families, Bruce and Stewart, signed a bond of loyalty to Edward I for their English land holdings and to whoever should end up as the legitimate new sovereign of Scotland. There was also an Irish element as both families had interests there – James and the youngest of the three Robert Bruces were later both to marry Irish wives – and agreed to help Richard de Burgh, the Earl of Ulster. This alliance of the two families reflected not only their joint interest in Ireland but also the fact that between them they now dominated Ayrshire, the Stewards in the north, the Bruces in the south. If Annandale and Renfrew were included plus the Stewart holdings in Galloway and the eastern borders this made a sizeable portion of Scotland.

This is not the place to go into the detail of the somewhat degrading competition for the Scottish throne which followed the death of the Maid of Norway in 1290. The eldest of the three Robert Bruces, John Balliol and another eleven competitors including Erik King of Norway all put forward their cases, none of which had any overwhelming credibility compared with the rest. Nor would any of the main players back down, so sadly there was an impasse in which Edward of England was called to arbitrate. For his own reasons he chose John Balliol as the most potentially pliable option. The three Bruces – the youngest one was now eighteen – all objected, but most other Scottish barons, including the Steward accepted the verdict, particularly when Edward I provided a cash hand-out. So King John Balliol was crowned at Scone.

James who had just become a father for the first time, was now the Steward of King John and his sheriff for Ayr and Kintyre where he was given an extra castle called Glasrog – location unknown. His Irish wife Egidia de Burgh had also brought him a castle on Lough Foyle and estates in Coleraine. Meanwhile the eldest of the three Bruces had resigned all his titles in disgust and died three years later. His son, the sixth Robert headed off to Norway for a couple of years to avoid having to do homage to King John Balliol and passed his earldom of Carrick on to his son the teenage Robert who kept out of the way on his estates in Yorkshire.

King John spent a perhaps underestimated three years doing his best to put the fractious kingdom of Scotland together, but by 1295 he had lost the confidence of his barons and in 1296 a council of twelve took over effective power. They sent James the Steward as ambassador to France which had just declared war on England so that they might keep Edward I of England busy on two fronts. When the overbearing Edward became aware of this he demanded the subservience of the Scots who in the name of John Balliol, now nicknamed Toom Tabard, refused. In his name they summoned the Scots feudal host and since it was in his name the two surviving Bruces refused to fight: the elder was by this time anyway following his father as governor of Carlisle for the English. Young Robert who for the time being had hopes of replacing Balliol, was being favourably treated by King Edward so he too headed for Carlisle.

The depleted Scots army wasted a lot of energy burning towns throughout northern England but nothing would stop Edward. He sacked Berwick which had been held by the Steward's brother-in-law William Douglas, and massacred the inhabitants. Then he easily outfought the less experienced Scottish army at Dunbar where amongst others the Steward's cousin, Alexander Stewart, Earl of Menteith was taken prisoner and put in the Tower of London. Scotland became a province of England. James the Steward had briefly held out at Roxburgh Castle but soon surrendered. Like most other surviving Scottish barons he signed the Ragman Roll as a symbol of accepting Edward as his king. Balliol was ceremonially dethroned, the coronation stone was shipped to Westminster, and the Bruces who had expected to replace him received no such reward.

James was by now no longer the Steward. He lost his sheriffdoms of Kintyre to Alexander MacDonald and of Ayr to Henry Percy. He was hemmed in by English garrisons at Bothwell, Ayr and Inverkip where the English kept a large siege engine and from which they creamed off the income from his confiscated estates. So we come to one of the most difficult questions about his career. Was he, as the English chroniclers suggested, an instigator of the rebellion begun by Wallace or just a half-hearted bystander who joined in when Wallace was winning but vanished when he was not? It was once assumed that Wallace was from the Elderslie branch of the family which would mean that he was part of the Steward's feudal retinue. But there is the alternative theory that William Wallace's father was an Alan Wallace and a royal tenant in Ayrshire, so the English assertion that he was a front man working for furtive behind-the-scenes manipulator James the Steward, is far from proven.

Either way Wallace was a guerrilla fighter of substantial flair and with his helper Sir William Douglas, James's brother-in-law, who made a base in Paisley forest which was owned by the Steward, he set the country alight with his daring attack on the English at Scone in 1297. At about this time both James the Steward and young Robert Bruce changed sides and aligned themselves with Wallace to face an English army under Percy at Irvine. But there was a lack of common ground among the leading Scots, for Wallace regarded himself as a supporter of Balliol and had no interest in promoting the career of Bruce, while neither Bruce nor James wanted to lose their estates for the sake of Balliol. The result was another surrender by James who capitulated a second time to Edward on fairly lenient terms in June 1297. Yet by September he seems to have reneged on this, for after offering to act as a peacemaker between the two opposing armies at Stirling Bridge he joined the winning Scots army in the last stages of the battle. As joint leader of the cavalry he reputedly chased the English baggage train when the real fighting had already been done by the infantry.

For nearly a year Wallace held supreme power as sole Guardian of Scotland and James played no significant part in affairs. But Edward I reappeared with a large army from Flanders and confronted the Scots under Wallace at Falkirk. This time Wallace's troops were too vulnerable to the longbow. There is no evidence that James Stewart was at the battle. He may have been inhibited by the fact that his eldest son Andrew had been taken off to England as a hostage – Andrew was never seen again, nor is there any evidence to suggest that Robert Bruce fought at this battle either. But the Stewart family was certainly represented by James's brother Sir John Stewart of Bunkle who led the Scots archers, mostly men from the Stewart estate on Bute. They were no match for their highly trained English opposite-numbers and Sir John, referred to by Bower as 'most valliant' died at his post. Luckily he had already fathered seven sons who between them were ancestors of a dozen new branches of the Stewart family such as the earls of Darnley, Buchan, Atholl, Galloway, Traquair and Blantyre. The fact that he himself had acquired Bunkle Castle and its border estates by marriage to Margaret of Bunkle and that due to his reputation his sons could in turn make good marriages meant a substantial accretion of new territories to the Stewart family and strengthened the position of the head of the house so that in the next generation a royal wedding was not out of the question. In addition John had been given Garlies by his father which he passed on to the next generation.

This time James was treated more harshly by King Edward. He lost all his lands and his offices and was lucky to be left alive. He joined with Bruce in a half-hearted attack on Roxburgh in 1299 and a couple of years later is found on another embassy to France to try to win help from that quarter. He is known to have stood up for the Bishop of St Andrews in 1300, but otherwise kept his head down except for another visit to Paris in 1303 to try to drum up French support.

It was not until about 1305 when Wallace had been captured by Sir John Stewart of Menteith, the younger son of Walter Ballach, and handed over to the English that James once more capitulated formally a third time to the English king and received back his estates. Bruce had capitulated three years earlier as once again he hoped that Edward would help him defeat his rivals the Comyns and win the crown of Scotland. But for a second time Bruce was disappointed and changed sides again for the last time. He had recently taken as his second wife Elizabeth de Burgh, daughter of the Earl of Ulster and niece of the Steward's wife Egidia, so it is possible that James had introduced them on one of their visits to Ireland. Running out of patience in February 1306, Bruce lost his temper and stabbed his main rival John Comyn in a church at Dumfries and two months later had himself crowned king at Scone. There followed his long hard struggle to establish himself, an effort which at last showed him as a resourceful and determined leader, for now there was no turning back.

Despite their long previous association James Stewart took some convincing to come to Bruce's aid. Though he seems to have allowed some of his Ulster knights to assist in the seaborne invasion of Ayrshire by Bruce in 1306, it was to be three years before he too officially changed sides for the last time and by then he had the comfort of knowing that Edward I was dead. An English army had been beaten at Loudoun and a MacDougall one at the Pass of Brander. So in 1309 James at last acknowledged King Robert I as his king, joined in this by his second son Walter, his cousins Sir Alexander Stewart of Bunkle and Alexander Stewart Earl of Menteith together with Bruce's own nephew Thomas Randolph. Menteith had spent time in the Tower of London after his capture at Dunbar, but then been released on condition that he fought for the English in France. Later he held the fords over the Forth for Edward but was captured by Douglas and brought to Bruce along with Randolph. He died soon after his return to the service of Bruce. James, now reinstated as Royal Steward, died shortly after he had attended Bruce's first Scottish parliament.

If both James the Steward and Robert the Bruce were guilty of changing allegiances several times during the course of these wars and their oaths of fealty meant little, the same was true of several other barons, including the Earl of Menteith's brother Sir John Stewart, the man later reviled for arresting Wallace and handing him over to the English. Sir John lived in a small castle on Loch Rusky near Callander but had also held Castle Sween and Skipness in the west so he had a lot to lose. Like his brother Alexander, Sir John was captured at Dunbar, only earning release by promising to fight for Edward who made him governor of Dumbarton Castle and rewarded him for his capture of Wallace by making him Earl of Lennox. Now he handed Dumbarton Castle over to Bruce and was restored by him to the lordship of Knapdale in return for giving up his earldom of Lennox. He is assumed to have fought at Bannockburn. His nephew Alan the third Earl of Menteith died after being captured fighting for Bruce at Methven eight years earlier and his son the fourth earl was killed at Dupplin Moor in 1332, so overall the patriotic pedigree of the family was respectable. The much maligned Sir John happened to be like many other Scots barons under oath to Edward at a particularly awkward juncture and his act of betrayal of Wallace did not at the time seem so horrendous to his fellow barons who regarded Wallace as a maverick.

Despite all his problems James the Steward had held on to the bulk of his estates and in some areas even added. Furthermore, the tentacles of the family had spread. His cousin the Earl of Menteith and his family dominated the Carse of Stirling, Arran and Kintyre. Sir John Stewart of Menteith the betrayer of Wallace had just received two extra properties, Glenbreackine in Kintyre and Aulisay which may have been Ailsa Craig. His nephews, the four sons of Sir John Stewart of Bunkle held a wide swathe of estates from Dreghorn in Ayrshire to Bunkle Castle and Jedburgh in the Borders, Garlies in Galloway and Crookston on the edge of Glasgow. James's three sisters had all made useful marriages: Euphemia, after the initial uproar about her marriage to Duncan of Galloway had come good when he was made Earl of Carrick, while Elizabeth had been the first wife of Sir William Douglas and thus mother of the Good Sir James. The house of Stewart was almost ready for its next great advance.

Chapter Six

Walter and the Royal Wedding

James the Steward's eldest son Andrew had died in England while a hostage for his father's good behaviour, so it was his younger son Walter (c.1294–1328) who now took over as Royal Steward at the age of about seventeen. He was half the age of his new master King Robert the Bruce and about six years younger than the Good Sir James Douglas (1286–1330) hero of the recent battle at the Pass of Brander and Sir Thomas Randolph (–1332) who became the king's foremost commanders along with the king's own brother Edward Bruce (1276–1318)

We know little of Walter's progress over the next five years but can assume it was a period of military apprenticeship in which he saw significant action. Edward II (1284–1327, king from 1307) of England was preoccupied with domestic squabbles, so Bruce had a relatively clear run in mopping up the pockets of English resistance that remained. In 1313 he himself led the capture of Perth, then Randolph took Edinburgh Castle, rapidly followed by a similar feat by Douglas at Roxburgh.

The Battle of Bannockburn was a confrontation with a full English army, which Bruce had always tried to avoid, but he was forced into it by the rash challenge of his brother Edward to the governor of Stirling Castle: unless he was rescued by the English army before midsummer 1314 he should surrender to the Scots. Edward II could not be seen to tolerate such insolence and Bruce could no longer put off the dreaded confrontation with a full-scale English army.

Walter the Steward was given nominal command of the third division of Bruce's army, a contingent of around a thousand men from the Clyde area, but as he was regarded as too young it was understood that his deputy James Douglas would give the orders.

A mychty god qha than mych see
The Steward Walter and his rout

There are hints in Barbour's account the Steward's role in the battle was concocted later as a piece of flattery to please the Stewarts. Both men, Walter and James Douglas were dubbed knights by Bruce on the eve of the battle and according to later chroniclers both acquitted themselves well.

Edward II escaped after his defeat and apart from the surrender of Stirling Castle still refused to acknowledge Bruce's right to the Scottish crown, but he did agree to hand over prisoners who had been held by him since Bruce's bad year in 1306. Among them were the Scots king's wife Elizabeth de Burgh, cousin of Walter's mother and so also was her step-daughter, Marjorie, Bruce's only child from his first marriage. Walter was given the task of escorting the released prisoners back from the border at Berwick where they were handed over. Whether his meeting with Marjorie resulted in immediate attraction or whether it was just politically expedient (Walter is alleged to have previously married or consorted with an Alice Ershe who produced a daughter for him called Jean) Bruce soon afterwards arranged a marriage between them which half a century later was to change the future lives of the Stewart family dramatically. From the king's point of view Walter represented not only a major land-owning family but also one which from its Clyde bases had the only fleet of galleys available to help satisfy the ambitions of his brother Edward to win a crown in Ireland.

Given that Bruce had a relatively young wife capable of bearing children and given that he still had a brother and several illegitimate children, no one would have expected the marriage of his daughter to produce a candidate for the throne of Scotland. But in 1200 when the fourth Robert the Bruce had married Isabel of Huntingdon, no one would have expected their great-grandson to be king either.

To add to the unlikelihood of the chances of a Stewart crown, Marjorie, according to legend, fell from her horse while in the final stages of pregnancy in 1316 (another version has her dying about eighteen months after the baby's birth). She had rashly decided to ride from her husband's castle at King's Inch to his hunting lodge at Blackhall. Traditionally the baby was only saved by the prompt action of a shepherd sometimes called Forrester who carried out a caesarean section. Marjorie died almost immediately but the baby was none the worse except for a bloodshot eye, which it was said had been touched by Forrester's knife. The boy Robert retained his bloodshot eye and since legend rearranged the facts the little monument erected on the spot came to be known as Queen Bleerie's Cross. It stood at Knock Hill near the spot where his ancestor the first Steward had helped defeat Somerled and a possible fragment of it has recently been discovered.

Walter meanwhile had accompanied his father-in-law on a naval campaign up the west coast, when they famously rolled their ships across the isthmus at Tarbert to avoid the risky passage round the Mull of Kintyre. In 1318 he joined Douglas in the capture and subsequent desperate defence of Berwick, then in 1322 in a raid on the Bishopric of Durham with further attacks on Hartlepool, Cleveland and Richmond. He married for a second or third time, and his new wife Isabel Graham had three children: Sir John Stewart of Ralston, Andrew and Egidia. He remained high in the royal councils and was briefly left in charge of Scotland when King Robert crossed to Ireland to help his brother Edward in 1317. Walter's brother John was killed alongside Edward Bruce (by this time briefly King of Ireland) at the disastrous Battle of Dundalk in 1318. Another Stewart casualty there was James, son of Sir John Stewart of Pearston (or Preston).

Walter was one of the thirty-nine Scottish magnates who signed the Declaration of Arbroath in 1320. In addition to all the traditional family estates, he had been given many more by the king, including the area round Bathgate Castle, Houston in West Lothian, Riccarton near Balerno and Dalswinton north of Dumfries, though its castle had just been demolished as part of Bruce's policy of leaving no strongholds capable of use by the English in order to regain a foothold in Scotland. The same had applied to Edinburgh, Stirling and many other major castles including Bruce's own home at Turnberry.

For the five years between the death of Edward Bruce the king's brother in 1318 and the birth of King Robert's son David in 1323, Walter's small son Robert, the king's only grandson, was the heir to the Scottish throne. But in 1326 both Walter and little Robert, now aged ten, had to swear fealty to the three-year-old Prince David. Soon afterwards in 1328 Walter died in his mid thirties at his castle in Bathgate:

> Walter Steward that
> At Bathket abe great sickness tais.

His death was followed a year later by that of Queen Elizabeth and soon after that King Robert himself.

Shortly before Bruce's death, Walter's friend and cousin Sir John Stewart of Preston, grandson of Sir John Stewart of Bunkle, the hero of Falkirk and son of the Stewart killed at Dundalk, was made Earl of Angus by King Robert, perhaps for his role as joint leader of the rescue contingent sent by Bruce in 1328 to help Sir James Douglas who had led one of his lightning expeditions deep into England and had been late coming back. This gave the family their second earldom, for despite a series of deaths, the Stewarts also still held Menteith with its Knapdale and Arran extensions. In addition, according to Barbour, Bruce gave the estate of Durisdeer with its castle commanding the route north from Dumfries to Sir James Stewart, Walter's brother, who now during young Robert's minority became head of the family.

As it turned out, both the Stewart earldoms were to die out over the next half century but in the short term, taken alongside Walter's extra territories, the Stewarts were the largest land-holders in Scotland apart from the king. The next nearest were probably the Black Douglases. Yet with Robert the Bruce having at last produced a healthy son there now seemed little likelihood that the crown would pass to a Stewart.

Part Four

KINGS AND ONE QUEEN OF SCOTLAND

Many Scots are accustomed to compare the Stewarts to horses in the district of
Mar which in youth are good but in their old age are bad.
— John Major or Mair, *History of Greater Britain*

Chapter One

King Robert II or King Blearie

At the time of his father's death, young Robert Stewart (1316–90) was the Bruce's only legitimate male descendant apart from Prince David. As we have seen, from the age of two when his uncle Edward Bruce was killed in Ireland, until the age of eight when his uncle David Bruce was born, he was the king's designated heir as upheld by a parliament at Cambuskenneth in 1320. So as a child he must have been aware of his possible future as a king. Bruce gave him properties at Methven, Kellie and Cunningham to reflect his importance. But for the next forty-four years after that he had to suffer at best uncertainty, at worst the feeling that the odds against his ever becoming king were very great. Right up to the moment when he was proclaimed king at the age of fifty-four it seemed much less likely that he would ever achieve his ultimate ambition. And at times it seemed as if he did not have all that much ambition anyway.

Robert's mother had died in childbirth or soon afterwards and his father Walter died when he was twelve. Thus he nominally became the old king's steward for a year before Robert I also died in 1329, but in practice he was under the guardianship of his uncle Sir James Stewart of Durisdeer. The new King David II (1324–70) was a child of five. Over the next couple of years a whole generation of able Scottish leaders were wiped out: Thomas Randolph the designated regent by disease, Sir James Douglas needlessly killed in a quixotic gesture of defiance among the Moors of Andalucia, two leading Stewarts at the Battle of Dupplin Moor in 1332 and four more Stewarts along with Archibald Douglas at the disastrous Battle of Halidon Hill the year after. Set against this cumulative loss of talent in Scotland there was an ominous improvement on the English side, for Edward II had met his end impaled on a red-hot poker in 1327 and his son, the extremely able Edward III (1312–77) had by 1330 rid himself of his minders. To make life for the Scots even more difficult, Edward was supporting an alternative

Scottish king, Edward Balliol (1286–1364), the son of Toom Tabard. This alternative king had won the battle at Dupplin and had himself crowned at Scone, King Edward I of Scotland.

The young steward Robert can hardly be blamed for the disasters of the 1330s. At seventeen he seems to have seen his first action in the skirmish at Annan when Balliol was temporarily driven back into England in 1332. He was also at Halidon Hill a year later when Archibald Douglas ignored the Bruce rules of engagement and tackled a full-scale English army head-on. Edward III's long-bows decimated the Scots, killing Douglas and three of Robert's Stewart cousins from the family of Bunkle whose father had died at Falkirk. Significantly all three of these cousins had founded important new branches of the family before they were killed. Sir Alan who had been given Dreghorn by Bruce and taken over the old Croc fief at Crookston founded the Darnley branch of the family which later held the Earldom of Lennox and produced a husband for Mary Queen of Scots. Sir James Stewart of Pearston, the second brother was ancestor of the Stewarts of Innermeath, Lorn, Rosyth, Galloway and Traquair. The only one of Bunkle's sons to survive Halidon Hill was Walter who founded the Garlies and Galloway wing of the family. Robert the Steward did survive the battle but not his guardian Sir James Stewart of Durisdeer.

As a result of the English victory at Halidon Hill, Robert was the second Royal Steward to be deprived of his office and his lands. Both were transferred by King Edward Balliol, the avowed vassal of Edward III, to one of the pro-English magnates disinherited by Bruce, David of Strathbogie. Robert Stewart joined with the new Earl of Moray John Randolph in a rebellion but Edward III counter-attacked so he fled first to Rothesay Castle, then escaped in a small boat (*litle cobil*) with his charters in a bag and sought refuge in Dumbarton Castle which was still held by the Scots loyalists. There he joined the young King David and Queen Joan who were soon smuggled out of Dumbarton to France for their greater safety. King Philip V of France (1293–1350, king from 1328) looked after them for the next few years in the massive Chateau Gaillard above the Seine.

John Randolph and Robert Stewart (still only eighteen but of course heir to the kingdom should David have no children) were appointed joint Guardians of Scotland – Robert was referred to by Fordun as 'a comely youth, tall, robust, modest, liberal with an innate sweetness.' With Campbell help he recaptured his own castles at Dunoon and Rothesay. The two Guardians then had some success in liberating the rest of Scotland as soon as Edward III's back was turned, but whenever he came back in force they could not withstand him. Strathbogie changed sides twice, the second time in 1335 arranging a truce for Robert Stewart as well as himself, but a year later was killed by a Douglas force in the Culblean Forest on Deeside. By a strange piece of reverse logic Robert's distant English cousin Richard Fitzalan, Earl of Arundel, Lord of Oswestry applied to Edward III for the vacant position of Royal Steward of Scotland. He was turned down but did visit Scotland to lead the English siege of Dunbar in 1338.

Randolph meanwhile had been captured by the English. With Robert at this point out of the picture, the resourceful Sir Andrew Moray was appointed sole Guardian and was quite effective until his capture by the English in 1335. In 1337–8 two events came together to bring a major change of fortune for the Scots and Robert Stewart in particular. In 1337 the row which had been simmering for some time between Philip VI of France and Edward III escalated into a war that was to last for the next hundred years. Edward argued that as Philip IV's grandson he had a better right to the French crown than Philip VI who was a mere grand-nephew a good excuse for the English to interfere. So with the burning of Southampton by the French, Edward had too much on his plate to bother with the unprofitable conquest of Scotland. The other event, nearly a year later, was the death of Sir Andrew Moray who had been released from captivity and retired to his castle at Avoch. Thus for the first time Robert Stewart, as heir to the throne, became sole Guardian of Scotland in 1338. He was by now twenty-two with considerable fighting experience behind him, even if he was not quite so well regarded as William Douglas of Liddesdale, the victor of Culblean, or Alexander Ramsay of Dalhousie, the two 'flowers of chivalry'.

With Edward III preoccupied it was not a bad time to be Guardian. Robert captured Perth from the English, called a parliament and began a siege of Stirling. John Randolph, now released from captivity added to the fighting capability and with Douglas and Ramsay started to clear the English from the Borders. Douglas managed to capture Edinburgh Castle by trickery – he disguised himself as a wine salesman to gain entry. But the very success of the Scots was to mean the end of Robert's career as Guardian, for things had gone so well by 1341 that it was safe for King David to return with his wife from his French exile. The King was now nearly eighteen and ready to take over personal control. Robert, now twenty-five had recently become a father, having married Elizabeth Muir of Rowallan, albeit without the blessing of the church – she was his cousin and he had also had an affair with another mutual cousin, Isabel. Thus he was spending more time at his favourite castle of Dundonald and reverted to the traditional role of Steward. Now that King David had a healthy adult bride Robert fully expected that he would also soon lose his position as heir to the crown. As consolation David gave him the earldom of Atholl which was kept by the Stewarts for many generations and gave Robert a vital base in the highlands which was to be a key part of his later power.

For the next five years, David, despite his youth, was to be a reasonably effective king, gradually removing the English from their last footholds in Scotland, sorting out the Lord of the Isles and generally bringing the country into line. In this he was helped by, among others, Sir John Stewart of Dalswinton who in 1342 was made warden of the West March. This split the Stewart leadership; part of David's strategy was clearly to weaken his most powerful subject, Robert the Steward. Properties at Bathgate, Dull and Durisdeer were taken out of his hands and he was eased away from the lordships of Fife and Atholl.

Everything was to change in 1346 when the English, at full strength, once more headed for Scotland. Edward III had just won a major victory over the French at Crécy in August and had besieged Calais, so by October he was free to deal with Scotland. David led a Scots army to meet him at Neville's Cross near Durham, ignoring maxims laid down by his father. Once more the English longbow proved superior to the Scots' and they took heavy casualties. Some fifty Scottish barons were killed, including several prominent Stewarts. Among them were Alexander of Dalswinton, Alan Stewart and three John Stewarts, one of them the Earl of Menteith who was executed. Robert the Steward along with the Earl of March led the third and largest division which was kept in reserve and once the English had dealt with the first two divisions he decided to save himself and his men. King David was injured in the eye and captured while Robert escaped unscathed. As the *Lanercost Chronicle* unkindly put it 'overwhelmed by coward-ice…he led off the dance, leaving David to caper as he wished.' Whether it was desertion, as the captured king understandably concluded, or common sense, or a mixture of the two, no one can really now judge. But Robert had many reasons for wanting rid of David, who had been steadily undermining his powers, and according to later pro-Stewart chroniclers, resented the impetuosity of the king in exposing a Scottish army to such danger. Certainly the result was that Robert had another opportunity to take over control of Scotland and this left a lasting rancour between David and the Steward, made worse by the fact that after five adult years of wedlock the king had still produced no heir, while the Steward had half a dozen.

So for the next eleven years King David was to be a prisoner in England and Robert as his heir apparent assumed the new title of Lieutenant of Scotland. Perhaps the most surprising feature of this tenure is not the fact that he made so little effort to pay David's ransom, but that he did not just seize the crown for himself. Such was the sense of genealogical legitimacy in Scotland compared with England, where there were several usurpations during the Middle Ages.

Robert perhaps simply did not want to make the extra effort needed if he was to make himself king. His regime, referred to by MacQuarrie as 'equally undis-tinguished' produced financial chaos, administrative carelessness and a situation where local barons were allowed to wield unsupervised, oppressive control of their districts, particularly if they were related to the Lieutenant, which meant most of them. Robert always seemed to choose the line of least resistance whether he was trying to impose justice, collect money or uphold the law. When Edward Balliol invaded Scotland in 1347 Robert bought him off rather than fight him. Two years later Scotland was hit by the Black Death, known up to this time as 'the foul death of the English' which affected particularly the crowded slums of the towns, but this at least could not be blamed on Robert.

Robert's most notable technique for controlling Scotland was to use his large family. In 1347 his eldest son John (c.1338–1406) was retrospectively legitimised by a papal dispensation which condoned Robert's allegedly incestuous marriage to his cousin Elizabeth, so there should be no problem over the succession. In 1350 his eldest daughter Margaret was married to the conveniently divorced John Lord of the Isles who at about this time was allowed to have that title officially, and at the same time as a peace offering acquired the Stewart territory of Kintyre and Knapdale. Robert's second son Walter married into the Earldom of Fife, thus acquiring Falkland and estates such as Murthly in Perthshire for the family, which after his death two years later went to the next brother, Robert junior. After the death of his first wife Elizabeth in 1355 Robert himself married the widow of John Randolph, Euphemia Ross, which helped him extend northwards from his Atholl properties into Badenoch. It also gave him a link to the Earl of Ross, the brother-in-law of the Lord of the Isles who had married Robert's daughter Margaret. Of his other daughters, Marjorie married the Earl of Menteith, Elizabeth the Constable Hay, Jean the Marshal and Isabella the Earl of Douglas. After that there were still four children to come from his second marriage plus at least eight bastards, including John the Black Stewart, Sheriff of Bute who was eventually to found the branch of the family that much later produced its only British Prime Minister.

Violence, including murder, was a symptom of the disorder which Robert's mild rule allowed to develop. Three Stewarts of Rusky, descendants of the betrayer of Wallace, were killed in a feud by the Drummonds in 1360 and Robert failed to punish the culprits. The most famous example of his laxity was when William Douglas of Liddesdale, the Flower of Chivalry, was ambushed and killed in 1353 by his cousin, William Lord of Douglas whose son married Robert's daughter. This allowed a conjunction of the vast Douglas estates under a single baron whose power was thus to create a real threat for the Stewarts in the years to follow. Other growing power-blocks at this time included the Lordship of the Isles and the Campbells. Even Edward Balliol persisted in trying to make his comeback but was finally expelled from Scotland in 1354 largely due to the efforts of Robert's cousin Alan Stewart of Crookston.

Robert had sabotaged two treaties that might have secured the King David's release in 1351 and 1355, but at last in 1357 the ransom was agreed and King David returned after eleven years in English custody. Several Scottish castles had to be dismantled as part of the terms of his freedom, including the Stewart castle at Dalswinton. The king was now thirty-four and his nephew the Steward over forty.

Having lost such a key period of his reign David returned full of resentment against his Lieutenant, the Steward, the man who was regrettably still his heir and who had deserted him at Neville's Cross. David, not surprisingly, still had no children. Queen Joan took the blame for this and was sent off back to her brother Edward III in 1357 to die five years later. This allowed David to marry one of his mistresses, the voluptuous widow Margaret Logie who already had a child and was therefore proved fertile. Meanwhile David's sister Margaret had produced a son, William, who was thus an alternative grandson of Robert the Bruce and for the time being a useful pawn to play off against the Steward. Robert was once more sent back to his estates and given a compensatory earldom in Strathearn to keep him quiet while David tried desperately to breed a new heir to replace him.

However both by the selection of junior barons to be his key advisers and by the financial burdens put on their seniors due to the need to collect his ransom money, David made himself unpopular with the old guard who had enjoyed such freedom while he was held captive. In 1360 there was a plot to kill the king's new mistress Katherine Mortimer at Soutra. Thomas Stewart (1330–62) Earl of Angus, Robert's cousin, was arrested for the crime despite the fact that he had helped King David's release from England and had led the daring night attack on Berwick in 1354. He was perhaps paying the price for being too close a henchman of Robert who had made him his lieutenant in the north east. He died soon afterwards in the dungeons of Dumbarton after a new outbreak of the Black Death hit Scotland and since he only left a daughter the earldom passed by virtue of a torrid love affair to the Douglases.

In 1363, just before David's marriage to Margaret Logie, the Steward Robert together with the Earls of March and Douglas instigated a new plot to purge the king's evil counsellors and prevent the marriage. Fordun calls it 'a great sedition and conspiracy', but Archibald Douglas the Grim stood by the king who wisely had acquired a war chest of money while collecting his ransom. The Earl of Douglas hesitated to fight a royal army and Robert the Steward backed down, as was becoming his habit when the odds were stacked against him. At the royal wedding which followed he was forced into a public humiliation. His name-sake Robert Stewart of Innermeath, a son of the Pearston branch, was given the lordship of Dalziel and later Durisdeer as if to spite him.

For the next seven years, King David tried his best to father an heir but Queen Margaret was no more successful than Joan. He also made continued improvements to revenue collection so that he could pay off his ransom and cut a bit of a dash in London where he maintained a relationship with Edward III and irritated the Scots barons by extravagant display. But he continued to demonstrate firm control: both the Campbell and MacDonald chiefs were forced to submit to him in 1369 while Robert the Steward and his eldest son John were each given a taste of the Loch Leven dungeons for daring to criticise the regime, in particular the lavish gifts to the king's latest mistress. After their release Robert was disciplined again by being deprived of the earldom of Strathearn while the Earl of Mar was marooned on the Bass Rock.

David had still failed to produce an heir and in 1369 started to divorce Queen Margaret but she outwitted him by escaping to Avignon where she could twist Pope Gregory XI round her little finger. David intended his third attempt at paternity to be with Agnes Dunbar but without papal approval of the divorce it would be impossible and in the midst of this crisis he died. He was only forty-seven.

Robert Stewart had been heir to the throne for forty-two years, yet had always expected to be displaced. He had made surprisingly little effort to pre-empt that eventuality other than to build up such a massive portfolio of property that he virtually controlled Scotland anyway. Now aged fifty-five, old for that period, he suddenly became king. More than 330 years after Walter Fitzalan's arrival in Scotland the Stewart family at last had their hands on their first crown. For Robert it was a remarkable tale of survival. As Stephen Boardman puts it he was 'the most successful, ambitious and ruthless of the Scottish magnates.'

Yet the rest of King Robert II's life was to be an anti-climax. According to the pro-Stewart Abbot Bower he was 'impressive, humble, mild, affable, cheerful and honourable.' Only his bloodshot eye, a relic of his remarkable birth, marred an otherwise commanding appearance. But even now he faced opposition. William the Earl of Douglas, his old ally, claimed the crown for himself and brought a substantial army to Linlithgow to back up his claim. Robert had his own troops ready and a combination of the age-old reluctance of rebels to fight against the royal standard together with a bit of judicious bribery persuaded Douglas to back down. He was given the princess Isabella for his son to marry, the justiciarship of the north and wardenship of the East March. Negotiation rather than confrontation had always been Robert's trademark. He dispensed with seven earldoms to keep his own sons quiet and had five of the other great Scottish lords as sons-in-law. He had no strategy for dealing with the English but stopped paying his predecessor's ransom instalments in 1377 and allowed his border barons to make unofficial raids against the English when they felt like it. The Earl of March sacked English-held Roxburgh in 1379. He and Archibald the Grim followed that up in 1384 by attacking Lochmaben and with a raid into England the following year.

The main features of Robert's reign were weakness in finance and in law and order. His two eldest sons were given high office: the eldest John had supervision of justice but failed lamentably to discipline high ranking law-breakers. The second surviving son, young Robert, was given charge of finance but after the tighter discipline of David he made no effort to budget properly or audit the collection system. King Robert II acquired a taste for delegation and in the last six years of his reign slid sadly into senility. It was suggested by his heir and the more aggressive southern barons that Robert had no stomach for war. Thus with council approval and in what amounted to a palace coup, Robert II was made to hand over executive power to his heir, John Earl of Carrick, in 1384. John was already in his mid-forties and had shown few significant signs of drive or ambition. A year later he was given the job of suppressing the marauding bandits or caterans of the north which included his own brother Alexander Stewart, the Wolf of Badenoch, but the campaign failed. He could not even get back Urquhart Castle for their half-brother David of Strathearn. Meanwhile the English, led by their new young king Richard II (1367–1400, king from 1377) were allowed to invade Scotland and burn Edinburgh and the border towns. The English only stopped short of total conquest because the Scots had burned their own countryside to deprive the English of a food supply.

A further loss of credibility came in 1388 when Robert was in his seventies and his son-in-law the new Earl of Douglas snatched a memorable victory against the English under Percy at Otterburn, dying heroically in the process. The only prominent Stewart present was Sir William Stewart of Jedworth (d.1402, son of Sir John Stewart of Jedworth, part of the Bunkle and Darnley branch of the family). Referred to as a knight banneret, a sign of conspicuous bravery in battle, he had also joined in the capture of Roxburgh Castle and was given Abercorn Castle. This and other military initiatives against England were part of the strategy of the Earl of Carrick, but ironically what might have been seen as a triumph was in fact a disaster for him, as the death of Douglas deprived him of his main political ally. At about this time he also suffered a severe injury when he was kicked by a horse owned by James Douglas of Dalkeith. He was permanently crippled and soon afterwards his younger brother Robert Earl of Fife, who had played a more robust part in the recent war, exploited his difficulties to stage another palace coup by which he was installed by the estates as Guardian or Governor in John's place. With a salary of a thousand marks a year he was not supposed to be tempted to pilfer the treasury but since he was chamberlain as well that was all too easy for him and the temptation proved too hard to resist.

Two years later at the age of seventy-four the first Stewart king died at his favourite castle of Dundonald. More by accident than design he left Scotland territorially stronger than it had been since the time of his grandfather Robert I, but its finances and justice system were in chaos. The chronicler John Major commented 'I cannot hold this aged king...to have been a skilful warrior or wise in counsel.' He had contributed very little to the enhancement of monarchy in Scotland but he had by the time of his death without doubt established the Stewarts as its unquestioned royal dynasty. In Ranald Nicholson's words he had 'stewartised the aristocracy'. That had partly been achieved by his own philoprogenitive tendencies, for with two sets of legitimate (or at least legitimised) children – more than twenty in total – his sons dominated the list of Scottish earldoms and almost monopolised the senior offices of state, while his daughters had married almost everyone else that mattered. The only problem was that such a large family created its own inner tensions. Over the coming years two of his sons were, in separate incidents, to kill two of his grandsons, one grandson to execute another along with two great grandsons, a great grandson to murder a son and a granddaughter-in-law to execute both a son and a grandson.

The fate of his bastard children was more varied. John of Bute, the Black Stewart, was made sheriff of Bute and founded a line that lasted into the twenty-first century, including Britain's only Stewart prime minister. Similarly his illegitimate son, another John born at Cardney, also founded a new line that lasted for many generations. A third John, John Stewart of Dundonald, was murdered by one of Robert's great-grandsons James the Gross when he tried to defend Dumbarton

Castle against him in 1425. A fourth bastard Alexander was given the important estate at Inverlunan which probably soon included Red Castle.

Robert II the great survivor who had perhaps in the end lived too long for his own good was buried at Scone under a stone sculpted by Nicholas Haen, though there is some suggestion that he had already had the handsome tomb which survives at St Mary's on Bute carved for himself. He had built up a huge portfolio of land and influence for his large extended family, but so many of his sons and sons-in-law had done so well out of it that it went to their heads and created jealousies which made the whole effort almost counterproductive. In particular he was leaving his crown to one son and his power to another.

It was a sign of the growing frustration of some of the lesser branches of the Stewart family that at about this time we see the first examples of them seeking military careers abroad. Sir Alexander Stewart of Darnley (a possible alternative is 'of Ralston') took part in the Barbary Crusade of 1390 in North Africa while Sir Robert Stewart of Durisdeer similarly took crusading vows to join the Teutonic Knights in their attack on East Prussia. With him were Alexander Stewart, perhaps the same one, and a John Stewart. Most mysterious of the Scottish crusaders were the Stewarts of Ardvorlich who cherished a magic armlet called the *clach dearg* or 'red stone' which one of the family had brought back from the crusades. However for the next generation it was not to be crusading but France that offered the best opportunities for soldiers of fortune, especially after the commencement of the Hundred Years War.

Chapter Two

Robert III or Faraneyier, Albany and the Wolf of Badenoch

The eventful history of the numerous children of Robert II is complicated by the fact that the eldest son, John Earl of Carrick changed his name to Robert, so he can be easily confused with his brother Robert, Earl of Fife and Menteith. John made the name-change on his accession to the throne because Scotland, France and England had all recently had unpopular King Johns: the Scots John Balliol because he had been weak, the French John because he allowed himself to be taken prisoner by the Black Prince, and the English John because he had deceitfully ignored the feudal rights of his barons. Thus John of Carrick became Robert III (c.1338–1406, king from 1390) but kept the mocking nickname Faraneyier (last year's John).

John had been born when his father Robert the High Steward was only twenty and struggling as the nominal stand-in for the child-king David II during the dark days after the English victory at Halidon Hill. Such was the chaos at that time that his parents' marriage had not been authorised by the church and was not to be so for another ten years. John was thus about ten when his father escaped from the debacle at Neville's Cross and left behind King David a prisoner of the English. There then followed the period of eleven years when his father was Lieutenant of Scotland, a period of plague and bad harvests. His mother had died when he was about sixteen and his father remarried, starting a new family which given the suspect nature of Robert's first marriage might well replace the first one.

Thus when David II returned from captivity and shortly sacked Robert as his Lieutenant, John had just come of age. Of his early activities we know very little, and there are only a few mentions of valiant exploits except in 1352 when he was a teenager and was sent with the army to win back Annandale from the Balliol supporters. So even before the accident which half crippled him thirty years later he was known as an experienced but not brilliant soldier though he was keen to adopt policies more warlike than those of his father.

In 1367 when John was about thirty he married Annabella Drummond (1350–1401) a cousin of King David's second wife Margaret Logie. She was seventeen, yet it was to be eleven years before they had their first child. In 1368 he was created Earl of Carrick and two years after his marriage he and his father were both imprisoned by King David in Lochleven Castle because of an alleged plot against him. Just how active John's role had been in such activities we do not know. Then after David's sudden death in 1371 the Steward became King Robert II and John in his mid-thirties became Steward himself, heir to the throne, earl of Atholl and governor of Edinburgh Castle.

A further fourteen years passed in which little is heard of John, other than the birth of his first son David in 1378. But then as his father was perceived as growing too old for active duties in 1384, John at the age of nearly fifty staged the palace coup that made him virtual regent, in charge of administering the law through-out Scotland. This was the peak period of his career but he failed to achieve sufficient success to impress either his father or his younger brother. Famously he condoned the murder of his own brother-in-law by one of his sheriffs and made no headway when given a remit by the Council in 1385 to suppress the caterans (light-armoured warriors) in the Highlands. He played only a background role in the victory against the English at Otterburn in 1388 and in that year was so badly kicked by a horse in the Linlithgow stable that he seems to have limped and suffered severe pain for the rest of his life. This injury combined with his poor recent record as a law-enforcer and the death of some of his ablest supporters at Otterburn, led to a coup in which he was replaced as regent by his able and ruthless younger brother Robert Earl of Fife (1340–1420).

Thus when their father died in 1390 Robert was in control of the kingdom. John took over as king in his mid-fifties as his father had done, but in name only and even that he changed to Robert III. His younger brother Robert Earl of Fife continued carrying out most of the duties except the ceremonial side of the job. He was more energetic and had more military experience than John, but was not dramatically more efficient. He had already shown signs of feathering his own nest at the expense of the treasury. Their other brother Alexander Stewart (1343–1405), Earl of Buchan since 1382 and known as the Wolf of Badenoch made his infamous raid on Elgin Cathedral just before their father's death but Robert found it hard to restrain him. Not long after that, the Wolf's bastard son Duncan and his caterans got away with murdering the Sheriff of Angus and his brother near Pitlochry late in 1391. Then came the judicial combat between two groups of thirty caterans at Perth in 1396, watched by the king, condoned by the dysfunctional legal system. The final outrage in this period was when a nephew of the two Roberts, Alastair Carrach MacDonald, brother of Donald Lord of the Isles and a son of the king's sister Margaret, invaded Moray to extract blackmail in 1398 and was allowed to retreat home with his booty. As Bower put it everywhere 'he who was stronger oppressed him who was weaker'. However Earl Robert did succeed where the king, his elder brother had failed, in gradually ending the scandal of their errant sibling the Wolf of Badenoch. That year Robert, as the man in charge of justice was promoted by his royal brother to be one of the first two Scottish dukes, taking the title Albany, an anglicised version of the Celtic Alba. The other new duke was Robert III's heir, the twenty-year-old David as Duke of Rothesay – a title retained to this day as one of those given to the heir of the British throne.

Robert III, now a benign old man with a long white beard was incapable of disciplining his brother but the same was not true of his Queen Annabella. With the help of Archibald Douglas the Grim and the veteran warrior Sir William Stewart of Jedworth who acted as sheriff and auditor of the Borders, she organised a small palace coup in which Albany was replaced by Rothesay as Lieutenant or de facto ruler on behalf of her husband. The charge against Albany was 'mysgouvernance of the realm'. The coup might have been more effective if it had not been bloodless, for Albany was too wily a schemer to be kept out of power for long. That same year the coup in England became much more permanent when Henry Bolingbroke dethroned Richard II, had him murdered soon afterwards and made himself Henry IV (1367–1413).

David Duke of Rothesay was too young and lacking in motivation to show any improvement on his uncle's easy-going conduct of affairs. He made three serious errors of judgement. The first was to underestimate the man he had replaced, thus failing to attack his power-base when he had the chance. The second mistake was to lead a life of unbridled extravagance and immature ostentation, good material for Albany to exploit for his comeback. As Walter Bower in his *Scotichronicon* put it 'all decency died in Scotland'. Like Albany, Rothesay failed to supervise the proper collection of taxes or auditing of expenditure and instead relied on filching custom duties and blackmail to fund his own extravagance. The third mistake was his ruthless jilting of his fiancée Agnes Dunbar in favour of the richer Margaret Douglas, daughter of his ally Archibald the Grim. To make it worse he failed to repay his ex-fiancée's dowry and when her father the Earl of March sought help in England, allowed his new father-in-law to seize his earldom.

The outraged father succeeded in winning English help and Henry IV invaded Scotland, accusing Rothesay of treason and demanding that Robert III do homage to him for Scotland. From the relative safety of Edinburgh Castle Rothesay offered to come out and fight three hundred English knights with the same number of Scots, but Henry refused. Having reached Edinburgh he spared the city and returned home, but it was a huge loss of face for Rothesay. He might have survived the consequences of these three mistakes had it not been for a further unfortunate coincidence. His two most important supporters, Queen Annabella his mother and Archibald the Grim, Earl of Douglas both died. The new Earl of Douglas was an Albany supporter and brother-in-law so the tide was set to turn.

Rothesay's continued aggressive behaviour lost him the support of the council while Albany orchestrated a campaign of dissatisfaction among the barons of Scotland. Rothesay was reputed to have seen a comet foretelling his own doom and was arrested on his way to St Andrews where he was heading to take over the coffers of the dead bishop. His captors were two Albany supporters, one of them the brother of yet another jilted sweetheart. He was imprisoned by Albany and Douglas in Falkland and died on 25 March 1402. Bower suggests that Albany's half-brother Walter Stewart was involved and as his reward was given the earldom of Atholl. Some accounts blamed dysentery, others starvation, but such was Robert III's weakness of character and the unpopularity of his son Rothesay that both Albany and Douglas were exonerated of charges of murder. The luckless heir to the throne was buried at Lindores Abbey which was later, according to folk memory, to be the scene of some remarkable miracles near his tomb. Sadly he had failed to produce anything remotely miraculous while he was alive.

Within two years of their coup, Albany and the Earl of Douglas made the disastrous error of judgement that led in 1404 to the defeat of the Scots army by the English under Percy at Homildon. It was Albany's over-confidence which exposed an army in open battle and the poor generalship of his son Murdoch and Archibald Douglas that led to such an abject defeat. It would have been even more disastrous if Percy had followed up on his victory, but he was about to launch his own rebellion against Henry IV. As it was there were heavy casualties. Both Douglas and Albany's eldest son Murdoch became prisoners with large ransoms on their heads. Sir William Stewart of Jedworth who had helped beat Percy at Otterburn and later invaded Northumberland, was captured and executed as a traitor by the vindictive Percy. The quarters of his body were then exposed in prominent places throughout northern England. His son John Stewart of Garlies was also taken prisoner but survived to seek his fortune fighting for the French and died at Orleans. The next generation of this family was to provide the favourite knight of James II and many years later their descendants became earls of Galloway.

Robert III had taken a long time to become a father in the first place but then had seven legitimate children (others which did not survive infancy) over a fifteen year period. James, the new heir to the throne had been born in 1394 after twenty-seven years of marriage when the queen was forty-three and the king nearly sixty – for this era in both cases medically significant feats. Robert must have been aware of the danger that his second son might also fall prey to Albany and in 1406 rather naïvely organised the despatch of the twelve-year-old prince to France for his own safety. He was sent to the Bass Rock to wait for a ship.

Just as the guilt for David Duke of Rothesay's death is uncertain so is the question of whether Albany and the Douglases tipped off the English that the new heir to the Scottish throne was crossing the North Sea. It was certainly a remarkable coincidence that English pirates waylaid the *Marienknyt* of Danzig off Flamborough Head and took James as a hostage to Henry IV. Robert III, a sad old widower, seems to have retreated to his favourite castle at Rothesay (or according to some accounts Dundonald) and when he heard the news collapsed over his supper and died. He was buried beside his grandmother Marjorie Bruce in the family abbey at Paisley having allegedly suggested his own epitaph 'Here lies the worst of kings and the most wretched of men in the whole realm.'

With one heir to the throne dead and the other a prisoner in England Robert Duke of Albany now embarked on a final fourteen years of power. The most obvious question is why did he not just have himself crowned king? In similar circumstances in England such usurpations had been quite common, yet in Scotland there was a remarkable respect for legitimacy throughout the Stewart period, with James IV as one of the few exceptions.

Albany, despite his apparent reluctance to go that last mile and make himself king was one of the most methodically ambitious and competent of the early Stewarts. He was already into his late sixties by the time he entered on his last fourteen year spell of absolute power and already had been virtual ruler of Scotland since 1388 with the one break from 1400–3 when Rothesay had displaced him. It was not lack of competence that led his system of rule to be ineffective so much as personal greed and the desire to better his own immediate family. He was illiterate like virtually all previous kings, but did not even encourage his clerical servants to maintain good paperwork. Accounts were unaudited, budgets unplanned, deeds neglected, but like his father he pursued a policy of binding other great barons to his allegiance by family ties or bribery.

As the younger son of Robert the Steward he had originally created a career for himself by his marriage in his early twenties to the Countess of Menteith who was already a widow three times over and as she held the title in her own right passed it on to him. He then also managed to manipulate Isabella his dead brother Walter's (d.1362) widow into handing over to him the Earldom of Fife which won his father's assent in 1371. These two earldoms gave him considerable territory including properties like Inchtulla on its island in the Lake of Menteith, Doune Castle which he built in the latest fashion, Falkland and possibly Tantallon. He used his extended family to continue what Ranald Nicholson calls the 'stewartisation' of the Highlands, making sure that he and his cronies had pensions – he himself enjoyed a 200 mark income from the customs duties of Cupar and Linlithgow as a personal perk. He had won booty from his raid into Cumberland in 1388 with Archibald the Grim. He also had a succession of lucrative appointments from governor of Stirling in 1372 to chamberlain for both Robert II and III. At the same time he handed over to his half-brother David the earldom of Strathearn which he had held since 1357.

Albany did enjoy some successes as Governor from 1406–20 but his financial administration remained chaotic and unruly, and barons still got away with murder. But having sustained less damage than he deserved after the defeat at Homildon Hill he was lucky again to survive a serious confrontation with the Islesmen seven years later in 1411. He had upset the MacDonalds by preventing Donald Lord of the Isles from taking the Earldom of Ross (he wanted it for his own younger son, John) to such an extent that Donald of the Isles invaded the mainland, burned Inverness and was only stopped from heading southwards by an army led by Albany's maverick nephew, Alexander Stewart, Earl of Mar, a bastard son of the Wolf of Badenoch. The Battle of Bloody Harlaw saw heavy casualties on both sides with neither achieving outright victory but Mar's generalship did enough damage to stop the Islesmen's advance and thus saved Albany from grave humiliation. Significantly another of the Wolf's bastard sons, William Stewart of Strathaven was knighted for his bravery during the battle and founded the new Stewart branch of Drumin and Ballechin.

On the positive side Albany did preside over the founding of Scotland's first university at St Andrews under Bishop Henry Wardlaw and wisely switched his allegiance back to the Pope in Rome from the Popes in Avignon, even though they had recently allowed Scotland to have its first cardinal in the shape of Wardlaw's uncle. With true ecclesiastical correctness he allowed the burning of Lollard heretics by the Inquisition at Lindores Abbey on the Tay. He also maintained a useful irritant against Henry IV of England by supporting the claims of the red-haired Richard II lookalike, but his final campaign against the English in 1420 was a disaster. He failed ignominiously to capture Berwick and the so-called 'foul raid' brought instant retaliation. When he died that year in his eighties at Stirling Castle, Albany was mourned by some as a great leader, but perhaps because he had been so generous with other people's money, his leniency to criminals seemed like kindness, and luck had frequently been on his side. Yet of all his failings the most blatant was his abject reluctance, like his father, to pay a ransom for the return of his rightful king, his nephew James from his prison in England. He paid up for the return of his own son Murdoch, but did virtually nothing to help free the king.

Besides Robert III and the Duke of Albany, Robert II had left three other surviving legitimate sons. The most colourful was Alexander Stewart (1345–1405), Earl of Buchan known as the Wolf of Badenoch, an estate that was given to him by his father in the 1360s and where he was known to the local caterans as Alasdair Mor Mac an Righ (Big Alastair son of the king). Like his father and elder brother he was imprisoned briefly in 1369 by King David, but when Robert became king two years later he was given various posts in charge of law and order in the Highlands, an opportunity he exploited to increase his own wealth. He aimed to acquire the Earldom of Ross in 1382 by marrying its heiress Euphemia, but it was a marriage purely of convenience since he was living and continued to live with his mistress Mairead of Eachan, the mother of his most famous son, Alexander, the hero of Harlaw. His neglect of his wife brought reprimands from the Bishop of Elgin which later turned into a major confrontation. Even his indulgent father would not let him take the Earldom of Ross but let him have Buchan instead. He was heading to be the largest landowner in Scotland of his day with new castles such as the two island strongholds of Lochindorb and Loch an Eilean near Aviemore, Garth near Aberfeldy, Ruthven where its vast mound is now crowned by the redcoat barracks, Kilnmaichlie and Castle King Edward. For a while he also held the imposing Urquhart Castle on Loch Ness which he leased from his brother David. Neither Robert II nor his son John had been able to control his depredations which reached their peak just before his father's death in 1390 when he burned the town of Forres and Elgin Cathedral whose bishop had dared to excommunicate him because of his adultery.

It was a step too far. Albany had taken action and deprived him of Castle Urquhart and the lands of Ross. This was endorsed when the Pope in Avignon annulled Alexander's marriage to Euphemia Ross, thus removing all his rights to her properties. In that year he was still carrying out raids on his neighbours, but his violent career had gone into steep decline. After a couple of years of belated repentance he died at the age of fifty and was buried in a fine tomb at Dunkeld Cathedral.

The elder of the Wolf's half-brothers, the sons of Robert II's second wife, Euphemia, was David (1357–86) who did not play any major role in affairs although he was made Earl of Strathearn by his father in 1371 at the age of twelve, and six years later also acquired Caithness. Apart from Urquhart Castle which he loaned to his more aggressive half-brother the Wolf, he held Braal in Caithness and Loch Leven. Unlike his siblings he failed to live into old age.

The youngest of Robert II's legitimate sons was Walter Lord of Brechin (1358–1437) who in later life was to suffer a terrible death as penance for the delusions of grandeur which came to obsess him. He was made Earl of Atholl by his father and after the death of David also took over Caithness. Referred to as 'the old serpent' by Pluscarden he was never tough enough to tackle his half-brother Albany, whose assistant he had probably been in contriving the death of their nephew, Rothesay. But once Albany was dead he began to think that he and his family should take over the throne rather than any of the progeny of Robert II's first wife: those children had only been legitimised long after birth by a belated papal dispensation. He thought his prospects were improved by the death of his elder brother David so that from 1420 he began a long-term plot which was to last for seventeen years and end both in failure and his excruciating execution.

Of King Robert's daughters, Isabella married the dashing James Douglas only to become an early widow when he was killed at Otterburn in 1388. Jean eloped with John Lion, Thane of Glamis, in 1376, but she too became a premature widow when he was murdered six years later.

The fates of Robert III's illegitimate brothers were as we have seen as varied as those of the official brood. Thomas went into the church, as illegitimate children often did, and rose to be an Archdeacon. Albany appointed him Bishop of St Andrews, the highest position in the Scottish church, but he failed to obtain papal approval. John the Red Stewart of Dundonald was murdered in 1425 by one of his half-brother Albany's grandsons, the violent James Stewart the Gross who had just burned Dumbarton. Robert II's mistress Marion of Cardney, sister of the Bishop of Dunkeld, had produced several sons for him including John Stewart, who in turn fathered a whole series of new Stewart families at Airntully, Dalguise and Murthly. Another of Robert's bastards was John Stewart, who was a fellow student of Sir Robert Graham, the future regicide, in Paris. The Stewarts of Bute prospered quietly in their own little enclave until bursting onto the British scene in 1760. Similarly Robert III's best-known bastard John Stewart of Ardgowan and Blackhall produced a new mini-dynasty which thrived into the twentieth century.

So far as the main line of Royal Stewarts is concerned the long regency of Albany had been a period of corruption, deception and lawlessness, dictated partly by the fact that Albany only clung to power until his death by refusing to ransom his nephew, the legitimate king. His only forms of discipline were self-aggrandisement and bribery, and his rule lacked legitimacy. He had an eldest son, Murdoch, who was even further down the route to chaos and grandsons who were worse still, so that in the next generation they were all but annihilated. The only real mystery about Albany's rule is that he did not take the final step of making himself king, but then the Royal Stewarts were still at this time *primus inter pares*. The dynasty itself seemed well entrenched but was still too fragile for its individual members to take the risk of challenging the accepted rules of succession.

Chapter Three

Duke Murdoch and King James I

With Albany's death in 1420, control of Scotland transferred seamlessly to his eldest son Sir Murdoch Stewart (1362–1425) who became both Governor and 2nd Duke of Albany at the age of fifty-eight. Good parental discipline had hardly been a feature either in his grandfather's or in his father's ménage, nor indeed in any branch of this now much extended family, and Murdoch inherited the corruption of his predecessor with much less of his talent and charm.

In 1388 young Murdoch had been made a justiciar during his father's first stint as regent and soon afterwards began to receive one of the lucrative pensions that his father could dispense. At the age of forty in 1402 he helped lead the Scots to a disastrous defeat at Homildon Hill and made things even worse by letting himself be captured, along with his friend the Earl of Douglas and many others. He was locked up in the Tower of London, where four years later his cousin King James I joined him as a prisoner, and was due to spend another eighteen years in English custody waiting for his huge ransom to be paid. Murdoch's incarceration was to be slightly shorter, a mere thirteen years. The first arrangement to release him in 1415 fell through and he was abducted by Lollards in Yorkshire on his attempted journey homewards. It was not until the following year that his ransom was paid, so he returned home in 1416 by which time his chief gaoler Henry V (1387–1422, king from 1413) had resoundingly defeated the French at Agincourt and mistakenly did not think that Scotland would cause him any trouble. Albany now promoted Murdoch to Lieutenant of Scotland and formally made him his heir in 1417, so he was second only to his father in the sad period of the Foul Raid when their joint attack on Berwick achieved nothing but contact with the bacilli of the Plague.

It was thus presumably the joint decision of Sir Murdoch and his father to send an army under his brother John Stewart of Coul (1380–1424) Earl of Buchan to fight the English in France – Coul was the castle on Deeside given to him by his indulgent father. Neither Murdoch nor his father had forgiven Henry V for keeping him a prisoner so long and John too had been captured at Homildon, though released much sooner. So he had acted as his father's main assistant during Murdoch's absence and was made chamberlain in 1406. Perhaps to get him out of Murdoch's way, perhaps because of his genuine ability, he was put in joint charge of the French expedition in 1419. He ignored the captive King James I who sent word from Rouen for the Scots not to fight, assuming that this was done at the behest of his English gaolers. Buchan and his men achieved a remarkable victory over an English army at Baugé, north of the Loire – the Scots were apparently playing football when the English made a surprise attack. Luckily Robert Stewart of Ralston and his archers delayed the English crossing the bridge with tactics closely resembling those of Wallace at Stirling. According to one chronicler, Buchan personally killed the English commander, Henry V's brother, the Duke of Clarence. Buchan was showered with honours and money by the dauphin, given Châtillon-sur-Indre and the title Constable of France. It was a considerable moral blow to Henry V who died unexpectedly not long afterwards, cursing the Scots. However John did not live long enough to enjoy his new status in France. Three years later he had joint command of a second large force of mainly Douglas mercenaries who were transported to La Rochelle by a Spanish fleet, but were badly defeated alongside their French allies at Verneuil. He was killed as was his fellow general and fellow ex-prisoner Archibald Earl of Douglas. Both were buried in the cathedral at Tours, as was another Stewart casualty Sir Robert Stewart of Ralston, the leader of the archers.

One of the few Scots survivors of Verneuil was one of Buchan's captains, John Stewart of Darnley (1380–1429), known in France as the Seigneur d'Arnley who after a peaceful pilgrimage to the Holy Land took over as Constable of France and leader of the Scots Guard in France, the now formalised *Garde Ecossaise* wearing their distinctive red, white and green uniforms and acting as the royal bodyguards. He fought under Charles VII at Montereau Bridge and Espailly. Subsequently he captured Chartres Castle, and besieged Alençon and Avranches in the year when Joan of Arc was making her name, but he lost an eye and was captured at Cravant. He was made Seigneur de Concressault and Aubigny, then Count of Evreux and so founded the remarkable branch of the Darnley Stuarts (this spelling came with their French base) who for several generations provided generals for the French army and split their time between France and Scotland. It was in 1425 that he came to Scotland looking for reinforcements and brought the promise of the county of Saintonge for James I as his reward as well as the offer of marriage between young princess Margaret and the French king's son Louis. By marrying a Lennox heiress (sister of Murdoch's wife) John also established the right of the family in due course to acquire that title. He himself was given the right to wear the lilies of France on his shield. Sadly he was killed at the Battle of the Herrings (so-called because the Scots attacked an English supply convoy carrying salted herring and led by Sir

John Falstaff), along with his brother William Stewart during Joan of Arc's campaign to raise the English siege of Orleans and was buried in Orleans Cathedral. It seems he had impetuously ordered his infantry to attack the English before his own side's artillery barrage was complete and suffered from the enemy longbows as a result. According to Fraser, he died vainly trying to save the life of his brother William, although one William did survive: William Stewart of Castlemilk. John's son John Stuart who married Beatrice d'Apchier followed in his footsteps and became a councillor to Louis XI. His grandson was the famous Marshal Bernard Stuart (see p.83, 100–2). Another relation, David Stewart of Rosyth, also fought with the French at this time, later returning home to be the patron of the chronicler Bower. Less respectable was the mysterious renegade Jacques Stewart '*chevalier batard d'escoce*' of unknown provenance who levied blackmail on the city of Tours in 1433.

The other able Stewart general of this generation, whom we have already encountered in connection with his very narrow and expensive victory at Harlaw, was Alexander Stewart (1380–1435), the illegitimate son of the Wolf of Badenoch who gained his first military experience as a highland cateran. The Albany family had refused to allow him to inherit his father's Earldom of Buchan so he was placated with Mar instead. He seems to have organised the murder of his predecessor there and married the widow, Isabella, in 1404, claiming Kildrummy Castle as his new home. He was versatile enough to command both land and sea forces, so 1405 saw him organising a naval blockade of Newcastle and being made an admiral. From 1407–8 he fought in the Low Countries for the Duke of Burgundy where he was both a big military and social success. Three years later he held the vital command at Harlaw where he saved the Albany regime from the Islesmen and then commanded the naval couterattack against the Lord of the Isles. Yet during the intervals between campaigns he resorted to piracy to maintain his extravagant lifestyle which seems to have included at one point three wives at the same time, one of them, Marie van Hoorn, based in Holland. Among the ships he captured during his career as a pirate was one belonging to Richard Whittington, the cat-loving mayor of London. The Hanseatic League issued complaints over his capture of one of their richest cargoes. He became rich, had no legitimate children but several bastards and, though a friend of Murdoch who made him briefly the Admiral of Scotland in 1423, he managed to make the dangerous transition to becoming a trusted general again under James I. In his last battle however he was outwitted by the MacDonalds under Donald Ballach at Inverlochy in 1431 and died a few years later. He was buried in the Dominican Friary at Inverness.

Duke Murdoch meanwhile in the middle of his short period in power, had entered his sixties. He had still naturally made no effort to pay the ransom for his former fellow-prisoner, King James I. But he seemed to be losing the will to sustain his governorship, let alone pass it on to his sons. Besides the concept of a third generation of the Albany dynasty was now beginning to disturb the rest of the Scottish nobility, even the Earl of Douglas, a long-term Albany supporter, and

Alexander Stewart of Mar, who had not been allowed to hand over his earldom to his bastard because one of Murdoch's sons wanted it. Murdoch made matters worse by condoning further financial mismanagement which exacerbated the crisis already brewing due to his father's similar conduct, but instead of grappling with the problem rejected all offers of auditing and hoped that it would go away.

To add to his problems Murdoch had fathered three particularly unruly sons, even by the standards of fifteenth-century Stewarts. The eldest Sir Walter had caused problems by misusing his governorship of Dumbarton Castle to waylay and blackmail customs officers in order to line his own pocket, and then by offending his father's best general Alexander of Mar. His two siblings, Alexander and James were equally rapacious and unpopular. As the government approached bankruptcy and as his family all defied him, Murdoch lost heart. He thus began to make preparations for the self-destruction of his branch of the dynasty and, if he had any imagination, for his own death. In 1423 he dictated – he was illiterate – what was in effect his suicide note. He at long last organised the down-payment for the release of James I and made a list of wealthy Scots hostages to be sent down to England to guarantee the payment of the rest.

James I (1394–1437), now aged thirty was to be released at last after eighteen years in English captivity. We last encoutered him as a young boy of twelve captured by pirates off Flamborough Head and handed over to Henry IV who immediately appreciated just what a politically and financially valuable prisoner had fallen into his hands. His mother had died when he was only six and his father whom he had only known as a doddering cripple, died after hearing the news of his capture. He was sixteen years younger than his eldest brother David Duke of Rothesay and was eight when Rothesay met his mysterious death at Falkland, while his only other brother Robert had died as a child.

James grew up deprived of any family warmth and any contact with people of his own kind. His teenage years of captivity under Henry IV were in the Tower of London, as a maximum security gaol, and he was put there again along with his older cousin Murdoch when Henry V took over in 1413, though he also spent nearly ten years in the relative comfort of Windsor. Despite such hardships however James probably had a much better education than he would have done at home. He was the first Scottish king to be able to read and write. He was even a poet of considerable talent - *The King's Quair* is a moving account of his imprisonment in the Tower

> Bewailing in my chamber thus alone
> Despeired of all my joye and remedye
> For-tiret of my thought and wo-begone.
> And to the window gan I walk in hye…

Though he was not given much military training he seems to have been physically tough. If there was a problem it was that inevitably he found it hard to relate to fellow humans and grew up in an English environment quite different to the conditions he had left behind in Scotland.

James was well enough aware of his situation to realise that he had been betrayed by Albany his uncle, and by his cousin, Murdoch. He knew that for eighteen years no one in Scotland had made any serious effort to obtain his release. Yet for all this inevitable bitterness his personality and intellect marked him out as one of the ablest royal Stewarts to date. In his twenties he was allowed out of the Tower on parole by Henry V who actually knighted him in France during one of his campaigns. He was also present at Henry's wedding to Catherine of France and at the execution for treason of Scottish soldiers caught fighting on the French side. Yet he must have realised that Henry was not patronising him without a devious motive. Clearly he had ideas for using James to bring Scotland inside his fast expanding empire. But for Henry's death and Murdoch's massive incompetence, the only way back for James might have been to let himself be used, like Edward Balliol, as an English puppet.

A key factor that contributed towards James's release from captivity was his choice of a wife. Joan Beaufort (c.1404–45) had in the poet king's own words 'Beautee eneuch to mak a world to dote' and he married her at Southwark in 1424. As niece of King Richard II and granddaughter of John of Gaunt she was extremely well-connected and in the political turmoil which followed the death of Henry V, the ducal family of Somerset would do what it could to have their daughter made a queen, even if it was only of Scotland. In addition, since Henry's death, the English under their regents were having more of a struggle to hold on to his French empire, difficulties which were partly due to the help given to the dauphin by groups of Scots mercenaries such as the Stewart-Douglas contingent which had won at Baugé. Consequently, the English regent, Humphrey Duke of Gloucester wanted Scotland taken out of the French wars.

Thus at last at the age of thirty James I returned to Scotland as its king, having been away for eighteen years. Murdoch immediately handed over all his powers and retired to his wife's castle on Inchmurrin in Loch Lomond. James was inexperienced both in war and in dealing with people but he had had the chance to watch the remarkable Henry V in action so Henry became his model, though perhaps a model not entirely suited to the less sophisticated environment of Scotland. His aim was to restore governmental discipline – 'I will make the key keep the castle, the bracken bush the cow.' So he embarked on a period of tougher, more centralised government than Scotland had ever experienced. Those who resisted were eliminated and he started understandably with the Albany Stewarts. Murdoch's eldest son Walter was arrested and imprisoned on the Bass Rock, then Murdoch himself, his second son Alexander of Kinclaven (a castle at Bridge of Isla in Perth provided to his grandson by Albany) and his father-in-law, the Earl of Lennox. All four were tried and executed at Stirling. Murdoch's only remaining son, James the Gross, had meanwhile burned the town of Dumbarton and murdered his uncle John the Red Stewart of Dundonald, the king's main enforcer on the west coast. Five of his companions were caught and torn limb from limb by horses outside

Stirling. James escaped to Ireland, leaving the king with a good additional excuse for the execution of his father and brothers. He was almost the sole survivor of the Albany dynasty, though he left seven illegitimate sons in Ireland. The only significant survivor was Walter's bastard son, Andrew Stewart of Morphie, later as Lord Avondale to have an impact on the next few reigns.

Naturally the Albany territories of Lennox, Menteith and Strathearn all passed to the crown which perhaps, when he realised how easy it was, gave James a taste for acquiring further wealth for himself. One Stewart who benefited was David of Rosyth who was given significant extra lands in Fife in 1428.

James's totalitarian approach to government was shown by the wide range of his acts: from destruction of rooks' nests to controlling the mesh of fish nets, imprisonment for the unemployed, a 4d fine for those caught playing football instead of doing archery practice, killing of wolves and poachers, conservation of forests, encouragement of agriculture and trade, exclusion of brothels from town centres, and above all, control of law and order. All these acts were processed through the Scots parliament to which he originally summoned all tenants-in-chief until he realised that any parliament building would be too small to accommodate them all, even the huge new hall he was building at Linlithgow.

He encouraged his barons to police their own territories, even in the furthest reaches of his kingdom, yet at the same time arrested some of the most senior of them and imprisoned them without trial. Even the new Earl of Douglas, his most powerful subject, suffered this indignity in the dungeons of Loch Leven for about a year, as did Kennedy of Cassilis in Stirling, until he managed to escape after four years. In addition to all of the Albany properties, James also confiscated the earldoms of Buchan, March and Mar for his own use. After such a long wait to take up his crown, he was clearly impatient for results, desperate to bring in the kind of governmental efficiencies he had seen during his stay in London, but gave the impression that he was greedy for money himself.

After the loss of John the Red Stewart of Dundonald, James had found other members of the wider family who would aid his policies. One was David Stewart of Rosyth who had gained fighting experience in France and also had some awareness of image as shown by his patronage of the chronicler Walter Bower, the Abbot of Inchcolm who polished the Stewart's dynastic credentials. Another surprising enforcer was a woman, the king's sister Margaret, widow of the 4th Black Douglas earl who with a firm hand managed the Stewart lands in Galloway and much of the Black Douglas territory from her castle at Threave. This formidable woman, who always styled herself Duchess of Touraine, one of the empty titles given to her husband by the French just before he was killed at Verneuil, lived until she was eighty and had a fine tomb built for herself at Lincluden. She also nurtured the career of her distant cousin Stewart of Garlies to whom she gave Glasserton Castle in Wigton for his help in controlling the south west.

The climax of James's new disciplinary policy came with his Highland visit four years after his return. This ruthlessness, combined with a measure of deceit, was eventually to undermine his credibility and threaten his success. Having invited all of his northern magnates to a parliament in Inverness he proceeded to ignore the laws of hospitality by arresting fifty of them, then executing the most recalcitrant without proper trial. While James satisfied his intellect by composing heroic Latin verses, the most important of the northern magnates, Alexander Macdonald, the new Lord of the Isles, was packed off in chains to Perth. He managed to make a daring escape (or ignored his parole) and furiously summoned his armies to attack the king. Once again the town of Inverness was burned and the army of the Islesmen confronted the royal army at Lochaber in what might have turned into a replay of Red Harlaw. This time however the king was present himself, and facing the prospect of a pitched battle with the royal standard on the other side, the MacDonald chief surrendered rather than risk losing. He was forced to grovel before the king and court at Holyrood wearing sackcloth and ashes. The beatific Queen Joan played her part in the propaganda spectacle by pleading with her proud husband to have mercy on the repentant Lord of the Isles. He was spared and condemned to a spell in the damp cliff-top dungeons of Tantallon. However it was in some ways a pyrrhic victory for James for he had stirred up deep resentment in the islands and was soon to pay the cost. In 1431 at Inverlochy the Islesmen under Donald Ballach MacDonald of Duniveg inflicted a humiliating defeat on the king's cousin Alexander Stewart of Mar, the former pirate and once highly successful general. One of the casualties was Alan Stewart, son of the Earl of Atholl who six years later was to be the king's murderer. James had to back down and release the Lord of the Isles from his prison.

While James had been a prisoner during his stay in Henry V's England he had been exposed to a more exotic standard of living than was yet common in Scotland and his taste for luxury contributed to the resentment felt by his barons. Given that his income from the royal estates was about £2,000 a year and his expenditure on the new palace at Linlithgow alone was £5,000, he was stretching his resources. As Nicholson points out 'he imported French floor tiles, ostrich feathers, purple velvet, sable mantles, spices, wine, tapestry and jewels' for his court, hired mimers from Holland and did not stint himself even in the plague-ridden years of 1431–2 nor during the dreadful winter of 1434. Then in 1436 he had the considerable expense attached to providing a dowry for his daughter Margaret (1424–45) when she went across to France at the age of eleven to marry the Dauphin Louis. This wedding was a major boost for the dynasty and had been organised by the Franco-Scottish mercenary John Stewart/Stuart of Darnley who had come to Scotland in 1425 to recruit more soldiers to help the French against the English. King James was offered the somewhat suspect reward of the French county of Saintonge for his help in encouraging recruitment. John Stuart of Darnley was to die in battle near Orlèans a few years later. By that time Joan of Arc was reported to have claimed, perhaps a little ungraciously, that she, not the Scots would save Orleans and the rest of France from the English. She was of course right, but the Scots had made a useful contribution.

In addition to wedding costs, James had a new expense previously unknown to Scottish kings, the purchase of guns and gunpowder. The fact that his system of revenue collection remained poor, combined with his failure to develop direct taxes meant that he resorted to forced loans and benevolences, thus increasing his unpopularity.

Now approaching the age of forty, he began to put on weight; he was harder, more ruthless and losing popularity amongst his peers. In 1436 he planned to besiege Roxburgh and drive the English out of southern Scotland, but his barons no longer trusted him and were reluctant to give their military service. The summons to arms ended in a humiliating loss of face, one of the worst fates that could befall any king.

Apart from his increasing general unpopularity there was one particular sense of injury which applied by this time to a number of noble families. This arose from the fact that so many of their eldest sons had been sent down to England to act as hostages for the long drawn out repayments on James's ransom. Two who had a special grudge in this respect were the king's elderly uncle Walter Earl of Atholl whose son David had died after ten years as a hostage in English captivity, and David's orphan son, Sir Robert Stewart. They blamed the king not only for letting David die in prison but also for taking away some of their properties and for not confirming a third earldom, Strathearn, which Walter had been given but was not allowed to pass on to his heirs. These grudges were further amplified by the idea that as descendants of Robert II's second, and legally less reproachable wife, they had a better right to the throne of Scotland than James who was descended from his first and allegedly incestuous marriage. Such speculation was made more interesting by the fact that Atholl had been one of James's most vociferous supporters in his efforts to wipe out the Albany dynasty, thus eliminating another entire family, except for one fugitive in Ireland, who still stood between the aging Atholl and the throne. Similarly a quarter of a century earlier he had perhaps played a part in the killing of David Duke of Rothesay at Falkland, in which case he was following a very long-term strategy, perhaps encouraged by the gypsy who allegedly prophesied that one day he would win the crown. It is possible too that Atholl resented the death of his other son, Alan Stewart who had been killed in royal service at the Battle of Inverlochy against the MacDonalds.

To add to all of this, the fact that James and his Queen Joan had been quite slow to produce healthy male heirs gave the Atholl Stewarts further encouragement in their devious plot. James had four daughters but the first of his twin sons Alexander died and the other, James, was at this stage an apparently delicate six-year-old at Stirling. What is more, any descendants of Robert II through his daughters were excluded from the succession by his law or tailzie passed in 1373.

The disgruntled Atholl Stewarts teamed up with another disgruntled baron, Sir Robert Graham who had been a fellow student in Paris of John Stewart, one of Robert II's bastards. Graham had further grievances, for his cousin Malise Graham was one of the hostages still held in England because James had stopped making the ransom repayments. As one of the rare Scots who had a university education he set himself up as a one-man opposition in the Scottish parliament accusing the king of 'cruel tyranny' and extortion. Against this background the regicide plot was hatched. Young Sir Robert Stewart, as a potential king was the keenest of all the plotters. He was the chamberlain and on guard duty when the royal couple were spending the night of 21 February 1437 at the Dominican Priory in Perth. He was thus able to let the other murderers into the priory. Famously the king had asked for the main drain of the cloisters to be blocked so that he could play real tennis without the balls being lost. When he heard the conspirators breaking in he raced to hide himself in the drain hole while Lady Douglas gave him time by placing her arm in the bolt of the inner door. But because the drain had been blocked it was impossible for him to escape. He was soon found and stabbed to death. The queen 'fled yn hir kirtill'.

The murderers made their escape but were captured eventually with the help of John Gorm Stewart of Garth, a grandson of the Wolf of Badenoch. The gentle Queen Joan made sure that the regicides died slowly: the elderly Walter Stewart of Atholl was ceremonially crowned with a red hot crown to emphasise his delusions of grandeur, the two Sir Roberts, his grandson and Graham, both after excruciating torture which they apparently suffered with resignation.

Thus with the help of one granddaughter-in-law, the proliferating sons and grandsons of Robert II had almost obliterated each other or died other violent deaths. James I had been the first Stewart king to take his role seriously and for all his errors of judgement had worked hard to be a professional with a deep sense of responsibility. But his very enthusiasm had led to impatience, a tendency to make the ends justify the means and stubbornness in the face of disagreement that led to his downfall. It was the basic problem of feudal monarchy that if the senior barons became too powerful, the king would try to reduce that power, but in doing so might well cause the whole system to collapse. There had to be mutual trust and respect. Nor is there any evidence that the king was using this policy for the benefit of the ordinary people of Scotland, though Ranald Nicholson suggests he did have 'a genuine concern for the poor'. The self-destructive streak evident in James was to reappear in a number of his successors. Yet perhaps the one key vice of this undoubtedly very able man was impatience.

Despite the self-decimation of the main royal Stewart dynasty at this time there had still been a proliferation of minor offshoots all descended from the original family at Renfrew, perhaps fifty branches by this time and multiplying at the rate of about two per generation. These included the Stewarts of Angus, Bute, Darnley and Lorn. The latter had been founded by John Stewart of Innermeath (or Invermay) with its castle on a rocky outcrop near Forteviot and had held Red Castle on the Montrose coast, as well as Durisdeer since 1328. In 1388 his grandson married Isabel MacDougal of Lorn and took Dunstaffnage Castle over from her with the lordship of Lorn. Their elder son Sir Robert (–1449) kept it in the family by marrying Albany's daughter Joanna, while her sister Marjorie was married to the Campbell chief, so the Stewarts were building up a nexus in the west. These Stewarts spawned the Stewarts of Appin who appear later in our narrative (see pp.105, 119, 193) as Sir Robert's son, known as John the Leper (1400–63) had a illegitimate son, Dougal who was their progenitor. Sadly John the Leper was to be murdered at the instigation of the Campbells so that they could in turn snatch the Lordship of Lorn. Meanwhile more important was Sir Robert's son James Stewart, known as the Black Knight of Lorn who two years after the murder of James I married his widow Queen Joan, so her two husbands confusingly shared the same name. Joan was ostracised from court after this marriage and removed from control of her son's education. She produced three more children, two earls and a bishop before she died in 1445 when her exiled husband forfeited all his lands. All three children were to play a significant part in the reign of their half-brother James II and his successor.

The Darnley branch of the family as we have seen first came to prominence with Sir John, the third of the fine Stewart/Stuart generals who appeared in this period. A son of Sir Alexander Stewart of Darnley he shared in the Scots victory over the English at Baugé, was made Count of Evreux in 1427 and helped broker the marriage of King James's daughter Margaret to the future King Louis XI. One of his grandsons later became Earl of Lennox while the younger John Stuart (–1469) remained in France as Seigneur d'Aubigny, became captain of the newly formed *Garde Ecossaise* which saved the king's life at La Reole in 1444 and generally proved its worth. John's son Bernard or Berault Stuart was later to become a marshal in the French army.

In addition to the new branches of the dynasty founded by spare sons there were also numerous new connections created by the daughters. Already two Macdonald chiefs, the Lords of the Isles and two Earls of Douglas had had Stewart brides. In addition there was Egidia Stewart, wife of de Meynes, founder of the Menzies, another Egidia, the lovely wife of William Douglas of Liddesdale, the Flower of Chivalry and Jean Stewart, wife of the Earl of Crawford, so as long as the family had any sense of corporate loyalty the tentacles ran deep. The behaviour of the Atholl branch had of course been a notable exception.

Without question James I had proved that the Stewart dynasty could produce abler kings than either his father or his grandfather, but sadly impatience and a touch of arrogance had invalidated some of his best efforts to strengthen the monarchy in Scotland. As Michael Brown puts it 'the thirteen years of his active rule transformed the goals and expectations of Scottish kingship.' Yet like three of his next four successors his greatest mistake was the failure to sense a threat to his own life at a time when his sons were far too young to take over, thus exposing Scotland to the rapacity and corruption of a regency.

Chapter Four

James II of the Fiery Face

The most miserable of James I's children was without question Margaret (1425–45), perhaps Scotland's first female poet and the neglected wife of the paranoid Dauphin Louis (1423–83) the Spider. He was made to marry her at Tours in 1436 when he was thirteen and she was eleven and he seems to have taken an instant dislike to her. But then he hated his father and most other people. Life for the '*dauphine melancolique*' was made more miserable by the famine and plague which hit France the next year. Despite several attempted coups against his own father, Louis did not succeed him on the French throne until 1461 by which time he had driven his childless bride to an early grave. She died the same year as her mother Joan Beaufort in 1445 and was buried in Thouars.

The fortunes of the other five daughters of James and Joan varied but all like Margaret were treated as bargaining counters in international diplomacy, so were lucky to find any personal happiness. Isabella was married in 1442 to Francis Duke of Brittany and so returned to the original home of the Fitzflaalds. Two years later her sister Mary married the Admiral of Burgundy, Wolfaert van Borselen of Campvere in Holland, a connection which was good for trade but not for Mary who died relatively young. Annabella was engaged soon afterwards to Count Louis of Geneva but after ten years of finishing school in Turin her marital value had declined and the wedding was called off. She reluctantly went back to Scotland to marry a local baron who also in due course annulled their marriage, perhaps for the same unspecified reason. Eleanor (d.1480) was sent to France to take over from her unlucky elder sister Margaret as a new wife for the unprepossessing Dauphin Louis, but she escaped that fate and in 1449 married Sigismund (1429–96) the Habsburg Archduke of the Tyrol, known as 'the Simple' due to a series of expensive military campaigns in which he lost most of his Swiss estates. Famous for his superb silver coinage and immaculate armour he was given

Carinthia as compensation and a home in Vienna where he became a champion performer at the tournaments, also later building castles on the Kuchelberg in what is now Italy. He did not father any heirs with either Eleanor or his second wife, but he did acknowledge fourteen bastards. In 1465 he sent some new artillery to his nephew James III, perhaps after Eleanor's half-brother Buchan's visit in 1465 (see p.96) the same year.

James I's least marriageable daughter, known as Dumb Joan, was also sent to France, but no husband was found for her there so she was palmed off on Douglas of Dalkeith who was promoted Earl of Morton as his reward for taking on the literally speechless princess. Their affectionate joint tomb can still be seen in the delightful Church of St Nicholas which they built at Dalkeith.

The single male child surviving to take over the throne of Scotland, James II (1431–60) was six when his father was murdered, so he had to survive a turbulent eleven year minority before he could assume power. Born at Holyrood he had a worrying babyhood because of the early death of his twin brother and was supposedly weaned on almonds at Stirling. His early childhood was at Albany's splendid new castle of Doune and he was made Duke of Rothesay at the age of four. Even at that stage the red birthmark on his face which led to his nickname seemed to augur an unpredictable temper.

Scotland now faced the first in a series of debilitating royal minorities, this one lasting more than ten years. As if in reaction to the authoritarian policies of James I, the barons were even more unruly than before and successive regents failed to keep order. The first was Archibald Earl of Douglas (also Duke of Touraine, one of the titles given to his father as a result of French service) who had been very badly treated by the dead king, despite being a first cousin – his mother Margaret was a daughter of Robert III. Though he had had a distinguished military career in France he was now older and in poor health so he made an ineffective ruler. He failed to protect the Queen and her young son who were imprisoned in Edinburgh Castle by its corrupt constable William Crichton. They escaped but then fell into the equally unscrupulous hands of Crichton's opposite number at Stirling Castle, Alexander Livingston. Both were ambitious men of lesser rank promoted by James I in his efforts to offset the power of the magnates, but both were to create a vicious rivalry over the next few years.

Meanwhile several other feuds were underway with Douglas unable to stop them. Alan Stuart of Darnley who had taken over command of the Scots troops in France from his brother John, came back to claim the Earldom of Lennox but was murdered by Sir Thomas Boyd, who was in turn murdered by Darnley's brothers, Alexander Buktuth Stewart and Matthew Stewart. This feud in turn spread to the Isles from which the MacDonalds sent a party of troops to massacre the Colquhouns at Luss on the edge of Lennox territory. Meanwhile the regent Douglas died and soon afterwards his two teenage sons were executed without proper trial after being lured to the Black Dinner at Edinburgh Castle by Crichton – the serving of a bull's head was a sign of impending death.

The nine-year-old king was made to watch the grim proceedings in Edinburgh Castle: to judge from his subsequent leniency to Crichton and his hatred of the Douglases he cannot have been too horrified.

It was against this background that Queen Joan, looking for a protector whom she could trust, married Sir James Stewart, the Black Knight of Lorn, quite a lowly rank for a queen dowager. This gave the Livingston faction the excuse they needed to snatch her son young James and finish his education without her influence. More extroverted, less intellectual, a more typically war-minded young man than his father, he became fond of jousting, fighting and hunting as was fashionable for men of his rank and background, as one French writer put it 'a valiant chevalier'.

The ten years 1439–49 were dominated by the power struggles of the Livingston and Crichton families, with other groupings like the Douglas faction switching loyalties on a regular basis while each tried to win control of the young king as he approached his coming of age. For the last four years of this period he was without any contact with his mother, who died in 1445. As his majority came closer a marriage was arranged for him that was designed further to improve the commercial interests of Scotland in the Low Countries and at the same time acquire a much needed continental dowry (60,000 crowns) for the Scottish treasury. The chosen bride was Mary, daughter of Duke Arnold of Guelders, a small semi-independent duchy lying across what is now the Dutch-German frontier on the Rhine. Mary of Guelders (1430–63) was the first non-British queen of Scotland since the reign of Alexander III. She was transported to Scotland by a fleet of fourteen Burgundian warships and the young couple were married in 1449. Mary was crowned queen soon afterwards.

James's first major task as an adult was to purge the Livingstons, now a much expanded family who had come out of the minority period well ahead of the other factions in the struggle for power. By this time they had gathered seven of the top governmental posts including governorships of five of the main royal castles: Doune, Stirling, Dumbarton, Dunoon and Methven, plus the constableship, the chancellorship and a marriage for one of their daughters to the new Lord of the Isles. James immediately had two of them arrested, Alexander and Robert. They were quickly tried and hanged before being beheaded, while two more of the family were imprisoned. All their rapidly acquired wealth was even more rapidly purloined by the king who needed it to help pay the expenses of his new Flemish queen. The pattern of the Livingstons, a rapid rise to power from humble beginnings followed by a sudden fall and the elimination of most if not all of the family, was to become a familiar one in future royal minorities in Scotland.

To some extent James II's action against the Livingstons was a retrograde step, for his father had been trying with difficulty to reduce the power of the landed magnates and place more reliance on salaried officials from the lower ranks. This was indeed the only effective way to distance the power of the monarch from that of the nobles and all the royal Stewarts were to follow that path. Yet James II's deviation from that policy can be understood given the corruption of the two families concerned and the indignities he had suffered during his minority.

James's next confrontation was to be much more in line with his father's strategy and much more difficult. It was to last five years and was with the Black Douglases who had become the largest landowners in Scotland with the possible exception of the king himself. Under the three Archibalds, the 3rd, 4th and 5th earls of Douglas, they had risen to command an army of up to six thousand retainers, such as the one that the 4th earl took to La Rochelle to fight the English in 1421. The Crichtons had eliminated one branch of the family at the Black Bull dinner but allowed an even more ruthless one to take over under James the Gross who brought Avondale and numerous other properties into the Black Douglas fold. Before his death he had made sure that three of his five sons would be earls, one a bishop and one a lord, and that the eldest would marry the Fair Maid of Galloway, his nephew's daughter who brought Galloway back into Black Douglas ownership – it had been the dowry of Margaret Stewart, wife of the accident-prone 4th earl and grandmother of the Black Bull victims.

So in 1450 the stage was set for a battle between the over-mighty subject William the new Earl of Douglas who was twenty-three and his fledgling king who was still not twenty. James made the first move and did so in a slightly under-hand way by waiting until Douglas left the country to attend the papal jubilee in Rome. He was entertained there most lavishly and received almost royal atten-tion when he visited England on his return journey six months later. The English at this point had just lost Normandy and Henry VI, ten years older than James, was still trying in vain to assert his authority.

The Scottish chancellor and chief adviser to the King James was the wily Sir William Crichton who had organised the judicial murder of the 6th earl only ten years earlier at the infamous Black Dinner. This remarkable survivor regarded the Black Douglas as unfinished business and an underhand attack while the victim was out of the country bears his hallmark. So the six month absence was exploited to besiege and destroy some key Douglas castles, particularly Craig Douglas in Yarrow. After this royal demonstration of strength there was no follow-up and Douglas when he returned from Rome was in no immediate position to retaliate, so there was an uneasy truce in which he was mollified by being recognised as Earl of Wigton.

The truce did not last long. Douglas decided to demonstrate his immunity from royal control by committing a series of atrocities against his enemies. John Sandilands, a relation of the king's was murdered. John Herries was hanged by Douglas for daring to object to handing over money to him. Similarly, Maclellan of Bombie was ostentatiously beheaded at Threave Castle for complaining about Douglas' arrogance and this in spite of a royal warrant for his release being pre-sented there by Patrick Grey. Then finally Douglas made a botched attempt to kidnap the Chancellor William Crichton.

James II was understandably furious at the deliberate flouting of his authority but to increase his alarm there were rumours that Douglas had made a secret defence pact with the Lord of the Isles, the Earl of Crawford and his own three brothers. James summoned Douglas under safe-conduct to negotiate with him at Stirling Castle. Douglas, despite the memory of the Black Dinner at Edinburgh Castle, accepted the safe conduct at face value and came. At twenty-two and twenty-seven respectively the king and his guest were still both relatively inexperienced. It is suggested that both ate and drank well, so that the subsequent discussions became even more heated. James lost his temper and stabbed Douglas. The wound was not fatal – 'in the collar and down the bodie' says the *Auchinleck Chronicle*, but the king's companions soon followed up the first thrust and Douglas was pushed from a window down the cliff. It had not been premeditated murder any more than that of Comyn by Bruce, but it was murder nonetheless and made more shameful by the safe conduct.

In this dangerous battle against the Douglases James had sought the help of some poor but ambitious members of his own family. Two of them shared the guilt of the earl's murder by using their own daggers to help finish him off. One was John Stewart (1424–95) the son of the Alan Stuart of Darnley who had been murdered in 1439 after his return from France. Immediately after his father's murder he was consoled by being made Lord Darnley and later (1473) won the prize his father had tried for in vain, the Earldom of Lennox. Having shared in the blame for the Douglas murder he went on to have a useful career during the next two reigns and was the ancestor of the man who married Mary Queen of Scots. He was governor of Rothesay Castle in 1465, in 1475 helped suppress the MacDonalds when he was Lieutenant of Renfrew and Ayr, then in 1482 he was Warden of the March. He stayed loyal to James III in the Lauder crisis (see p.98) but switched sides to join his rebel son at Sauchieburn in 1488. He was given charge of Dumbarton Castle in 1489 but then in his old age rebelled against James IV and was besieged in his own castle.

The second Stewart who was one of the stabbers at Stirling also received his reward. This was Andrew Stewart of Morphie (c.1420–87) bastard grandson of Murdoch Duke of Albany who had been executed by James I. Andrew came home from exile in Ireland and England in 1440 and received the former Black Douglas lordship of Avondale with Strathaven Castle as his share of the booty from the 1452 murder. Soon after that he was made chancellor and in 1468 negotiated the marriage settlement of James III which resulted later in Scotland acquiring the Orkney and Shetland Islands. He was to stay loyal to James III right to the end of his career. He died leaving no heir except his grand-nephew, another Andrew Stewart of Morphie.

Two other Stewarts who became loyal helpers of James in his time of need were his half-brothers John and James. John Stewart (1440–1512) was the eldest son of ex-Queen Joan and the Black Knight of Lorn. For his services during the Douglas crisis he was given the former Black Douglas lordship of Balvenie by James in 1460, ten years later also becoming Earl of Atholl. He too fought in the Isles campaign of 1475 and tried to stop the MacDonald civil war of 1481 that ended with the Battle of the Boody Bay. In a complicated fashion he remained loyal to James III on and off until 1488. The other half-brother James 'Hearty' Stewart (1441–1500) who had married the heiress of Auchterhouse was given Trabreath for his services to James II and was envoy to Burgundy in 1459 and again to their sister Eleanor in Austria in 1465, perhaps to help rescue her from a difficult marriage, perhaps to beg for the artillery which in due course Archduke Sigismund sent to Scotland. James was made Earl of Buchan in 1470 in the next reign, but fell out with James III in 1482, was exiled, stood by James III in 1488 but plotted against his son and ended up trusted by no one. It was one of the illegitimate children of this James who founded the Stewarts of Traquair.

In addition to these two half brothers there was the king's very distant cousin Sir William Stewart of Garlies (d.1479) one of the king's favourites and highly likely to have been involved in the destruction of the Black Douglases.

Thus at least five Stewarts benefited by supporting James II when he had endangered his own crown by the rash stabbing of William Earl of Douglas and at least two of them were involved in finishing off the Douglas by tossing him out of the castle window. He in turn benefited from their support then and afterwards. They doubtless represented five of the votes which helped exonerate the king from murder charges when parliament was asked to make judgement. The Red Douglases, jealous of their Black cousins would also vote for the king's acquittal as would all the bishops. To make sure, the king awarded seven new peerages, including ones to both the Boyds and the Lyles who had originally come from Shropshire to Scotland with his ancestors. As Christine McGladdery puts it 'James had a remarkable aptitude for redeeming potentially dangerous situations.'

Meanwhile James had rid himself of one Black Douglas brother only to be faced by the remaining four. Even the advantage of causing them temporarily to lose Galloway – held by William only through his marriage to the Fair Maid – was removed when the new (and last) Black Douglas Earl, James, won leave to marry his widowed sister-in-law. As it turned out, neither of the brothers managed to make her pregnant, though strangely her third husband John Stewart of Atholl, the half-brother of James II, succeeded many times.

James, the university-educated last Black Douglas Earl had been bishop designate of Aberdeen but was a champion in the tournament lists and with his three brothers had as many troops at his disposal as the king. After his brother's murder he charged with them ostentatiously into Stirling dragging the infamous safeconduct behind his horse. The king had to look on helplessly but smuggled his pregnant queen Mary of Guelders away to St Andrews where she gave birth to the future James III.

James Douglas meanwhile was let down by his most important allies. The Earl of Crawford was beaten in a skirmish by the Earl of Huntly and the Lord of the Isles started a rebellion to help him, but did so without any clear strategy. Douglas however was in no hurry as he had needed a truce with the king while he gained papal permission to marry his ex-sister-in-law. Once his territory was back to its maximum size again he could renew his quest for revenge.

The situation was now complicated by the start of the Wars of the Roses in England. King James II's mother Joan Beaufort had been part of the Lancastrian connexion so he sided with the Red Rose party, while Douglas therefore found a natural ally in the House of York. Thus, King James chose a moment to resume his attack on the Douglases when Henry VI had briefly recovered his sanity and the Yorkists were on the run. Using his expensive new artillery, including almost certainly the famous cannon, Mons Meg, he began to besiege Black Douglas castles, starting with the massive Abercorn on the shores of the Forth. He captured it, executed the defenders and destroyed the castle, thus challenging Douglas to make an appearance. Douglas brought an army to confront the king at Carron, but hesitated at the sight of the royal standard and lost support, including that of previously loyal supporters like the Hamiltons. The humiliated Douglas fled to his White Rose friends in England, but his three brothers put up more of a fight.

The two younger Black Douglas brothers, the earls of Ormond and Moray together with the Douglas Lord of Balvenie were defeated by a royal force under their arch-rival the Red Douglas at Arkinholm. Moray was killed outright, Ormond wounded and later executed, Balvenie escaped to England. Threave Castle was besieged and captured. Numerous Douglas estates were put to the torch leaving many of the ordinary people starving. This was the opportunity for the king to confiscate the entire Black Douglas inheritance except for the Fair Maid's land in Galloway – she had refused to follow her husband to his English exile and eventually took as her third husband the Stewart Earl of Atholl, the king's half brother.

Some of the Douglas titles James could now redistribute amongst his loyal allies, particularly the other Stewarts and the Red Douglases. The revenues he largely kept for a much-needed contribution to his own expenses. It was a major victory only marred by the fact that James did not apparently foresee that in future times the Red Douglases would become just as great a menace to his dynasty as the Black had been. James the 9th and last Earl of Douglas spent the next thirty years in fruitless plots for his restoration and was to die a sad old man at Lindores.

Meanwhile the Wars of the Roses so weakened the English that they gave James II an excellent opportunity to recover lost ground in the Borders. The first major success was the recovery of Berwick which had been in English hands almost permanently since the days of Balliol. The acquisition of this important trading port helped boost the Scottish economy and there was a general improvement in prosperity. With his increased wealth King James felt able to send embassies to Italy, Spain and Denmark. There was a new trend in church-building with fine collegiate churches being put up by the Scottish magnates, Rosslyn by the Sinclairs, Dalkeith by the Douglases, Kilmun by the Campbells, Bothwell by the Douglases and Lincluden by Margaret, the Stewart Duchess of Touraine. Literature took a step forward with works like the *Buke of the Ordre of Knechthede* written in Rosslyn.

But the crowning achievement of James II's short reign came at great cost. According to legend there had been a prophecy that a dead man would capture

Roxburgh, the last great castle still held by the English north of the Scottish border. James was accompanied to the siege in 1460 by all the Scottish magnates in a rare display of cooperation, including even John MacDonald Lord of the Isles. A special salvo was ordered to greet the arrival of Queen Mary on a visit to the besieging army. King James 'mair curious nor became him' stood too close to an artillery piece which blew up and sent a splinter into his thigh. He died at the age of twenty-nine, his army captured Roxburgh and the crown was left to his eldest son James who was eight.

A stone in the grounds of Floors Castle marks the spot where James died of his wound beside the huge fortress which was shortly captured and demolished. James had ruled effectively for little over ten years, half of which had been spent on his feud with the Black Douglas. His achievement in clearing the Borders of English troops was considerable, as was his elimination of the Black Douglas, but all his successes were put at risk by that final piece of rashness which cost him his life, leaving Scotland to yet another minority. It also left a young and very unhappy widow, Mary of Guelders, the mother of six small children.

There is no evidence to suggest that James II's period of rule was damaged by the fact that he got away with murder. But there are signs that he could have achieved more than he did by a more consistent policy which could have gradually eroded the power of the Black Douglases without leaving a vacuum, particularly one which might be filled by their Red cousins. That flash of temper in 1452 might easily have cost him his throne, but for the support of his two half-brothers and other Stewarts who formed the core of the anti-Douglas party. Without their backing in parliament it might also have brought about the end of his dynasty. So might his impetuosity and ostentation in standing so close to his still highly unpredictable artillery eight years later. As McGladdery sums him up he was a man of 'shrewd calculation, fierce personal pride and strong passionate temper.'

Chapter Five

James III and the Hanging Bridge

James III was crowned in 1460 at Kelso at the age of eight, so it would be ten years before he could legally wield power. The government of Scotland was to be rendered toothless by a third successive period of minority in three reigns. Even when James took over executive power, he was to use it in an erratic, self-indulgent manner which in due course after two decades caused his rule to come to an abrupt end. Both fratricide and parricide were to be themes of this extraordinary reign by a Renaissance man in a country where there was still no Renaissance. Sadly, however talented he may have been, he seems to have had the respect of neither of his two brothers, his two sisters nor his eldest son.

The first three years of his minority were dominated by the widowed Queen Mary who was not yet thirty, but pretty, able and ambitious, both for her children and herself. She was aided by her husband's two half-brothers, the two Stewarts of Lorn, shortly to become earls of Atholl and Buchan. After a brief period of mourning she offered asylum to her fellow ex-queen, Margaret of Anjou, the wife of Henry VI of England who was deposed by Edward IV (1442–83) in 1461. The Yorkists had finally ousted the Lancastrians. Henry after his deposition had the grace to surrender Berwick formally to the Scots as a token of his need for help. Mary also went on a visit to France to meet King Louis XI who had been married to her husband's sister Margaret of Scotland. She even organised an invasion of Northumbria to support her Lancastrian friends but this came to nothing.

Queen Mary showed her religious devotion by endowing a large new church and hospital at Trinity College Edinburgh and another at Stirling, but her private life began to deteriorate. She was using her undoubted charms to assist her ambitious schemes, seducing, it seems fairly certain, at least the Duke of Somerset and Adam Hepburn of Hailes, the ancestor of Bothwell (starting what became in his family a traditional penchant for royal widows) with whom her affair was so blatant and her political plotting so convoluted that even her most loyal allies began to desert her. Within four years of her husband's death when she was still in her early thirties she too died.

The king, by this time aged thirteen, was handed over to Bishop Kennedy of St Andrews who had sheltered the pregnant queen during the Douglas crisis of 1452. Kennedy who was a grandson of Robert II, had had a long apprenticeship for the brief eighteen months of supreme power which he was now to enjoy. He thrust all his considerable talents into the administration and maintenance of justice which was restored to the reasonable standard achieved by the two previous King Jameses at their height. Then sadly he succumbed to overwork and died. The remaining three years of James III's minority were dominated by a new upstart family, the Boyds of Kilmarnock, descended ironically from the same Breton stock as the Stewarts. Their bid for power depended on having control of the young king, so they kidnapped him. Sir Alexander Boyd, constable of Edinburgh Castle and riding instructor to James snatched him on a hunting trip near Linlithgow. Lord Boyd, his elder and more devious brother then extracted the regency from the captive prince and got rid of the remaining members of the Kennedy family who still had positions of power.

Having used his younger brother to do the dirty work and made no arrangements for his legal exoneration, Lord Boyd now dispensed with his services and proceeded to the full enjoyment of his new powers. He mortified young James by arranging the marriage of his own son to the king's sister, Mary, but she does not seem to have been too unhappy. The main achievement of the Boyd regency was to finalise the arrangements already started by Andrew Stewart Lord Avondale for James himself to marry Margaret of Denmark (1457–87) at Holyrood in 1469. He was eighteen and she was twelve. The pledges for her dowry were the islands of Orkney and Shetland, still at that time part of the Danish kingdom, pledges which King Christian (1428–81) must in all honesty have known then that he would have to surrender, for his finances were in chaos. Besides he had bigger prey in mind such as Sweden and Norway. The Boyds would undoubtedly have preferred to see the cash rather than the islands, as they would have taken their percentage and used it to bolster their regime.

Margaret was the first of three Stewart consorts to come from the Oldenburg dynasty: James VI also took his queen from them, and Queen Anne her husband. More recently Edward VII had an Oldenburg wife, Alexandra, and the Greek branch of the Oldenburgs provided Queen Elizabeth II with her consort, Prince Philip.

The marriage ceremony heralded James III's arrival at adulthood and he was now in a position to wreak revenge on the Boyds who had kidnapped him and run his life for the past three years. Just as the Livingstons had been purged in 1440 so now it was the turn of the Boyds. The son, now Earl of Arran had barely disembarked on his return from Denmark with the new queen when his wife the princess Mary came to warn him of his impending arrest, the first example of one of the king's siblings defying his wishes. The young couple fled to Denmark and Arran's father Lord Boyd also made his escape, leaving behind his brother the luckless Sir Alexander Boyd to be beheaded for treason. The Boyd lands around Kilmarnock were confiscated for the benefit of the crown and to help support the new Queen Margaret who was also given Doune Castle and Linlithgow as 'a token of James's great affection and love.' The two uncles, John who now became Earl of Atholl and James, soon afterwards Chamberlain and Earl of Buchan, returned as his chief advisers along with Andrew Stewart of Avondale.

Given the chaotic nature of his minority it is not surprising that James III's education as a potential king had been spasmodic. The Boyds had shown no interest in training him to rule since it was to their advantage to keep him away from state affairs as much as possible. But it would be unfair to blame them for the fact that he became interested in subjects other than statecraft. After all not everyone is fascinated by politics, and it is the fate of hereditary monarchs to be thrust into many roles which they may not particularly enjoy. Unfortunately James III was in many respects ahead of his time, for he had the interest in music, dance and the visual arts which we expect to find in a Renaissance prince, yet the Renaissance had barely started in Italy – James was the same age as Leonardo de Vinci – let alone Scotland. He also had an unfashionable flair for business, perhaps inherited from his Dutch-German mother.

The problems of Scotland stemmed mainly from an unruly and greedy set of landed magnates who were in need of a strong king to keep them in order, and James had little stomach for that. He did to some extent pursue the now traditional policy of his dynasty by employing men of lower birth as bureaucrats and courtiers, but his choice of men like his architect Thomas or Robert Cochrane and the musician William Roger seemed totally outrageous to the average, semi-literate Scottish earl, even if this may have been exaggerated by subsequent propaganda. James was very fond of hunting – he had a valuable collection of falcons and greyhounds – but apart from an interest in artillery he was not passionate about soldiering in the way expected of a late medieval monarch. So he had difficulty in commanding the respect of his nobles, something he still needed if he was to exercise real control over his kingdom. It was also an accepted fact at this time that kings needed to make regular appearances in all corners of their kingdoms in order to assert their authority, and James showed great reluctance to travel. Thus murder and robbery were 'sa common throughout the hale realme' and went largely unpunished. Besides the legal system was still chaotic and James was little interested in any effort to codify the laws of Scotland or establish clear standards of justice.

The king's entrepreneurial flair certainly enabled him to make money. He developed his own profitable salt-pans and had his own private merchant fleet serving the leather trade, remarkable achievements for a man of his background. But he was also a very big spender as was Queen Margaret who came from a German-Danish family renowned for its extravagance. His own wardrobe bill was just marginally lower than hers. Then there was the considerable expenditure on new palaces at Linlithgow and the new great hall at Stirling, with building work of a very high standard supervised by Cochrane. The hiring of foreign musicians, his purchases of tapestries, falcons, dogs and fine horses all contrasted with the now fairly grim state of the Scottish economy. Even with the restoration of the port of Berwick trade was depressed. The Edinburgh wool trade was stagnant and even the advent of a new herring industry in the North Sea failed to halt the decline.

The contrast between the apparent self-indulgence of the court and the problems of his subjects began to undermine the king's popularity. As Pitscottie put it 'He lovit solitarness and desynit mair in musik and polliecie of begin nor he did the government of his realme.' He admitted to being 'wondrous covetous' and there were rumours of his 'big black kist' full of gold, though a frantic search for it after his death proved to be in vain.

The combination of courtly extravagance and poor trading conditions had for some time been leading to a shortage of gold and silver in Scotland which meant that too few coins could be issued to meet the needs of normal business. James III's response to this crisis was ineffective. He issued a bastardised coinage, halfpennies with copper and silver which could easily be forged and were of uncertain value. James made matters even worse by minting extra copper coins on the sly to boost his own coffers. This caused a further crisis in 1472–3 when the country faced virtual bankruptcy. In Nicholson's words 'There can be little doubt that in this matter as in law enforcement James III constantly failed to fulfil the expectations of his parliaments' or as the author of *The Lion and the Mouse* put it he

Takis no labour
To reull nor steir the land nor justice keip
Lyis in lustis, slewth and sleip.

James also like his father and grandfather before him resolutely purloined the estates of recalcitrant barons and kept their revenues for himself. He already had those of the Boyds and later took the earldoms of Ross, March and Annandale. The big prize was Ross which came into his hands when talks with the English in 1474 brought about the leaking of the treacherous pact made twelve years earlier at Ardtornish by John Lord of the Isles with the English and the exiled Black Douglas. The ousting of the MacDonald from his earldom of Ross was managed by the king's cousin Andrew Stewart, Lord Avondale who as chancellor was one of the chief royal advisors. This was followed up on the ground by the king's uncle John Stewart Earl of Atholl who led a campaign to pacify the north west in 1475. He was further involved in preventing any resurgence of the Lordship of the Isles when he tried to mediate in the struggle between the Lord and his bastard son Angus Og in 1481, but was beaten by him in a skirmish at Lagabrad. He then borrowed some ships from the Campbells and kidnapped Angus Og's baby son, Donald Dhu, from the family home on Islay, handing him over for incarceration to the boy's grandfather, the Campbell Earl of Argyll, who kept him for decades in his prison fortress on Loch Awe. Not surprisingly therefore the following year Stewart of Atholl was in turn abducted by Angus Og from Blair along with his wife and all his treasure, but the raiding party was mysteriously struck down by storms and plague on its way back to Islay, so the Stewart prisoners were released unharmed. Angus Og was murdered soon afterwards but Donald Dhu was to spend most of the next fifty years as a prisoner.

Meanwhile the king's financial problems were not helped by the fact that his father-in-law Christian of Denmark predictably failed to pay over Margaret's dowry, so the Northern Isles were transferred to Scotland and while this brought in some revenue from Orkney and Shetland it was not immediately very significant. The acquisition of these islands was nevertheless seen as a useful achievement, particularly as at this time Orkney was a major agricultural producer.

Another area of ongoing bullion seepage from Scotland lay in the dues paid by the Scottish church to the papacy in Rome. This led to a triangular row between King James III, Pope Sixtus IV and Scotland's senior clergyman Bishop Graham of St Andrews. James objected to Graham being promoted by the Pope to the rank of archbishop because it gave him greater control over Scotland's other bishoprics and James wanted this for himself so that he could keep a grip on their considerable wealth. In this he was no different from most other European monarchs of the time. The unfortunate Graham eventually died in the dungeons of Loch Leven without ever being installed as Scotland's first official archbishop.

Meanwhile James did at least provide the kingdom with an heir and a spare, both called James (born 1473 and 1476) so that even if one died there should still be another King James. He seemed devoted to Queen Margaret; after her death he tried to have her canonised as a saint, though he was not immune to the less saintly charms of 'a whore called Daisie'. Some writers draw cynical conclusions from the fact that for several years James and his queen appeared to lead separate lives, the king in Edinburgh and Margaret with her son in Stirling, but others point to this as a precaution against possible coups. Surprisingly in 1482 she seems to have sided briefly with his brother when the king was imprisoned but then also took part in his release. So it is not easy to assess her true feelings.

Yet with all these difficulties it was to be in another area that James finally began to lose all support for his regime. It appealed to his vanity to play the game of empire-building and though he rarely strayed far from Edinburgh, James now began to pursue the illusion of overseas territories. There were three to which he had a vague claim and it suited some of his fellow kings to let him think so. There was the county of Saintonge in France which had been promised by the French to the Stewarts back in 1425 when the Scots were helping them resist their English conquerors (and the thought of keeping such a promise was purely theoretical). The second area was even larger: Brittany, where James's aunt, Isabella Stewart had been the Duchess but had left no sons. The third was Guelders in western Germany where there had been a coup against James's grandfather, the Duke. How realistic any of these acquisitions might have been is questionable, but James's confidence as a player on the European stage may well have been boosted by the gift of some fancy new artillery from his uncle (by marriage) Archduke Sigismund of Tyrol.

On the strength of his new ambitions James had the Scottish crown remodelled as for an emperor and embarked on a policy of seeking English backing. At the same time as part of his icon-building programme he had the emblem of the thistle adopted by the dynasty and incorporated into its image. Unfortunately his policy of cultivating friendship with the English ran counter to the ideas of many Scots lairds, particularly those who made their living by raids over the border. So it was around this time that the anti-English party in Scotland hired the poet Blind Harry to write a patriotic epic about William Wallace.

The negotiations for rapprochement with England focussed on two potential marriages: one between James, Duke of Rothesay, the king's heir, and Cicely the daughter of Edward IV; the other was between the Scots king's sister Margaret and an English earl, Lord Rivers. In some respects the idea heralded what turned out to be the real match of young James with a later king of England's daughter, Margaret Tudor, so in his way James III might be given some credit for setting in motion the union of the crowns. All seemed to go smoothly until early in 1479 when Margaret embarrassingly gave birth to a bastard daughter, fathered by her secret lover, Lord Crichton. It was the second time that James had been let down by one of his sisters and it sabotaged his entire imperial policy.

Norman Macdougall sums up James unsparingly with 'a clear portrait of an aloof, overbearing and vindictive ruler whose dangerously exalted concept of Scottish kingship astonished his friends and eventually proved a godsend to his enemies.' It was in this atmosphere that James now fell out with his two brothers, both of whom had shared at least tacitly in the anti-English stance of most of the Scottish nobles over recent years, and both of whom James clearly suspected of plotting. Thomas Cochrane, the king's favourite, sought to exploit these suspicions and found a witch to persuade the credulous king that the supposed plots were a reality, particularly when an astrologer was brought in to corroborate. Both the royal brothers were arrested in midnight raids on their homes.

Alexander Duke of Albany (1454-85) the elder of the two had been brought up for four years in Guelders, suffered capture by pirates but kept out of politics until frustrations with the king began to surface in the mid-1470s. His image was much more that of the traditional medieval knight than King James. After being locked up in Edinburgh Castle he made the king look foolish by escaping down a rope made of sheets. His image was further enhanced when his servant broke a leg when jumping down the last bit of rock and Alexander gallantly carried him all the way to Leith on his back. He then defied the king from his castle in Dunbar before heading to France to prepare for a couterattack. At the same time he divorced his first wife, a Sinclair who had given him four children and married a rich French heiress, Anne de la Tour in the Auvergne.

The younger of the brothers, John Earl of Mar (1457–79) – 'young , fair, lustie and broad was he' – who was accused of dabbling in witchcraft was taken to Craigmillar and later died mysteriously at the Canongate, apparently after being bled by doctors in his bath. It was suspicious enough to add the label of fratricide to those already applied to James III. Whatever the truth of what may at least partially be anti-James propaganda he had only himself to blame.

Meanwhile the inevitable confrontation with the English gradually approached and in 1482 for the first time James had to summon his feudal host. Given his increasing unpopularity it came with great reluctance and once assembled at Lauder showed great truculence. The main grievance now was against the king's favourites, men despised by the Scots nobles but given wealth and titles by the king. Top of the list was Cochrane, the architect, who according to some versions had been created Earl of Mar. But the entourage also included Foulis the harpist, Brown the lute player, Bennet the hunch-backed fiddler, a tambourine-playing Moor, William Roger the musical squire, Stobo the court poet, Leonard the shoe maker and Torpichen the fencing master. Roger had been given the lordship of Traquair but that had been taken away in an earlier confrontation and given to James Stewart, Earl of Buchan, the king's uncle, who later passed it on to his illegitimate son.

The events at Lauder have been described often enough although the details remain far from certain and the accounts are clouded by propaganda. The Red Douglas leader, Archibald Earl of Angus may have deliberately provoked the crisis by raiding across the English border so that Richard Duke of Gloucester (later Richard III) was forced to retaliate, meaning that the Scottish army would have to be called up and thus creating a critical mass to confront the king. Famously Douglas played the role of Bell-the-Cat and achieved his brief moment of fame by leading a lynching party to execute Cochrane, Roger and some of the other favourites. The king was arrested and taken back to Edinburgh under escort, to be warded apparently with his wife's approval in the castle by his two Stewart uncles, the earls of Atholl and Buchan who thus had the whip hand along with the governor of the castle John Stewart of Darnley. Just why the two uncles had fallen out with him is not clear, but at some point he had arraigned them with an incident from ten years earlier, also to do with holding Edinburgh Castle. So they were among his opposition at Lauder as were the two Darnley Stewarts, John soon (in 1488) to be rewarded with the earldom of Lennox and Matthew his heir, but not Andrew Stewart of Avondale who now after twenty-two years lost his job as chancellor.

Meanwhile the army disbanded, making no effort to save Berwick when it was attacked by the English under Richard of Gloucester. The town was never recovered by the Scots. Nor did the Scots make any effort to stop Gloucester from occupying all of Edinburgh except the castle which he had no siege equipment to deal with.

Alexander, Duke of Albany, described by Macdougall as 'a feckless conspirator' now made his comeback, proclaiming himself with English backing as King Alexander IV of Scotland by right of his brother's misconduct. He was supported initially by his two uncles, Atholl and Buchan who now also wanted preferment for their brother Andrew Stewart to be Archbishop of St Andrews. Such an appoint-ment needed a payment to the Vatican of 6,000 duckets to be collected from the citizens of Edinburgh. But the rebel lords had no real desire to replace the weak James with his stronger brother, particularly when he was backed by the English, so Alexander was bought off by the return of all his confiscated estates round Dunbar. The two Stewart uncles Atholl and Buchan changed sides after saving face by undergoing a staged siege of Edinburgh Castle and Buchan went into temporary exile in England which became his base for future troublemaking. John Stewart of

Darnley, the governor of the castle took it upon himself to release the king from captivity and Albany's last real chance of displacing his brother vanished when his chief ally, Edward IV of England died in 1483. He was to make one final ill-judged attempt to invade Scotland along with the exiled Black Douglas, but they were easily defeated at Lochmaben. Albany returned to France, died soon afterwards in a tournament and was buried in Paris, but his new French wife had produced a son who was to make an impact on Scotland thirty years later (see p. 112–3).

Remarkably James III was given another chance. Things in Scotland were improving because the plague had passed and food was more abundant. Angus and his fellow rebels were keeping a low profile. The death of Edward IV of England and of his two young sons in the Tower was soon followed by that of his brother Richard III. Henry VII the new Tudor king was playing a cautious hand. But James's newfound authority did not last for long. Three misfortunes hit him just when his confidence was on the mend. The first was the death in 1487 of his wife Queen Margaret aged only thirty, whom in spite of the competitive ministrations of the pliant Daisie, he missed very deeply. The second was a messy and drawn-out row about the riches of Coldingham Priory in the Borders. The third was the king's declining relationship with his own elder son, a problem largely of his own making.

James, Duke of Rothesay, the teenage heir was beginning to rebel against his father's perceived lack of the manly virtues most admired in the middle ages and his preference for things musical and artistic. The humiliations of Lauder and the fact that James might easily have lost his position as heir if Alexander of Albany had been allowed to become king must have caused him considerable alarm. Then on top of this the king began to show obvious favouritism towards his younger brother and namesake the younger James, who had just been unnecessarily promoted from Earl to Duke of Ross. The jealousies and insecurities of Rothesay were worked on by those around him, particularly the governor of Stirling Castle where the young duke was housed. The governor was one of the plotters trying to win the revenues of Coldingham who needed James as a figurehead for their proposed coup against his father.

This time the king's two old uncles, John Stewart of Atholl and James Stewart of Buchan who had returned from his English exile, sided with their nephew against their grandnephew. The devious Buchan played a particularly prominent role by urging the king to break a truce he had made with the rebels and organising his armies at Blackness Castle by the Forth ready for a showdown, though by the time of the actual battle he had been handed over as a hostage. He and his brother Atholl who now led the army's front line were suspected of creaming off some of the bullion from the king's black war chest. Thomas Stewart of Innermeath was also on the king's side (though he later died fighting for his son at Flodden) but the Stewarts of Lennox were with the Duke of Rothesay against his father.

Two armies both under the Royal Standard met at Sauchieburn (Sauchinford Burn), very close to the neighbouring battle site of Bannockburn. The king's army had initially been larger than his son's but the balance shifted. James, wearing the sword of Robert the Bruce, was apparently confident but in the end his army was easily defeated by the now larger one supporting his son. James III, according to various conflicting sources, fled the field. He was thrown from his horse near Crichton's Mill and stunned. He apparently asked for a priest and was sent a man dressed as such who stabbed him to death. He was still only thirty-six. The murderer according to some versions was Lord Grey, who had been one of the Lauder rebels, but others suggest that against the specific orders of young James the king was killed in the mopping-up operations following the battle. James was buried beside his wife at Cambuskenneth Abbey, Stirling, where their tomb was many years later restored by Queen Victoria.

Thus all the sons of James II were dead and only the two feisty daughters survived. Mary, who had returned from her Danish exile in 1471, was now remarried as Lady Hamilton and making money as her brother had done out of the leather trade. Margaret, whose illicit pregnancy had caused such problems in 1479, now became the effervescent chief hostess for her nephew King James IV. Of the other Stewarts who had played a leading part behind the scenes under James III, Andrew of Avonside had died without a direct heir, the two old uncles Atholl and Buchan lingered on into the next reign as did the father and son Lennox who soon regretted their support for the new young king.

Ironically the Tudor dynasty which had just taken over in England had been helped significantly in its access to power by a group of Franco-Scottish mercenaries fighting at Bosworth under the command of another member of the Lennox family, Bernard or Berault Stuart, 3rd Lord Aubigny (1452–1508). Bernard had upheld the tradition of the Darnley Stewarts in letting their younger sons have their French estates at Aubigny and make a living as mercenaries in the French royal service. He rose to command the *Garde Ecossaise* and made his name as a teenager by helping to save the life of Louis XI of France at the Battle of Monthlery in 1465 just as he later saved the future Louis XII after a failed coup in 1496. He was made Castellan of Bois de Vincennes, Bailie of Berry and Captain of Harfleur, and then became count of Beaumont-le-Roger by marriage. He continued to prosper in Louis XI's wars with Burgundy until the paranoid king died in 1483. He soon afterwards made his first visit to Scotland to negotiate a renewal of the 'auld alliance'.

Then in 1485 came Bernard's opportunity to aid the destruction of Richard III of England at Bosworth, after which he took part with Ferdinand of Aragon in the capture of Granada from the Moors in 1492 (he may well have met Christopher Columbus at Santa Fe) and became a trusted general of Charles VII the Affable (1493–8) of France. Famed for his exceptional courage and his brilliance at spying out the land for ambushes he invaded Italy, captured Florence and, along with his ally the infamous Cesare Borgia, led the French to victory at the First Battle of Seminara in 1495. After some setbacks and despite chronic gout he was back fighting in Italy in 1499, this time for Louis XII when he drove the Sforzas from Milan in a three-week war, and then became its governor. At the same time he hired Leonardo da Vinci, who had just completed *The Last Supper*, as field engineer for his and Cesare's next campaign. He was welcomed in Rome by Cesare's father Pope Alexander VI and won a good reputation for preventing his troops from looting captured cities, only to lose it when his men committed dreadful atrocities at the capture of Capua. He defeated the Spanish army on Christmas Day 1502 at Terranuova near the heel of Italy, a victory which earned him the title of Duke of Terranuova, but he lost a second or third battle at Seminara, partly because his grandnephew John Stuart attacked the wrong target. He wanted to die on the battlefield but was persuaded to retreat and was later trapped at Angistola after which he spent some time in the dungeons of Castel Nuovo in Naples. Leonardo da Vinci was meanwhile packed off to entertain the French court at Amboise.

Bernard was accompanied to Italy by three of his Darnley Stuart nephews, one of whom, John Stuart of Darnley, the Seigneur d'Oizon (d.1567) later took over command of the *Garde Ecossaise*, fought in the Italian campaign but also spent three years in the Bastille (1544–7). He had saved Bernard's life at the Battle of Terranuova and later became his heir at Aubigny and Homme de l'Armes of France in 1505. His brother was William Stuart of Darnley, Seigneur d'Oizon (d.1543) who fought in Italy and a third brother was Bernard's son-in-law Robert Stuart (1470–1544), who ingeniously found a new pass over the Alps by using chamois hunters as guides. By aiding the French victory of Marignano and capturing Prospero Colonna at Villa Franca he helped conquer Milan again in 1515. Part of his reward was the cash to extend the magnificent Chateau la Verrerie near Aubigny which Berault had started with an audacious mixture of French and Italian styles. Its chapel was decorated with both the fleur-de-lys and thistles.

Robert Stuart later became a Marshal of France and, wearing the white doublet with crowned salamander, fought in 1525 at the disastrous Battle of Pavia under Francis I (1515–47). Like his king he was captured by the imperial army, but ransomed sooner, so that he became a viceroy and helped negotiate the king's release. His successor in the *Garde* was Matthew Stuart (1516–71) who was sent to France after his father's murder at Linlithgow and acquired the polish which later earned him both a half-royal bride (see p.122) and a pension from Henry VIII. When he left the *Garde* to go to England it so annoyed Francis I that he put Matthew's unfortunate brother John, also an officer in the *Garde*, into the Bastille for a couple of years. John, though not regarded as very astute, nevertheless rose through the ranks after his release and took part in France's capture of Calais from the English in 1558. He later encouraged his nephew Henry Lord Darnley in his pursuit of Mary Queen of Scots.

Bernard Stuart's victories in Italy had won him the titles of Marshal of France, Duke of Terranuova, Marquis of Giraccio, Governor of Calabria and of Milan. He later came to Scotland as ambassador to James IV in 1508 and a tournament was held in his honour in Edinburgh. The court poet William Dunbar was briefed to produce a special ballad for the old warrior, 'most strong, incomparable knyght, the fame of armys and the the flour of vassalaye' (*Ballad of Lord Bernard Stewart*). Soon afterwards he died in Corstorphine en route to a pilgrimage at Whithorn. He was buried in Blackfriars, Edinburgh. Other French Stuarts at this time included Alexander Stuart Lord of St Quentin who was put in charge of La Rocca in 1507, and John Stuart, Seigneur de la Mothe who was killed at Marignano.

Chapter Six

James IV of the Iron Belt

Ethnically speaking, James IV (1473–1513) was half German (the Oldenburgs of Denmark came from what is now Lower Saxony) quarter Fleming and quarter Anglo-Norman so all this perhaps accounts for the complexity of his character. It perhaps also explains his international outlook. He had seized the throne illegally from his father and presided over the battle which led to the old king's death. For this at least he seems to have had genuine feelings of remorse. Yet at the age of fifteen he showed no great impatience to take over the duties of power.

In many respects James was the ablest member of his dynasty to date and had many of the qualities of a hero king, though sadly also some of the vices. On the positive side he could leap into the saddle without putting a foot in the stir-rups, could speak six languages including Latin, Gaelic and English, was a keen tennis player, was fascinated by archery, played the clavichord, loved hunting in Glenartney and Glenfinglas, loved hawks, dogs and pretty women and had a charismatic personality. He was both generous to others and extravagant for his own delight, as well as ruthless and deeply religious.

After the death of his father at Sauchieburn he suffered feelings of patricidal guilt and condemned himself to wear an iron belt at least during Lent for the rest of his life. He would not ride on Sundays, ate fish on Wednesdays and Fridays and occasionally donned monk's clothing to join the friars at the Observantine friary at Stirling. He said two masses before all major occasions and made pilgrimages each year to the shrines of both St Ninian at Whithorn and St Duthac at Tain, albeit en route to the latter he passed the castle of one of his favourite mistresses.

His attitude to the church of his day was ambivalent; on the one hand he condemned its corruptions and was determined to lead a new crusade against the Turks, yet at the same time he was quite cynical in demanding an archbishopric for one illegitimate son and lesser ecclesiastical posts for several others.

At the same time he consistently increased the amount of money he extracted from the church so that along with similar increased exploitation of feudal dues he managed to triple the royal income without having to impose new taxes. Thus he was under little pressure to summon parliaments and rarely did so.

The Battle of Sauchieburn had achieved nothing in terms of settling Scotland. It was a victory of one faction of barons over another; the winners expected their teenage figurehead to be a pliant puppet in their hands, but did not have any coherent policy other than to pursue their own greedy ambitions without interference. So the first few years of James IV's reign consisted of a series of minor rebellions which simply gave him the experience to cope and the confidence to assert his authority. The first was by those two Stewart/Stuart stalwarts John Earl of Lennox and his son Matthew who had so far been his ardent supporters but were unhappy with their share in the spoils of victory. Most of those had gone to James's close associates the Homes and Hepburns. The Lennox pair produced the late king's bloody shirt or 'bludy sark' and under this banner held Dumbarton and other castles against the martyr's son. James brought the great cannon Mons Meg to the west and captured the Darnley stronghold of Crookston. Then he beat the rebels in a battle on the Moss of Gartalunane near Aberfoyle. Dumbarton was taken in due course and Lennox with his colleagues was let off with a warning.

Harsher treatment was the lot of the king's grand-uncle James Stewart Earl of Buchan who had been consorting with the English (his mother had been Queen Joan, the Beaufort so he had a close relationship with the Tudors) and he was driven deeper into treason. He had also been in harness with Archibald Bell-the-Cat, the Red Douglas Earl of Angus who had initiated the first deposition of the old king and as the largest land-owner in Scotland was still the biggest threat to the crown. James approached his castle of Tantallon with his artillery and Angus backed down. He accepted a deal in which he swapped some of his strategic castles near the border for other less important ones. By thus weakening his hold on his feudal retinue and scattering his estates over a wider area James did something to reduce his power. Then he promoted Angus to Chancellor to save his face and keep him part of the establishment. Stewart of Buchan on the other hand remained what Macdougall calls 'a compulsive conspirator' and was involved in a failed English plot to kidnap the king and his brother in 1491.

Throughout this time, James kept moving and this was a key difference between him and his father who had rarely ventured beyond Edinburgh and Stirling. Thus he stamped his authority on every area, at the same time conveniently extending the geographical spread of his mistresses.

James also soon showed a great interest in sea-power and the expansion of Scotland's modest navy which could now carry serious cannons. This was particularly relevant to the need to bring order on the west coast where the MacDonalds, under the Lord of the Isles had always been able to rely on their superiority at sea to elude capture even when they had been defeated on the mainland. Since John Lord of the Isles had lost the Earldom of Ross back in 1473 he had kept a fairly low profile but his bastard son Angus Og had regularly attacked areas on the mainland almost with impunity. As we have seen, after the abduction of his son Donald Dhu he attacked Blair, kidnapping John Stewart of Atholl, the man responsible. However in 1491 he was murdered by an Irish harpist in Inverness and was succeeded as semi-official leader of the MacDonalds by an even more violent pair, Alexander MacDonald of Lochalsh and James MacDonald of Dunyveg and the Glens (of Antrim). James IV and the Scottish parliament decided that since the Lord of the Isles could not control his vassals he should lose his status and he was made to abdicate his powers in 1493. This was the easy bit, as John offered no resistance, retired and died in obscurity, to be buried alongside his Stewart ancestors in Paisley Abbey.

There then followed a series of naval campaigns led by the king to bring the west coast of Scotland under his direct rule and thus consolidate his kingdom. The first in 1493 took him to Dunstaffnage which was by this time a Campbell stronghold and where he made peace with the two MacDonald leaders, Alexander of Lochalsh and James of Dunyveg. He knighted them both as a token of their absorption into his regime but this proved fairly ineffective. The next year with his fleet in the Firth of Clyde he created a base at Tarbert and captured the ancient MacDonald castle of Dunaverty on its own precipitous rock near the Mull of Kintyre. Yet almost as soon as he had set sail leaving a royal governor in charge, MacDonald of Dunyveg recaptured the castle by storm and hanged the new governor from its ramparts, supposedly within sight of the departing fleet. This huge insult was only avenged when MacDonald was inveigled into a trap by the bounty-hunting MacIains and handed over for execution.

The next year saw James conduct a third naval campaign, this time taking Ardnamurchan with its castle at Mingary, followed by landings on Tiree and Islay. A new royal castle was built in what was later called Campbeltown as a base for controlling Kintyre and the southern Hebrides. But after five years James was perhaps beginning to tire of his west coast adventures and to look for a larger stage on which to display his military prowess. So from 1499 he delegated the task to the Earl of Argyll with his Campbells for the west and the Earl of Huntly with his Gordons for the north. The Campbell was given a three year command based at the refurbished royal castle of Tarbert and together with Huntly began to marginalise the island and west highland clans. The MacIains and the MacGregors were almost wiped out. The only major setback was when the desperate MacGregors managed to snatch Donald Dhu, son of Angus Og, from his island dungeon and coordinate a serious come-back. But Scotland's new royal navy under Admiral Wood, who had already achieved considerable success against the North Sea pirates, was now able for the first time to deploy artillery against the island fortresses. Even remote Cairnaburgh Castle on the Treshnish Islands off Mull which had been used as a pirate base by the MacIains, was captured soon afterwards in 1506 as was Stornoway where Donald Dhu the phantom Lord of the Isles was finally retaken. The Dunad Commission that year began a process of converting the west from Celtic to Scottish law and similarly the church in the west was put under a strengthened bishopric based on Iona.

As the MacDonalds and their kindred clans found themselves pushed to the fringes of their former lands it was the Campbells who with the approval of Edinburgh moved in to replace them. Three more castles were rebuilt or fitted out as government bases: Stornoway on Lewis, Inverlochy at Fort William and Castle Urquhart on Loch Ness. Duncan Stewart of Appin, the builder of Castle Stalker in Loch Laich and a descendant of the last Stewart Lord of Lorn, was made Chamberlain of the Isles for his help throughout the campaign.

Meanwhile James IV had begun to dabble in English politics. Within a year of his succession he had been involved in Yorkist plots against Henry VII and these took a more serious turn when he was able to exploit the presence of Perkin Warbeck, a young hopeful masquerading as Edward V who had somehow managed to avoid being murdered in the Tower of London. Warbeck was given one of the James's cousins, Catherine Gordon, as a bride and treating him as if he really was Edward V, James organised a lavish tournament in which he himself suffered an accidental injury. This strategy ended in 1495 when after one failed attempt at kidnap by the rascally James Stewart, Earl of Buchan the unfortunate Warbeck was captured and executed by Henry VII. But James persisted with goading the Tudor and launched an attack over the English border in 1497 to collect what was traditionally called 'spear money'.

Now a headstrong twenty-four with reasonable experience of tackling semi-professional armies James ostentatiously challenged the English commander, Thomas Howard, Earl of Surrey to single combat as a way of settling the issue. It was during the Scots' siege of Norham in Northumbria that the Spanish ambassador Ayala who had been checking him out as a possible husband for the Spanish princess, made the fateful observation that James 'is courageous even more than a king should be, but is not a good captain because he begins to fight before he has given orders.' Surrey who sixteen years later was to prove James's nemesis, refused the offer of single combat, but James still managed to avoid a pitched battle with him which could, as it did in 1513, have proved to be disastrous. As it was he nearly drowned on his way back over the Tweed and founded a church there at Ladykirk to celebrate his survival.

The fact that he had got away with his invasion of England and suffered no retaliation from Henry VII perhaps gave James an inaccurately high estimation of his own military skills and a dangerous underestimation of the English. He came away with a seven year truce and agreement that he should marry the English king's nine-year-old daughter Margaret Tudor. As was usual in royal marriages she was a distant cousin through his Beaufort grandmother, so papal dispensation was required. This might not at the time have seemed more than a very good diplomatic match but it was in due course to turn out very much more than that and to take the Stewart dynasty to a whole new level of power and wealth.

James IV had not been without female companionship. Presiding at court was his feisty aunt Margaret Stewart, whose secret pregnancy had scuppered James III's pro-English plans back in 1472. James had met one of his first mistresses, Margaret

Boyd during the siege of Duchall back in 1489. She bore him the son Alexander Stewart who was later to become a brilliant scholar under Erasmus at Padua and was archbishop designate of St Andrews before dying at his father's side at Flodden. His second notable mistress was Margaret Drummond with whom he lived for a time at Falkland until she and her two sisters all died in 1502, perhaps of food poisoning, but in circumstances that gave rise to rumours of skulduggery. Food poisoning was nevertheless common enough in the royal palaces for as the court grew larger so did the number of hangers-on and after a few weeks residence at Falkland, Linlithgow or Holyrood the crude arrangements for sanitation became totally overloaded, with pollution of the water supply a natural consequence. Even James's policy of moving regularly round his kingdom, taking furniture, trappings and entourage with him, still ran the risk of illness from poor hygiene. The king himself was unusual for his age in occasionally taking a bath – even his royal cousin Henry in England wore a piece of fur to trap his body lice.

The third important mistress was Janet Kennedy, who had her own suite at Stirling Castle until she was obliged to move out to make way for the king's wife. As compensation she was given Darnaway Castle and the Earldom of Moray for her son by him, James Stewart (1500–44), destined to have a distinguished career in the next reign. Significantly, two of James's other mistresses were Stewarts: Isabel the daughter of his uncle the rascally Earl of Buchan, and Agnes, the daughter of Buchan's bastard son, Stewart of Traquair. Another of Buchan's granddaughters was the Janet Stewart who became a mistress of Henri II of France.

After a three year negotiation the wedding by proxy of the twelve-year-old English princess Margaret and the twenty-eight-year-old King James took place in 1502 accompanied by promises of perpetual peace between the two nations. James would get a substantial cash dowry and Margaret three castles. While he waited for his bride to arrive he ordered large quantities of cloth of gold for her bed of state and his horses, together with crimson and gold cushions, gold gowns and furs.

Eleven pages were fitted out in gold and blue. He also commissioned a replacement palace at Holyrood and went to meet her at Dalkeith with a lavish wedding party to follow. He sported a huge ruby on his black hat and gave Margaret a tame hart as a present. There was a five day pageant and feast at Holyrood with roast crane and other delicacies, fire-eaters, conjurers and rope-dancers. But despite all his efforts the new bride was homesick and uncomfortable. To make matters worse James still spent much time away with his mistresses and the first three children Margaret bore him before she was twenty all died in infancy.

James like his father began to nourish imperial ambitions. At this time European kings were all trying to raise themselves to the rank of emperor as an adjunct to their self-esteem. Three areas interested James: Guelders, the home of his grandmother Mary remained a possible dream acquisition just as it had been for James III; nearby Veere which had had a Stewart countess was also attractive and was one of the major markets for Scottish wool and dried fish, and finally his mother's home, Denmark where his cousin Johan (1459–1513) was now king and was having a perpetual struggle to keep control of his other kingdoms in Norway and Sweden. James organised his first foreign expedition to help King Johan in Denmark and then attempted to rescue his queen, Kristina, from Stockholm where the locals had risen against her. The Scots navy under the brothers Andrew and Robert Barton made its first voyage into the Baltic in 1507. Denmark along with France became part of a triangular alliance with Scotland which might at some point threaten the perpetual peace already agreed with England. For the time being the new pope Julius II was so impressed by James that he sent him a sword of state and golden rose (now in Edinburgh Castle).

This papal approval perhaps did not stretch to some of James IV's other activities. Like his father he had been trying to prevent the wealth of the Scottish church being creamed off by Rome. The power of St Andrews had been weakened by turning Glasgow into an archbishopric in 1492 with control of all the western sees. Then in 1497 the king put forward his younger brother James Duke of Ross aged twenty as the archbishop designate for St Andrews. When he died seven years later, still too young to be consecrated, he was replaced by the king's illegitimate son Alexander, at this point aged eleven, so that the king got his hands on the revenues. Bishop Andrew Stewart of Caithness was another royal appointee as was John Damien, Abbot of Tongland who was given the job simply because he was the king's tame alchemist employed in 1507 to discover the fabled elixir of life, the '*quinta essencia*'. This would-be scientist lost some credibility when he tried disastrously to fly from the battlements of Stirling Castle using wings made of feathers.

To justify his virtual nationalisation of the church in Scotland James encouraged a whole new cult of Scottish saints and the building of fine new collegiate churches at Seton, Lochwinnoch, Edinburgh and the Chapel Royal at Stirling. He also made clear his special devotion to the more ascetic orders and joined in the persecution of heretics. On a personal level he still kept up his annual pilgrimages to the shrines at Whithorn and Tain.

In his personal life however he was far from a saint. Despite a continued trade recession he was lavish in his courtly expenditure. On one night he lost £70 at cards - Matthew Stuart of Lennox was one of his regular card partners. Near starving peasants were ruthlessly cleared from the land. He expanded the number of Scottish burghs in a decade that saw both the first venereal disease arrive in Scotland and the first distillation of *aqua vitae* i.e. the water of life, *uisque beatha* or whisky. The royal tournaments were particularly ostentatious to fit the new image of James as a King Arthur or a Richard Lionheart, the crusader and he himself appeared in elaborate disguises. He was very liberal when his liberality would be noticed: to the mendicant friars, fools, falconers, musicians, the sick and insane. He gave every appearance of encouraging justice yet used it as a source of cash for himself and his grandiose schemes. He encouraged the cultural life of the court by patronising poets and scholars. Indeed there was a flowering of literature during his reign with poets like Robert Henryson, William Dunbar and Gavin Douglas, scholars like John Major and Hector Boece, and musicians such as

Robert Carver. James encouraged the first printing presses in Edinburgh to help further his nationalist propaganda.

James IV still however had his dreams of imperial glory. He built the new naval dockyard at Newhaven in 1505 and ordered massive new warships like the *Great Michael* which at 240 feet long was one of the strongest of its day and needed a crew of four hundred men. In this, his efforts were subsidised by Louis XII of France who supplied money, timber and skilled shipwrights. The ships were fitted with the latest cannons forged by imported French craftsmen who now toiled in the arsenals of Stirling and Edinburgh Castles. Such ships were not just to keep down the MacDonalds or the east coast pirates but were to justify his greater ambitions which now began to focus on leading a crusade against the Turks, a plan that perhaps began to crystallise after Archbishop Blackadder's visit to the Holy Land in 1508.

Then in 1509 came an event which changed the picture considerably, the death of James's father-in-law Henry VII at the relatively young age of fifty-two. As he was succeeded by his only surviving son, Henry VIII (1491–1547) who as yet had no children, the Scots queen Margaret Tudor suddenly became for a period the heir apparent of England, Ireland and Wales. This situation was to last for seven crucial years before Henry at last produced a daughter of his own, Mary (1516–58) and was made even more irritating for Henry by the fact that the Scottish royal couple produced a healthy boy in 1512. Henry was so disgusted that he would not even pass over to his sister their father's legacy to her. At the same time it must have given James a dream of fabulous new wealth and power just a single life away.

Henry VIII, though at eighteen half the age of his Scots brother-in-law, had imperial ambitions of his own, so more than mere genetic rivalry was soon evident between the two of them. On the one hand Henry in the mode of many earlier English kings wanted to recover some wealthy tracts of France such as Aquitaine. James on the other hand was now less interested in territory but wanted desperately to be the leader of a glorious crusade against the Turks. His cousin Johan of Denmark was on his deathbed; Louis XII of France was entangled in a short-lived conquest of Italy in which a number of the French Stuarts played a significant part. Henry VIII was still too young, so James felt that he alone should be recognised as Europe's premier leader and the natural choice as commander of the coming crusade against the aggressive Selim the Grim of Turkey.

An unfortunate series of events led gradually to the peace with England being less than perpetual. First in 1511 there was an unofficial skirmish between a Scots fleet under Andrew Barton, supposedly sent as a privateer against the Portuguese, and an English one under the brothers Edward and Thomas Howard which met them unexpectedly in the Channel. Barton was killed and two Scots ships captured. It was a mixture of misunderstanding, farce and tragedy.

Next James succumbed to some flattering suggestions from Louis XII who was desperate for allies in his vain attempt to hold onto his Italian conquests against a coalition of England, Spain and Austria. In return for possible help against the English he offered James two tantalizing rewards: support of his claim for the crown of England and massive French assistance once James set off on his crusade. It was too much for James to turn down.

Meanwhile Henry VIII had lost face in a failed raid on Guienne and was determined to make some gains. The French added to his frustration by seizing Navarre. In May 1513 the Scots navy was mobilised for an attack on England if Henry attacked France. In June 1513 the French were defeated by Henry's allies at Novara in Italy and Queen Anne of France sent a personal appeal to James to come to France's aid by making an attack on England. The Scots bishop Forman was offered a French archbishopric for persuading his king to undertake the attack.

James not only agreed to the request but for some reason decided on a two-pronged attack, thus dividing his forces. His fleet with his best guns and gunners under Andrew Wood and the Earl of Arran was sent to annoy the English by attacking them in northern Ireland. The Scots army was summoned to meet for a cross-border raid down the east coast. Meanwhile an unofficial Scots raid led by the Homes had ended in humiliation not far from Flodden, so there was potential loss of face for the Scots unless this was avenged.

The pace of events now accelerated. James left Edinburgh to join his army on 19 August. Three days later he was over the border attacking Norham Castle which was captured within a week. At the same time unknown to James the main English army under Henry had captured Thérouanne some twenty-five miles inland from Boulogne, a serious blow for the French. James captured another three English border castles. The English commander in the north, Thomas Howard, set out from his base at Pontefract, with an extra thousand men going by sea to the Tyne. Howard had almost humiliated James back in 1489 and again had attacked the Scots fleet under Barton two years earlier, so he had the psychological edge when as a mere earl he challenged a king to meet him on the field of battle on a fixed day, 9 September. James accepted the challenge, dug his army into a good position and waited with chivalrous naivety for 9 September, turning down his gunners' offer to destroy the Twizel Bridge as he wanted a fair fight with the English. Howard on the other hand exploited the delay to sneak between James and his route back to Scotland.

None of this need have been disastrous for the Scots. The numbers on both sides were about even, around 20,000. The Scots still had the better position. But now the weapons differential began to take effect. With Scotland's best guns and gunners away with the fleet, the Scots artillery at Flodden consisted mainly of cumbersome siege cannons which could not quickly be moved on rough ground or easily re-trained and aimed. The English had lighter artillery which was much more flexible and with it their skilled mercenary gunners rained such fire on the Scots that they were forced to leave their defensive position and attack the English over uneven, boggy ground.

In the next stage of the battle a second weapons differential took effect. The Scots infantry relied for close combat on pikes over 17ft long which suited a tight formation on flat ground. The English had 9ft halberds which could be used much more flexibly. Finally the Scots barons with heavy armour and big swords could cope with short battles but not long ones, so if their first efforts failed they soon became too tired to fight. Matthew Stuart Earl of Lennox who had for some reason been given joint command of the right wing along with the Earl of Argyll, died beside his colleague trying in vain to stop the highland contingent from running away. Such was the mixture of human error, lack of planning and a bit of bad luck which led to the comprehensive Scottish defeat at Flodden. In a few hours James IV threw away all the good which he had achieved by the strengthening of his dynasty and the Scottish kingdom.

The body of James IV was found apparently under a pile of others, dragged off to Berwick and later buried without any of the promised ceremony at Richmond. He was barely forty. His wife was twenty-four and his son James was one. With him died many of the nobles of Scotland including his bastard son Alexander Stewart, the archbishop designate, Matthew Stuart Earl of Lennox , young Andrew Stewart of Avondale, Alexander Stewart of Garlies and James Stewart of Minto.

Few historians have questioned the overall qualities of James IV as king but there is the irritating conundrum of why he undertook an unnecessary war against the English and whether after a military career that had been mainly to do with suppressing his own rebels he had the expertise necessary to fight troops with continental experience. Mackie's verdict is 'fearless but ultimately stupid', Nicholson's 'shrewd, occasionally devious' and Macdougall's that 'James was simply pursuing an anti-English policy which was widely popular with his own people, which started well with his capture of Norham and might on a better day have ended successfully.'

James IV had at least succeeded where his forbears had failed: he had eliminated any serious rivalry to his own authority by over-ambitious barons or undisciplined clans. He had been able, unlike both James I and James III to lead an army into battle, but by succumbing to vague dreams of glory, lured by false promises and paying too little attention to the pragmatic needs of war he had thrown everything he had worked for away.

> But now they are moaning on ilka green loaning
> The Flowers of the Forest are a' wede away.

Thus the king who had dreamed of leading a European crusade died in what should have been no more than a minor skirmish and ironically having employed an alchemist to find the secret of eternal life and even to fly he had been killed not very gloriously by a better equipped army led only by an English earl.

Not all the Stewarts were privileged to throw their lives away in such glorious gestures as did James IV. In 1499 one George Stewart had been employed at 1s per day to clear Edinburgh's plague-ridden streets of bodies, a job that would almost certainly have led to him catching the dreaded disease himself.

Chapter Seven

James V and Self-Destruction

In many respects the life of James V (1510–40) who was crowned in the Church of the Holy Rude at Stirling in 1513 was the most depressing of all the Stewarts. He was an infant of barely eighteen months when his father was killed at Flodden. His mother Queen Margaret bore a posthumous son for the dead king, but he died before he was two. Perhaps because she had become a widow at the young age of twenty-four, and perhaps because her first three children all died as infants, Margaret was a very indulgent mother to James and spoiled him, yet added to his sense of insecurity by rapidly throwing herself at a replacement husband. Partly due to her poor choice of men James became a political pawn in the hands of successive regents whose main aim in life was to exploit him for their own ends and to prevent him from developing the kind of character that would make him a strong king. To this end they did their best to corrupt him and thwart his education.

Yet whether it was his unorthodox upbringing or some genetic fault that ultimately weakened his character it is now impossible to tell.

Initially Margaret did her best, but with early widowhood followed by the birth of an ailing baby, she could not have found it easy to maintain her position as regent. Her eight years of marriage to James IV had often been times of humiliation for he had ruthlessly made use of her to produce an heir but then often left her to consort with his many mistresses. For the sister of Henry VIII this was hard to take. Now freed from the dominant personality of such a charismatic but older first husband, she emerged from his shadow to look for personal happiness even though the will of James IV had stipulated that she should no longer be regent if she remarried. Her choice of second husband was impetuous: Archibald Douglas (1489–1557), Earl of Angus. The new chief of the Red Douglas faction was only nineteen, handsome, vain, ambitious and unreliable, but Margaret Tudor seems to have been besotted with him. In their brief marriage they produced a daughter, Margaret, who married Matthew Stuart (1516–71)Earl of Lennox so that Margaret was not only the grandmother of Mary Queen of Scots but also of Henry Darnley, the coupling that two decades later resulted in James VI having a double dose of Tudor blood in his veins.

The unofficial regency of Margaret aided by her new husband did not last long and was against the terms of her first husband's will. The Scots parliament soon found a candidate with superior claims. This was John Stuart, Duke of Albany (1484–1536) eldest son of the boy king's uncle Alexander Duke of Albany who had himself acted as regent after the coup against James III in 1482 and who had briefly claimed the throne himself as Alexander IV. Born and brought up in France, he had just added to his French properties – he was already Count of Auvergne and an Admiral of France – by marrying Anne de la Tour, his first cousin, as his second wife. On the continent his career prospects were excellent – he had Lorenzo de Medici, head of the Florentine banking family as his brother-in-law, and was on good terms with King Francis I of France, Pope Leo and the Emperor Maximilian. He had helped in the capture of Milan as a teenager in 1499 alongside the famous Marshal Bernard Stuart and two years later took part in the international crusade against the Turks after which he was shipwrecked and rescued by a Venetian ship.

The question arises therefore as to just how appealing it was for this French Stuart to be the Governor of Scotland, when even the throne itself probably offered poorer pickings than his rich lands in France. For a brief period between the death of his cousin James IV until the birth of the latter's posthumous son the Duke of Ross, he was next in line, and again after the latter's early death, but the role of wicked uncle adopted by the earlier Duke of Albany did not suit him. He seems to have accepted the task as a duty rather than an honour, found the work frustrating and was reputed to toss his expensive hats into the fire in exasperation.

Albany arrived in Scotland in 1515 and immediately ran into difficulties when Margaret refused to hand over the young king to his care. Albany had to besiege Stirling Castle to gain control of the boy. If nothing else, the siege had the effect of showing Margaret what a poor choice she had made in her second husband, the fickle Angus. He deserted her in her time of need and soon acquired a mistress in the shape of Janet Stewart of Traquair who bore him a child. Not only was Margaret still nursing the ailing Duke of Ross, the current heir to the throne, but she was pregnant with the first child of the new marriage. She now found herself losing not only her political power to Albany, but both of her sons. The elder she was not to see again for two years and the younger she never saw again – she accused Albany of having him poisoned.

Albany was governor of Scotland for nearly nine years and by no means incompetent. The Scots barons, led by the embittered Angus, circulated bad propaganda about him, recalling his father's attempted betrayal of Scotland to the English back in 1485, ironic since Angus was himself in the pay of Henry VIII. Albany succumbed to an error of judgement in organising small ineffective raids against the English as he felt obliged to keep up the anti-English alliance. This was made the more complicated by the fact that Margaret was using her brother's help to intrigue against him and trying to recapture the boy king, even if it meant taking him to England. Albany also surrendered to his own ambition by deserting his post on several occasions to visit his lusher pastures in France, taking time off for example to lead a French attack on Naples in 1525, and fighting alongside other French Stuarts of the *Garde Ecossaise* in the disastrous Battle of Pavia. During one of these absences in 1524 Margaret managed a counter-coup with the aid of James Hamilton, Earl of Arran (1477–1529) who as a grandson of James II was himself not far from the throne. But Arran and his adherents were beaten by the Douglases in an Edinburgh street battle known as Cleanse the Causeways.

Meanwhile the boy king was developing into an elegant youth with long reddish hair and blue-grey eyes. Ethnically speaking he was the most British king of Scotland for some generations, since of his four grandparents one was the Anglo-Welsh Henry Tudor, the second his wife Elizabeth of York, the third the half-Flemish James III and the fourth the Germano-Danish queen Margaret. As an infant he had notionally been second in line for the English throne, as it was not until 1516 that Henry VIII had his first daughter, Mary. Young James had a smattering of Latin and French but was the first Scots king to have no Gaelic. He played the lute and could sight-read music; enjoyed riding and hunting but occasionally displayed bouts of bad temper. At twelve he knifed a porter at Stirling Castle for refusing to open the gates for him.

In 1526 his situation worsened. Albany had been manoeuvred by Margaret and her brother Henry VIII into a rash winter invasion of Northumberland which ended in failure. This gave the Scots barons a good excuse for declaring him unfit to continue and soon afterwards he returned to France. He remained heir to the Scots throne until his death at his castle of Mirefleurs near Clermont in 1536, but left no children of his own to continue that branch of the Stuart line.

Margaret Tudor had meanwhile divorced Angus and rushed into yet another unsuitable marriage. Her new husband was another Stewart, her young bodyguard Henry Stewart of Avondale (1495–1553 later Lord Methven) whom 'she employed more freely than wisely' and who had helped her and Arran regain control of the king in 1524. This was a marriage seen by her peers as even less suitable than that with Angus, particularly as Henry was twelve years her junior and scandal spread about her 'amorous propensities' or what Fraser called 'ungodlie living'. Even her brother Henry VIII who was just developing as a serial monogamist was shocked and ceased to support her. She retired to her castle at Methven.

Without English support Margaret's power base was too weak for her to hold on for long. It was now the turn of her ex-husband, the fickle Earl of Angus, who had managed to escape from the prison in France to which he had been sent by the Duke of Albany. Though officially now one of four alternate guardians for the king he effectively made himself the sole regent by refusing to surrender the boy to his three colleagues. One attempt to rescue the king was mounted in 1526 by his friend John Stuart Earl of Lennox (–1526), but it was defeated at Manuel near Linlithgow. The young king was told that he would be killed before the Douglas would let him be taken by any other faction, so the boy acquired a most virulent hatred for his former step-father. The unfortunate Lennox was murdered soon afterwards, probably by Sir James Hamilton of Finart, an Arran bastard who made himself notorious as a freelance hit-man, first for the Douglases and later for the king himself. Finnart had visited many of the latest fortresses in France and brought back ideas for improved fortification of Scottish castles which he was soon to put to good use.

The main objective of Angus now that the king was a teenager was to thwart his escape and to prevent him from learning too much about kingship in case he tried to assert his own authority. So the boy's education was abruptly halted and replaced by a regime which sought to undermine his character by plying him with money, exotic clothes, hunting trips, gambling, drink, wenches and other temptations. The government was packed with Douglases and for nearly three years Angus managed to maintain his position as effective ruler of Scotland. But it could not last. Eventually in 1528 James at seventeen was wily enough during a stay at St Andrews to lure his current minder, Douglas of Parkhead, into organising a short hunting expedition at Falkland. James escaped from the palace at night dressed as one of his own servants and sought sanctuary at Stirling Castle. From there with the support of his mother and the anti-Douglas faction he announced that he was taking over the rule of his country. Angus fled first to his huge castle at Tantallon and when James and his artillery approached he headed for the English border.

As king the first priority for James was to restore the royal finances which had been depleted by years of corruption and chaos. The task was made easier since the church was a more vulnerable target than it had been in the past. This was due to the fact that there was widespread panic in Catholic circles at the rapid spread of the Reformation since the launch of Luther's *Ninety-five Theses* just eleven years earlier. Pope Leo X was already alarmed by the beginnings of religious rebellion in England where Henry VIII soon afterwards began pressing Cardinal Wolsey to help him divorce Queen Catherine. Scotland's first major reformist Patrick Hamilton had already been preaching so successfully in St Andrews that he had been driven briefly into exile. By a strange quirk, Hamilton was in fact a cousin of King James, for his mother Catherine Stewart was an illegitimate half sister of the Duke of Albany. When the charismatic preacher returned to Scotland in 1528 he was arrested by Archbishop Beaton and became the first Scot to be burned at the stake for his beliefs, a punishment which did much more to encourage than discourage the mood for religious change. So it was against this background that James was able to assert his authority over the Catholic Church in Scotland and extract from it at least a portion of the money he needed. Among his aides in this activity was William Stewart of Minto (1479–1545) who was bishop of Aberdeen where he built the King's College Library.

His other potential source of quick cash was to look for a bride with a large dowry, but the first candidate, Mary the daughter of Henry VIII appeared to be part of a plot to absorb Scotland into the English empire, so he dismissed the idea. In the meantime he indulged himself with a range of mistresses, the longest-lasting being Mary Erskine. She bore him a couple of sons who were later found rich sinecures in the church. At one point he thought of marrying her, changed his mind to let her marry someone else, then changed it back again and tried to get her a divorce. In modern parlance he also had a penchant for a bit of rough and earned a reputation for wandering the streets at night in disguise looking for adventure, a theme romantically expanded by Sir Walter Scott in his *Lady of the Lake:*

> Yes Ellen when disguised I stray
> In life's more low but happier way
> Tis under name which veils my power
> Nor falsely veils, for Stirling's tower
> Of yore the name of Snowdon claims
> And Normans call me James Fitzjames

Under his favourite aliases as the Gudeman of Ballengeich (the street below Stirling Castle) or the Knight of Snowdon (a district of Paisley) James would join in hunting thieves, help beggars and on one occasion had a vat of beer thrown over him by a serving maid so that he could seduce her in the steaming puddle. It was this kind of behaviour which led John Knox, at this time still a student at St Andrews to write later about the king's debaucheries 'most vicious we shall call him.'

In the end it was several years before James made serious efforts to secure an appropriate match. After being rejected by the King Francis I of France as a suitor for his delicate daughter Madeleine, James had settled on Marie, daughter of the Duke de Vendome. However on seeing Madeleine while he was in France he pressed her father to change his mind and eventually got his way, helped by his ambassador David Beaton (1494–1546, later Cardinal). A royal wedding in Notre Dame with a dowry of 100,000 livres did much to enhance his image. The king's illegitimate half-brother James Stewart, Earl of Moray acted as Lieutenant General of Scotland while he was away in France. Sadly, just as her father had predicted, Madeleine only survived the wedding by a few months, even though James made the effort to build a hospice for her at Balmerino.

By this time in his mid-twenties and conscious of his need for a legitimate heir James was quick to replace Madeleine and arranged for the new cardinal David Beaton to negotiate for a rich widow, Mary of Guise (1515–60) whose husband the Duke of Longueville had recently died. In 1538 James married his much more robust second queen by proxy in France. The organiser of this event was William Stewart of Minto, Bishop of Aberdeen who had also acted as his ambassador to England. Mary was forced to leave behind her three-year-old son as part of the contract, but was treated to a forty day celebration at St Andrews once she arrived in Scotland.

The third major source for adding to the royal treasury was in the confiscation of lands belonging to errant barons and in this area too James was active. The most obvious examples were the Red Douglases who now lost everything just as their Black cousins had done seventy years before. James made a habit of having senior lords imprisoned for no specific reason, particularly if they had a Douglas connection. Even the sister and brother-in-law of the exiled Angus were most harshly treated, the sister Lady Glamis burned at the stake on a trumped-up charge of witchcraft and her husband Campbell of Skipness imprisoned in Edinburgh Castle until he died while trying to escape. Another Douglas agent called Forbes was executed as was the vicious Hamilton of Finnart who had for a while resumed his hitman role under a new master, the king. Even such a normally pro-government figure as the Earl of Argyll was deprived of half his lieutenancy in the west and had a spell in prison to emphasise the king's power. Thus rather like his great-grandfather James I the new king acquired a reputation for abusing the rights of his subjects and snatching enemies by stealth rather than open confrontation. This was exemplified in his treatment of the border freebooter Johnnie Armstrong and his followers in 1530. Normally there might have been little sympathy for such men, but the way James invited them to a meeting at Langholm, under trust, and then arrested and hanged them without proper trial recalled both the behaviour of James I at Inverness and James II when he invited the Black Douglas to Stirling. It was this unpredictable treatment of his feudal inferiors which gradually undermined trust in James V and meant that some of his more powerful subjects became reluctant to support him. This was made worse by the fact that he later dismissed his more competent generals, replacing them with lower-ranked men such as Oliver Sinclair whose abilities would not outshine his own. So long as affairs went smoothly he would get away with it, but in a crisis his position would be weak.

If these three strands to his policy – attacking the church, acquiring a prestigious bride and undermining the aristocracy – were originally dictated by a desire to replenish the Scots treasury, they also became part of a general strategy to centralise the monarchy and enhance its image. In this he had a lot in common with other Renaissance monarchs but perhaps did not have quite the mental stamina required to pull it off. Besides, like many of them including his uncle Henry VIII he was as much concerned with show as with reality. Thus having made all this effort to sort out the royal finances he embarked on lavish expenditure. His staff of three hundred included a Keeper of the King's Parrots. The rebuilding of palaces at Falkland, Linlithgow, Stirling and Holyrood continued with exquisitely painted ceilings, carved medallions and elegant halls. The fortifications of royal bases like Blackness were modernised. In one hunting party laid on for him by his cousin John Stewart Earl Atholl (1507–42) he is recorded as having personally killed six hundred harts and hinds before a feast of crane and swan in a specially constructed mini-palace which was burned to the ground when he departed. Similarly Queen Mary at great cost imported pear and plum trees from France, and brought in qualified stone masons, doctors, apothecaries, armourers and tailors from Lorraine to improve life at court. She even optimistically imported gold miners to help tap the vein which had been discovered at Crawford Muir.

The ultimate extravagance was another restyling of the Scottish regalia with the symbolism of empire rather than mere monarchy on the new crown and sceptre. Perhaps James had in mind the fact that because of his Tudor mother only three individuals stood between him and the English throne if Henry VIII should die: the princess Mary Tudor, Elizabeth (born 1533) still classified as a bastard and one sickly boy, Edward (born 1537).

The other area where James showed imperial pretensions was in Ireland where his interest was a dangerous provocation to his uncle. Meanwhile to boost his dynastic image he gave a pension to William Stewart (1481–1550) his former tutor and a descendant of the Wolf of Badenoch who was to write a poetic history of Scotland lauding the achievements of the Stewarts.

Similar signs of extravagance were shown when in 1540 he went on his naval expedition with twelve gunships to bring royal control to the Northern Isles and Hebrides. He had gold plate and an orchestra on board to impress the clan chiefs whom he visited. His landing on Skye was commemorated by the renaming of the town Portree (Port of the King). At least some political advantage was gained by this expedition as hostages were taken for the good behaviour of the clans and parliament was told to erase the concept of the Lordship of the Isles. The MacLean and MacDonald chiefs were both arrested and royal garrisons put into Dunaverty and Dunyveg. He even commissioned the first hydrographic survey of the west coast, all worthwhile projects in terms of his consolidation of the Scottish monarchy.

On Twelfth Night 1540 at Linlithgow James and his queen watched the performance of a daring new play *The Thrie Estaitis* written by his herald and court poet Sir David Lindsay in which he himself was probably the model for the character King Humanitie and his mistress for Sensualitie. This satire on the corruption of the church would cause him mild amusement but not serious grounds for concern, as no doubt was the case when his other court poet William Stewart demanded the 'banishment of falseheid and ignorance.' For James had made sure his five illegitimate sons were appointed to good livings in Perth, St Andrews, Melrose, Coldingham and Holyrood. George Wishart, the second of the pioneering Scots Protestants had recently been sacked from his post in Montrose Grammar School and sent into exile for explaining the New Testament from the Greek. John Knox was still working as a notary in Haddington and had yet to make his move. But reform of the church was not of any interest to James V other than hypocritical demands that the clergy should be less corrupt. His friend Cardinal David Beaton had just succeeded his uncle, James Beaton, as Archbishop of St Andrews and himself needed several extra benefices to maintain his lavish lifestyle which included a resident mistress.

Meanwhile the downfall of James V was approaching. It is possible that a hunting accident in 1537 had damaged his health and there is the theory that his mixture of charisma and depression reflected a hereditary strain of porphyria which was observed later in a number of his descendants right down to George III. It was also suggested that he was haunted by guilt over his execution of Hamilton of Finnart who had done some of his early dirty work. He was depressed perhaps both by the death of his first wife and of the first two sons produced by his second, Mary of Guise. His grandiose architectural schemes had failed to satisfy his insatiable vanity and his conspicuous levels of consumption must have placed a considerable strain on the economy. All these circumstances added to the fragility of his mental state as at the age of thirty he approached the first real test of his kingship, a confrontation with his uncle, Henry VIII.

James had indulged in some unsubtle diplomacy with the English and had caused his uncle offence by his pretensions in Ireland where Henry was making himself very unpopular by taking over the church. When a meeting was arranged between the two kings at York James failed to turn up – perhaps on advice from his council because of recent unavenged raids across the border by English wardens. Thus he snubbed his uncle who was just about to execute his fifth wife for adultery and was not in the best of moods.

Angered by the insult and worried about another Franco-Scottish pincer movement Henry decided to make a pre-emptive strike against the Scots. Knowing how best to hurt James's vanity and recalling the submission of William the Lion to Henry II he announced his imperial suzerainty over the Scottish kingdom and sent his armies north to put it into effect. James wisely refused a request from the Irish to take over as their king but this just added to the irritation of Henry.

The long-term traitor Archibald Earl of Angus joined one of the English forces raiding the Borders but they were defeated by a Scottish force under Huntly at Hadden Rig. Henry retaliated by demanding the return of all prisoners and total submission by James V or he would invade Scotland. Henry used Thomas Howard, Duke of Norfolk, known as Scourge of the Scots, son of the man who had beaten James IV at Flodden and manipulative uncle of both Henry's second and fifth wives, to attack with 40,000 men.

James had no alternative but to reject his uncle's demands and muster his forces. But this was where his past insensitivities began to catch up with him. Just as the gathering of troops at Lauder by James III had led to his virtual deposition so nearby Fala Muir was the turning point for James V. According to some chroniclers the feudal barons who formed the backbone of his army refused to accept his orders. Nor did they like the fact that Cardinal Beaton had been put in command, turning the campaign into a virtual crusade against the English who had just been excommunicated for their rejection of papal authority. So the army began to desert, leaving James humiliated and unable to attack Norfolk's force. An alternative explanation championed by Jamie Cameron plays down the humiliation and suggests that because the season was late James V just decided to halt operations for the winter. If so his actions still came across as weak.

Whatever the truth of Fala Muir, James scraped together another army and headed westwards where Lord Maxwell was Warden of the March. At this point the king succumbed to some sort of illness and decided that the army should head on southwards without him. But instead of letting Maxwell take command he unwisely removed him when the army approached English territory at

Solway Moss. He handed the command instead to his courtier friend Oliver Sinclair of Pitcairn whom the border troops refused to obey. The result was that a Scots army was caught in total confusion by an English force a quarter its size under Sir Thomas Wharton. The outcome was panic, many of the Scots were stuck in the bog or drowned, large numbers of the officers, including Sinclair, captured by the English and many killed.

Though there was no subsequent invasion of Scotland by the English it was an unnecessary, avoidable and humiliating defeat for which James V had to accept a substantial share of the blame. This coupled with the humiliation at Fala Muir was enough to destroy much of his authority and all of his confidence. Perhaps still not recovered from whatever illness had affected him (Norman McDougall has suggested dysentery or even cholera) he spent the next two weeks wandering from one of his palaces to another, finally settling at Falkland where he learned the news that his wife Mary whose company and exhortations at this point he seems to have been avoiding, had produced a daughter at Linlithgow Palace. Then 'he spak little from then forth bot turned his bak to his lordis and his face to the wall' and a week later 'held vp his hands to God and yieldit the spirit.' Reputedly also at some point according to Pitscottie he commented on his daughter's birth 'it cam wi a lass and it'll gang wi a lass', but this suggests a surprisingly acute sense of history for someone in his semi-hysterical condition.

He was only thirty. He died five years before his syphilitic old uncle Henry VIII leaving only a nine day old daughter to carry on the dynasty. It was the first time in fourteen generations that the Stewarts had failed to produce a surviving male heir and ironically James had produced nine bastards of whom at least five were healthy boys. Whether he had a serious illness or whether the supposed porphyria strain induced an exaggerated depression after his two setbacks it is now impossible to tell. After six generations on the throne the Stewarts were beginning to feel insecure amongst their richer peers: mixing with the gilded royalty of France bred dissatisfaction as did being neighbour to a larger, richer kingdom south of the border.

Among the lesser branches of the dynasty this period saw the beginning of a feud that was to last for two centuries, between the Appin Stewarts and the Campbells who had snatched from them the lordship of Lorn. In 1520 Stewart of Invernahayle was murdered by Green Colin Campbell while fishing off the new Stewart base of Castle Stalker. Stewart's baby son Donald was rescued and brought up on Tiree by an elderly couple, then grew into a stalwart warrior who in due course achieved vengeance by murdering Green Colin at Dunstaffnage. This was followed by another murder of a Campbell by the Stewarts in 1590 and then the alleged confidence trick by which the Campbells snatched Castle Stalker from the Stewarts thirty years later. The two families were to remain on opposite sides in the civil wars of the 1640s and again during the Jacobite rebellions. It was an early example of the clear divide that was emerging between the poor relation branches of the Stewarts who were now stranded in the Highlands and those who prospered by clinging to the coat-tails of the monarchy.

Chapter Eight

Mary Queen of Scots, King Henry and Her Other Two Husbands

Numerous excellent accounts have been written of the chaotic life of Mary Stuart, Queen of Scots (1542–87), whom Alison Weir describes as 'one of the most wronged women in history', Michael Lynch as 'a tragic enigma and one of the chief assets of the Scottish tourist industry', Antonia Fraser as 'famed for being personally fearless' and Harry Potter rather harshly as 'impetuous and inadequate.' There have also been numerous investigations into her level of guilt for the murder of her second husband, most of which are inconclusive, but range from accusations of outright complicity to compliant non-intervention or lack of judgement. The purpose of this short version is therefore not to supplant any of these but more to consider her career in the context of her dynasty and in particular to look at the contribution made to it by other members of the Stewart/Stuart family.

The four other members of her family who figured most importantly in the first half of her life were her cousin and second husband Henry Stuart, Lord Darnley (1545–67) and her three illegitimate half-brothers James Stewart Earl of Moray (1530–70), the most serious and politically active of the three, Lord Robert Stewart (1533–93 later Earl of Orkney), the most profligate, and Lord John Stewart (1531–63), her favourite. In addition there was also the manipulative figure of Darnley's father, Matthew Stuart, Earl of Lennox (1516–71) and his ally the solid but not very daring John Stewart (–1579) Earl of Atholl, who was her leading Catholic supporter. Among the female relations were Jean Stewart (wife of the Earl of Argyll) her half-sister and best friend and Janet Stewart Lady Fleming, her aunt and early mentor. In the second half of her life the two most important members of her family were her understandably disloyal son James Stuart (1566–1625) who did nothing to try to save her, and her niece Arabella Stuart (1575–1615) who though never able to meet her in the flesh brought a little comfort to Mary in her final years but was soon afterwards to ruin her own life.

Outwith the main royal line there were a number of other Stewarts who contributed to the drama of her life. John Stewart of Traquair was her chief bodyguard. The fiercest Protestant among her relatives was Andrew Stewart, Lord Ochiltree (1520–94) a descendant of Murdoch Duke of Albany, who had survived charges of heresy back in 1553 (alongside John Stewart of Methven) and was now one of the pillars of the new church and father of John Knox's second and much younger wife, Margaret. In the last stages of her life there was her faithful groom Hannibal Stuart. On top of this there were numerous cousins such as the Earls of Huntly, Arran and Morton. It would certainly be untrue to suggest that the family all came together to help save the Stewart monarchy, but equally if is not unreasonable to suggest that this scattering of Stewarts did in spite of their occasional differences contribute to the overall capacity of the dynasty to survive and prove false the dying prophesy of James V 'it'll gang wi' a lass'.

Of all the minorities of the Stewart royal house, and there were six in total, Mary's was the longest. For a start Mary was just a week old when her father died and she was the youngest to inherit the throne. To make things more awkward when she came of age she was living abroad and had other employment as queen of France. Her minority was also the most troublesome, partly because she was female, and a female head of state was as yet a novelty for the Scots, and also because the usual rivalries of great families, each one thinking it had the right to provide regents, were exacerbated by the new ingredient of religious division as the hostility between Catholic and Protestant became more virulent.

In addition, her minority was made more complex by the fact that not only was she the queen of Scotland from her infancy but by 1559 she was queen consort of France, and from 1558 there was only one life between her and the throne of England, that of her Tudor cousin Elizabeth I. She was therefore a political pawn of very substantial significance.

Ethnically speaking Mary Queen of Scots, born at Linlithgow, had two French grandparents (the Duke and Duchess of Guise), one English (Margaret Tudor) and one half Danish, quarter Flemish Anglo-Norman (James IV) so she was hardly Scottish at all.

Mary spent the first six years of her life (1542–8) in Scotland, a period generally known as that of 'the rough wooing'. This phrase coined by the Earl of Huntly referred to the efforts of Henry VIII to unite Britain under the Tudor dynasty by forcing the Scots to let Mary marry Henry's son Prince Edward (1537–53, king from 1547). It was of course also a pre-emptive move by Henry since Mary represented not only an opportunity for English expansion but also a threat to Tudor succession, for she was next in line to the English throne after his none-too-healthy son and his two more or less discarded daughters. Initially the Scots under the regency of James Hamilton the Earl of Arran (1515–75), himself next in line for the Scottish throne after Mary (he was the grandson of James III's wayward sister Mary and her second husband, a Hamilton), played along with the idea and thus delayed the onset of war until 1544 when Arran reneged on the marriage Treaty of Greenwich, backed very much by Mary's mother, Mary of Guise. Three years later Henry VIII died but the 'rough wooing' was continued in earnest by the English regent, Edward Seymour, Duke of Somerset. In effect the Scots lost nearly all of the battles (an exception was Archibald Douglas's victory at Ancrum Moor in 1545) but won the war, for at the end of it Mary was shipped out to France. The long-term outcome (and it is difficult to guess whether it was a benefit) was that instead of Britain being united under the Tudors in 1548 it was united fifty-five years later under the Stuarts. The cost to the Scots of achieving this outcome was not just the Battle of Pinkie in 1547 when 10,000 of them were killed, but the sacking of Edinburgh in 1544, the total destruction of Dundee, the massive devastation of the borders by Seymour, the burning of most border towns and destruction of farms and abbeys which probably led to another 10,000 deaths in 1545, and in 1547 the threat of a massive invasion of the west coast from Ireland under the token leadership of Donald Dhu the resurrected Lord of the Isles.

Mary had spent some of this terrible period at the island Priory of Inchmahome on the Lake of Menteith and was at the end of it shipped out from Dumbarton to Roscoff, then on to St Germain to meet her prospective husband the Dauphin Francis and his father Henri II. The next thirteen years of her life were to be spent in France (1549–61) and were probably her happiest. The outcome was a triumph for the Earl of Arran who was given the French dukedom of Châtellerault as his reward and kept the regency in Scotland for another six years till 1554, despite his ambition for his son to become the husband of Elizabeth of England remaining unfulfilled. It was also a triumph for Mary of Guise who had not only secured the safety of her daughter but a brilliant match. In addition she was provided with French money and troops to help bolster her own position as the new regent for her daughter from 1554 till her death in 1560.

One ambitious Stewart did make an appearance at this time to try to extract some advantage from the potential power vacuum. This was Matthew Stuart (1516–71) Earl of Lennox, son of the Lennox who had been murdered by Finnart in 1526, himself born in Dumbarton and close enough as a descendant of James II to have vague pretensions to the throne. He had acquired both polish and military experience as a captain of the royal guard in France (alongside Mary's half-brother Robert) when he achieved significant success in the campaigns of 1532–36 under Francis I. He had returned from France in 1543 and helped to organise the coronation of Mary at the same time using his French-honed charms to try to captivate her widowed mother, but for whatever reason without success. He almost irretrievably damaged his image in Scotland and possibly also his later mental health by the unnecessary slaughter in 1545 of eleven child hostages, sons of opposing Scots barons who never forgave him. The subsequent period saw him exiled to England where after a spell in the Tower he managed to win an alternative half-royal wife, Margaret, daughter of Margaret Tudor and her second husband Angus. They settled near Leeds at Temple Newsham for most of the next two decades and produced eight children, one of them the future Lord Darnley, who was thus regarded as an English subject.

Meanwhile Lennox himself put his military experience at the disposal of the English and it was to be a long time before he resumed his career in Scotland.

Mary now enjoyed an education befitting a princess. At the palaces of Fontainebleau and Chambord she had the best of everything. The style of the court was hedonistic if not totally permissive but she was still perhaps too young to know what was going on. King Henri II even had an affair in 1551 with her aunt, Janet Stewart (Lady Fleming), an illegitimate daughter of James IV and Isabella Stewart (daughter of 'Hearty' James Earl of Buchan) and she bore him a son, Henri le Batarde d'Angouleme (1551–86), a poet, abbot and soldier who took a notorious part in the Massacre of St Bartholemew's Day in 1572. He also led an army to capture the Provencal fortress of Menerbes in 1577 before being killed in a duel. Meanwhile by contrast in 1550 a Robert Stuart of the *Garde Ecossaise* in Paris was accused of being a Protestant agent and of trying to poison the young queen. He was executed.

Mary was tall and erect like the mother she had not seen for years, warm, witty, vivacious rather perhaps than conventionally pretty. She was given the finest, most fashionable clothes to wear and sometimes liked to dress up as a man for outdoor sports. She still enjoyed the friendship of her companions like Janet Stewart, her new confidante Elizabeth de Valois, later queen of Spain and her brothers Robert and John who took posts in the *Garde Ecossaise*. She spoke four languages: Italian, Spanish, French and English and could cope with some Latin and a little Greek. She played the lute and the virginal, loved music, was passionately fond of dancing and embroidery, fine clothes, jewellery and wigs, and enjoyed archery and golf. As was to be expected of a young woman brought up away from the influence of Luther and the other reformers she was a sincere but not over-fanatical believer in the Roman Catholic Church.

From the moment Mary arrived in France she was well treated by Henri II and his court but her presence was immediately also exploited for the benefit of French diplomacy. Her fiancé the Dauphin Francis (1544–60) was undersized and suffered both skin and breathing problems, all possibly the result of Valois inbreeding or his father's syphilis. Her engagement to him made it possible for France to prepare a one-sided treaty which involved the virtual annexation of Scotland by the French, so that the couple's children, if they had any, would inherit both kingdoms, but Mary would inherit no part of France if they had none. In addition it was asserted in French propaganda that Mary was the heir to England so that the Capet-Valois could add England and Ireland to their list of thrones.

The very year (1558) that the young couple were married in Notre Dame Cathedral, the disillusioned Queen Mary I of England died and was replaced by her half-sister Elizabeth. Since Mary had been aggressively Catholic and Elizabeth was a Protestant this brought about a significant change of direction. It was therefore an ideal opportunity for the French to assert that Francis and Mary were not only already king and queen of Scotland as well as being heirs to France but should also be rulers of England. A year later when Henri II was killed in a jousting accident the sickly dauphin and his Stuart wife did actually become king and queen of France, but the claim to England was never more than posturing.

This point was perhaps the peak of Mary's career but in some respects it was all an illusion. She heard distant rumblings of disaffection in Scotland and in the manner expected of an absolute monarch after the French style she commented 'My subjects in Scotland do their duty in nothing ... they must be taught to know their duties.' But the French troops in Scotland who had been supporting the regime of her mother grew increasingly unpopular and incapable of preventing the drift towards Protestantism, so such rhetoric became all but meaningless. In fact Scotland in 1559–60 enjoyed a mini-revolution in which a self-appointed parliament, the Lords of Congregation, made its decision to abandon the Catholic Church, to reject the government of Mary of Guise and expel French troops from Scotland by the Treaty of Leith. Scone Abbey was destroyed by a Protestant mob and Mary's half-brother, James Stewart, the future Earl of Moray established himself as regent. It would be very difficult to turn the clock back.

If this was potentially an ominous situation for Mary Queen of Scots it was soon followed by a greater disaster. This was the death of her husband Francis II in December 1560 aged only eighteen and after only eighteen months on the throne. Theirs had been an affectionate, probably unconsummated marriage and real power had been in the hands of her Guise cousins, but now unexpectedly Mary became a mere dowager queen with no particular rights. Insultingly perhaps there was no effort to persuade her to marry her brother-in-law, the new young King Charles IX, but he was only nine years old. Despite this Mary was still, along with her cousin Queen Elizabeth, one of the two most eligible single women in Europe and if Elizabeth who was nearly ten years her senior died childless before her she would stand to inherit the crown of England. Yet alongside this potential game of dynastic musical chairs there had been the onset of much increased religious turmoil which shortly plunged France into civil war. England, having gone from Protestant back to Catholic in 1553 under Mary reverted back in 1558 to the Protestant side with Elizabeth. Scotland having welcomed back John Knox in 1559 had converted with particular enthusiasm because of the identification of the catholic cause with its French armies of occupation, so its approach was all the more radical.

It was perhaps the wealth of marital opportunities which dissuaded Mary from a rapid return to Scotland. But it was now that the members of her own family began to play a major part in her career. Her eldest half-brother Lord James Stewart was one of the leaders of the new Protestant government in Scotland, along with her cousin Arran. As the eldest son of James V, Lord James might have made a move to snatch the throne for himself despite his illegitimacy (he was officially legitimised in 1551), but instead he chose reluctantly to support his legitimate sister and came to France to fetch her home. Along with him (if they were not already in France) came two of her other half-brothers, Robert and John, both of them much less politically active than the hardworking James, but as lovers of a good time quite likely to endear themselves to Mary and make a return to Scotland more palatable. Besides both were relatively cultured men, having studied at St Andrews to justify their promotion to positions in the church, the usual career for royal bastards.

As the English ambassador Throckmorton commented Mary had 'both a great wisdom for her years, modesty and also of great judgement in the wise handling of herself and her matters, which increasing with her years cannot but turn greatly to her commendation, reputation, honour and the great benefit of her and her country'. Yet despite her many qualities, as Alison Weir sums her up, 'she lacked prudence and common sense and was a notoriously bad judge of character … ever at the mercy of her emotions … and subject to storms of hysterical weeping and periods of nervous prostration.' Yet there is no doubt also that she was a person who loved fun, so while James appealed to one side of her nature the playboy lords Robert and John did to the other. Between them they smoothed the road for her return to Scotland in August 1561.

Scotland had used the breathing space after the death of Mary of Guise and the departure of the French troops to put its informal protestant church onto a firmer footing – the Confession of Faith was agreed in 1560 – so that its newly arrived Catholic queen would be less tempted to restore her own form of worship by force. In fact when she arrived back in Scotland seven months after the death of her husband, Mary at eighteen behaved very much like her cousin Elizabeth had at the age of twenty-five a few years earlier in England. She adopted a shrewd and tolerant attitude in religious matters and made no effort to overturn the new Church of Scotland as long as she was allowed to celebrate Mass in private. Mary was remarkably similar to her English cousin: in appearance, in her broadminded attitude to religion, in her tendency to be half-compromised by flirting with numerous suitors, yet perhaps a small underlying streak of misandry. Both were to have a lover suspected of using murder to get closer to them – Leicester in the case of Elizabeth and Bothwell with Mary. Yet Elizabeth had the double advantage not only that she came to the throne with an extra seven years of life-experience but also of having spent all of it at home not abroad, so she knew much more about the workings of her own country. She had also known fear, a useful antidote to over-confidence, whereas Mary had lived in the cushioned luxury of the French court, where most people did as they were ordered.

In spite of this Mary, with the backing of her brother James, made a good start to her personal rule. Unlike her great-grandson James VII & II and his two male would-be successors she refused to let religion stand in the way of her political security. Despite generating a fair amount of righteous anger by her secret Masses she maintained a calm working relationship with the Protestants, including their spiritual leader John Knox. She rejected the offer of her cousin George Gordon, Earl of Huntly, the country's leading Catholic baron, to organise a Catholic coup, and instead taunted him by giving the Earldom of Moray to her brother James, then allowed her aides to engage him in a battle which resulted in Huntly's death at Corrichie. There were even signs that she might have a meeting with Elizabeth to discuss the English succession, but after 1563 such a prospect ebbed away.

Mary's greatest weakness was perhaps her taste in men. Her first marriage which had been arranged for her when she was too young to know any better had provided her with experience as a nurse rather than as a wife, but it had perhaps alerted her to the importance of dynastic links. Now she was presented with a bewildering array of suitors and her relationship with at least two of them must have been distressing. The younger James Hamilton, now Earl of Arran since his father had become Duke of Châtellerault was her cousin, a childhood friend who had been a hostage in France and was a possible second in line to the Scottish throne after his father. Latterly he had been pressing his suit to Elizabeth but when that was rejected turned to Mary with whom he became totally obsessed. Sadly he was neurotic and unstable, a condition that worsened in 1562 when he was the object of a series of drunken pranks by Mary's playboy brother John (whom she made Lord Darnley till he died to her great distress in 1563 leaving this title free for her future husband) and his friend Bothwell who kept trying to surprise Arran in bed with his low-life mistress. Soon afterwards he seemed to go completely off the rails and was locked away by his father.

The other problem suitor was Don Carlos, the heir to the Spanish throne and a Catholic who was just as unstable and whose potential alliance with Mary caused Elizabeth of England very serious alarm. As it turned out Don Carlos, like Arran, became totally insane and was shut away by his family for the rest of his life. Elizabeth instead put forward her own reject, the Earl of Leicester, still under suspicion for the murder of his wife at Kenilworth, but Mary was not interested in a second Elizabethan cast-off.

In at least one respect Mary was a notably effective monarch – she obeyed the adage that kings or queens should keep moving round their realms, so unlike James III she was constantly journeying round her various palaces and staying with friends or relatives like the Earl of Argyll at Castle Campbell and Inveraray, her cousin Atholl at Blair or John Stewart at Traquair. She was also reasonably conscientious in doing her paperwork, but this did not diminish the generally indulgent atmosphere of the court where pleasures were enjoyed to the full, flirtation was the norm and to the horror of John Knox, music and dancing were enjoyed on a regular basis. It was this kind of atmosphere which perhaps gave false encouragement to unlikely wooers such as the French courtier and poet Pierre de Châtelard who twice hid himself under the queen's bed. The first time was at Holyrood for which he was banished, the second time in 1563 at Rossend in Fife for which he was executed. Mary was forced by her brother, now Earl of Moray, to be present so that she would see the harsh consequences of her coquetry.

The impasse over suitors was only resolved when Henry Stuart, now made Lord Darnley, appeared in Scotland in February 1565. Born in England, the son of Matthew Stuart the unpopular Earl of Lennox who had been in exile there since 1544, he had inherited Tudor blood from the second marriage of his grandmother the ex-Queen Margaret to the Earl of Angus, and at the same time Stewart blood going back to James II and beyond. He was thus Mary's full cousin, next in line to the English throne after Mary herself and even a remote contender for the Scottish throne after the two Hamiltons, so in some ways it is remarkable that

Elizabeth did not do more to prevent the match, as it was potentially a serious threat to her own safety.

Two years earlier as soon as news arrived in England of Mary's widowhood, young Darnley had been sent to France by his ambitious mother, but at that time when he was just seventeen and he seems to have made no impression. Now at nineteen, though two years younger than Mary he was tall and good looking and she quickly fell in love. In fact good first impressions seem to have been his speciality for many of those who now met him for the first time found him charming and intelligent. Sadly most of them were soon to be disillusioned.

Darnley was ambitious in a sort of indolent fashion and expected all the rewards without any of the effort. He was already drinking more than was advisable, sexually permissive and of indeterminate religion. The fact that he was brought up entirely in England by very manipulative parents who were aware of his huge potential as a gene bank did not help. He sulked when Mary delayed until July 1565 before making him Duke of Albany and again when she gave him the title Henry King of Scots only one day before their wedding. His impatience to have the full rights of kingship as King Henry I of Scotland was cringe-making for his new subjects and he rapidly acquired the intense dislike of what until a few weeks before had been his peer group, particularly Mary's two surviving half-brothers, James Stewart, whose ambitions were now seriously reduced, and Robert though he had been knighted by Darnley – John her favourite half-brother had died in 1563 – and all of her cousins, including Andrew Stewart of Ochiltree who was exiled for his recalcitrance. Mary herself soon became aware of her new husband's shallowness and began to turn back for consolation to her younger half-brother, Robert.

Mary's eldest half-brother James, who had been made Earl of Moray (he preferred this to the offer of a cardinal's hat) in 1562, had been deeply disturbed by the marriage to Darnley, for any child that it produced would put an end to any hopes he still had of seizing the throne for himself. So after first retiring to his mother's castle on Loch Leven he felt driven to attempt a coup against Mary, but it failed miserably and he went into exile, hoping for English help. Amongst her key supporters now were James Hepburn, the swashbuckling Earl of Bothwell and two key Stewarts: Lennox, Darnley's father, and John Stewart the Catholic Earl of Atholl, a natural peacemaker and one of the few nobles definitely not involved in either of the two murders which were shortly to shake the Scottish establishment.

With the powerful influence of Moray removed and her husband increasingly neglectful, Mary now turned to the talented Piedmontese courtier David Riccio who acted as part diplomat, part secretary and part entertainer. Her show of affection to Riccio, though it probably meant no more than the coquetry she had practiced on de Châtelard, was enough to drive the petty-minded Darnley into paroxysms of jealousy and provided good material for the Protestant lords to spread malicious gossip. So it was easy for the more corrupt element of the Douglas faction to lure Darnley into supporting a plot to murder Riccio which also perhaps could have led to a coup against Mary herself, for in her advanced state of pregnancy such shock treatment could have easily proved fatal. If so the plot partly misfired for Mary survived and Darnley was not given the promised reward of being made a real king.

Darnley, on whose future as founder of a new royal Stuart dynasty his parents had lavished so much effort, threw it all away with his impatience and arrogance. He had alienated nearly all of the most powerful Scots barons by his petty insistence on the crown matrimonial. He had impressed neither the Catholics nor the Protestants by pretending to support both sides at the same time. He had ruined his relationship with Mary by his flagrant womanising if not also by signs of bisexuality – he sometimes shared a bed with Riccio and even the tolerant Robert Stewart was shocked by some unmentionable lewd behaviour on a trip to Inchkeith. Now having joined in the Riccio plot because the plotters had promised him the crown, he soon found that he had been used by them and the real winner was to be one of the old Stewart line, the bastard James Earl of Moray, who now reappeared from his exile.

Mary's cousin John Stewart of Atholl and her half-brother Robert were present during the Riccio incident, as was her half-sister Jean, now the ex-countess of Argyll. In the aftermath Mary was held in Holyrood under house arrest but managed to escape with a remorseful Darnley by pretending that she was on the verge of a miscarriage. John Stewart of Traquair took the initiative in leading the royal couple away from Holyrood to Dunbar Castle where they were soon joined by Bothwell. Darnley who had shown his cowardly streak during the escape from Edinburgh, seems hardly to have been sure which side he was on, was fully implicated in the plot by his co-conspirators (his dagger was used by one of the murderers), but chose to betray them soon afterwards. By doing so he created a major additional motive for his own murder.

Whether Mary blessed the plot to murder Darnley, was aware of it but chose to ignore it or was totally innocent is in the end unfathomable and not particularly important. How often she quarrelled with him, how often she slept with him in the eleven months between March 1566 and February 1567 are also the subject of endless debate. There was talk of their rows on a hunting weekend at Traquair in July 1566. Certainly Darnley treated her badly: he had whores, he probably caught syphilis, he was deplorably inconsiderate during her often difficult pregnancy (the baby James was born in Edinburgh Castle in June 1566) and almost malignant towards his offspring – he sulkily refused to attend the baptism at Stirling in December 1566. There can be no doubt that she latterly found him verging on the repulsive. But the so-called Casket Letters produced to show her complicity in the plot to kill him were almost certainly forgeries and the accusation that she did nothing to arrest the culprits is unfair, for Atholl and his colleagues certainly put such a plan into effect. Equally unfair is the suggestion that her affair with Bothwell started as early as the famous ride from Jedburgh to Hermitage, for at this point Bothwell had been badly wounded and was not expected to live.

Darnley had alienated virtually all his potential allies in Scotland, with the possible exception of Mary's other half-brother, the maverick Robert who warned

1. The Cathedral of Dol, Brittany.

2. The remains of Oswestry Castle, Shropshire, from which the Fitzalans emigrated to Scotland.

3. Dundonald Castle, Ayrshire, birthplace of the first Stewart king.

4. Rothesay castle

5. Lochindorb Castle

6. The tomb of the Wolf of Badenoch

7. Chateau
Aubigny, France

8. Chateau La Verrerie

9. The cannon, *Mons Meg*

10. Linlithgow Palace

11. Stirling Castle Great Hall

12. Castle Stalker

13. John Stewart, Constable of France.

IACOBVS DEI GRATIA. SCOTOR &c. REX.

14. James II

15. James III

16. James IV

17. James V

18. Mary Queen of Scots and the poet de Châtelard.

Iacobus 1*mus* *D.G. Mag. Brit. Fra. et Hib. Rex*

19. James VI of Scotland and I of Great Britain.

20. Charles I

21. Charles II

22. James VII and II.

23. Queen Anne.

24. Bonnie Prince Charlie in middle age.

25. Charlotte, daughter of
Bonnie Prince Charlie.

26. John Stuart, Earl of Bute and Prime Minister.

27. Robert Stewart, Viscount Castlereagh, Foreign Secretary.

28. General J.E.B. Stuart, Confederate Army.

29. John MacDouall Stewart, explorer of central Australia.

him that there was a plot against his life. He still seemed to be devising his own counter-plot, to rid himself of Mary, Moray and Bothwell so that he could reign as King Henry. He treacherously sought Spanish help. Thus the three most important members of the dynasty, Mary, Darnley and Moray continued on a path of triangular self-destruction and Darnley being the least intelligent was the first to be trapped. Having recuperated from a bout of syphilis he survived the gunpowder plot of Kirk o' Field but was strangled in its garden.

Mary's huge error of judgement was to become so rapidly involved in an affair with anyone, let alone the chief suspect for the murder of her husband. Bothwell's error was his overconfidence and impatience. With indecent haste he started divorce proceedings against his relatively new wife so that he could marry Mary, exulted in his new dukedom of Orkney and was too blatant about his impending elevation above his old peer group. All this allowed the scandalmongers of Edinburgh to set up a fast moving campaign of anti-Marian propaganda.

James Stewart, Earl of Moray meanwhile had been restored to favour – he had returned from his English exile the day after Riccio's murder, thus giving some credence to the idea that he had been one of the many conspirators. He stood by Mary during the awkward period of her disillusionment in Darnley and she perhaps even hoped that Moray would get rid of Darnley for her, but he could see that others would do the dirty work while he manipulated affairs from behind the scenes. Yet when the aggressive Bothwell took the lead Moray was once more sidelined. On the verge of trying another counter-coup against Mary and Bothwell or just waiting for them to self-destruct, he headed off to France.

Similarly Matthew Stuart, Earl of Lennox decided to keep well away from Edinburgh and in due course also headed for London where the idea was mooted by Elizabeth of abducting the baby James so that he could be brought up in England by his half-Tudor grandmother, Margaret of Lennox. At this point there was no longer any question in her eyes of Mary being recognised as successor to the English throne.

Bothwell meanwhile was acquitted by friendly jurors of the charges of murder and revelling in his title as High Admiral. In April he took the queen by force near Cramond and according to some sources raped her so that she had no alternative but to marry him when his divorce came through in April. By June the vast majority of the barons and the Edinburgh crowd had turned against her, so after some brief confrontations when she was in Borthwick Castle the climax came at Carberry Hill by the Esk. When the two forces met the rebel lords who included John Stewart, Earl of Atholl simply asked her to hand over Bothwell but she indignantly refused. Her own troops were not convinced that her refusal was genuine and began to desert, as did Bothwell's. Bothwell though outnumbered would have made a fight of it but Mary who was pregnant chose to surrender so long as Bothwell was allowed to make his escape. Bothwell wanted to refuse but had no alternative in the end but to accept. Atholl and Morton led the moves to make her a prisoner in Loch Leven Castle and force her to abdicate. Knox was still ranting away about destroying 'the whore in her whoredom.' In July she miscarried of twins, almost certainly fathered by Bothwell, but just possibly by Darnley. By August Mary's brother, James Stewart, Earl of Moray had returned from London and confronted her with no sign of fraternal sympathy at Loch Leven.

Already the richest landowner in Scotland (as Mary's brother Robert had once mischievously pointed out to Darnley) Moray even took some of her jewels to give to his wife and had the rest sold. The baby James was crowned King of Scotland and Moray was appointed regent, a position which he had covertly been working towards for several years and which he was to hold until his murder less than three years later. There is little doubt about his ability and he was still only in his mid-thirties. He may have thought of disposing of his nephew the baby king, but perhaps felt rightly that his power base was too small, there were too many other rival factions such as the Douglases, Hamiltons and Campbells to make anything easy for him. There was also still the religious divide as John Knox, no doubt invigorated by his teenage Stewart second wife, pressed a more radical approach while much of rural Scotland still adhered to the old faith.

Thus when Mary managed to make her escape from Loch Leven in May 1568 there was plenty of support for her. If her troops had not been so ineptly handled at Langside by the epileptic Earl of Argyll there is every possibility that she might have recovered her throne. Even after the battle her cause was by no means doomed but having watched the battle from Crookston Castle, the old Darnley stronghold near Glasgow, she lost heart and decided to seek help in England. She headed south to the Solway, crossed to Workington and most unwisely surrendered to the English. Once she was there Moray and his colleagues supplied the evidence, much of it probably false which allowed Elizabeth to organise an abortive trial for complicity in Darnley's murder. There was no verdict but Mary spent the next nineteen years in a succession of English fortresses: Sheffield, Chatsworth, Tutbury and Fotheringhay.

Mary was almost certainly innocent of plotting Elizabeth's downfall when her imprisonment started, but it is hardly surprising if she was guilty of it as the years wore on. She used her old charm to write flirtatious letters to possible suitors like the Duke of Norfolk, the great soldier Don John of Austria and the Duke of Anjou. She became involved through the Florentine banker Ridolfi in a hair-brained plan for a Spanish invasion in 1571, then in an amateurish plot to murder Elizabeth in 1586 organised by a less than competent Derbyshire farmer called Babbington. Her involvement was stupid, particularly as it was probably encouraged by the English administration which was desperate for an excuse to execute her. She gave them two. At the time of her execution she was still only forty-four, overweight and grey-haired beneath her auburn wig. She died with great dignity in February 1587; twenty years almost to the day after the murder of Darnley and nine years after Bothwell finally succumbed to his demons in a Danish dungeon. With her on that day was her faithful groom Hannibal Stuart.

Meanwhile Moray had managed one more year as regent of Scotland on behalf of Mary's son James. With the help of John Knox he moved the Church of

Scotland further down the Calvinist route, but in 1570 at the age of thirty-nine he was murdered in Linlithgow by James Hamilton of Bothwellhaugh, a man whose lands he had taken away from him and whose wife had been driven out destitute as a result. As a Stewart bastard Moray had done much to ensure the continuity of the dynasty back in 1560 when Mary might just have stayed in France, then again in 1568 after she was forced to abdicate had held things together as regent. Yet like previous Stewart regents he had stopped short of the final step of usurpation. And like so many Royal Stewarts he courted an early death by pandering to his own weakness, in his case greed.

The same year that Moray died another Stewart was suffering on the other side of Scotland. This was Alan Stewart (−1587) the commendator or abbot of Crossraguel Abbey in Ayrshire who was roasted on a spit at Dunure Castle by the Earl of Cassilis until he agreed to sign a document passing over church property. Even more drastic was the fate of William Stewart, appointed the Lyon Herald in 1568, sacked a year later and burned at the stake. But on the whole the Stewarts, especially the illegitimate royal ones, were on the winning side when it came to taking over church properties.

Moray's successor as regent was another Stewart who had every reason to make sure that the inheritance of James VI was taken care of; the boy's grandfather Matthew Stuart, Earl of Lennox. But Lennox too had an uneasy passage and was killed within a few months in his mid-fifties in a skirmish at Stirling. Then after another brief regency under Mar it was the turn at last of the Douglases, who under Morton terrorised the country into submission for the next eight years. By the end of that time King James was fifteen and sufficiently aware of his position to look around for allies to topple the Morton regime. Significantly, three of the key leaders of his coup were to be Stewarts: Esmé Stuart (1542–83) Lord of Aubigny and the protestant stalwart, Andrew Stewart of Ochiltree, the father-in-law of John Knox together with his son Captain James Stewart. Between them these three organised the impeachment of Morton for his part in the Darnley murder and set the stage for James to make his first faltering steps towards asserting himself. So once again the more remote members of the dynasty had come forward when needed to ensure its continuity.

Meanwhile Mary's surviving brother Robert (1533–93) had carved out a totally new career for himself. He had been knighted by Darnley in 1565 and at about the same time been given the Orkney Isles, so he had taken himself off there after Darnley's murder and spent the next twenty-five years turning them and the Shetlands into a little empire for his new branch of the dynasty. Initially this effort impressed his young nephew James VI who made him Earl of Orkney in 1581, though he came to regret it when he found out the level of extortion and oppression which Robert had used to make his mark. But Robert could not be dislodged and in due course was to pass on his inheritance to his even more notorious son Black Patie (see p. 145). He also had three mistresses and a string of bastards, built the charming Birsay Palace which still survives and when he died was buried in St Magnus Cathedral, Kirkwall.

The Stuarts had by this time been holding senior positions in the French army for nearly two centuries and this had come to a climax with the significant contribution of Stuarts to the ultimately unsuccessful conquest of Italy that obsessed the last of the Valois kings. In the sixteenth century we find Stewarts extending their service into other parts of Europe. A number of Stewarts were in the Danish army and James Stewart of Ardgowan was so disgusted by his part in the murder of Swedish nobles in Stockholm in 1519 that he resigned. Later David Stewart was second in command of the Danish force at the storming of Halmstad.

The other area that attracted Stewart mercenaries was Holland where William the Silent of Orange was conducting a heroic war against Spanish Catholic domination. Captain James Stewart (1548–96) of Ochiltree transferred from the French to the Dutch service until 1582 and gained useful experience which enabled him to take a key part in the toppling of the Regent Morton and win himself the earldom of Arran. His younger brother Sir William Stewart (1550–88) of Monkton and Carstairs had also fought in Holland. Both brothers were reputed to have committed 'sundry odious murders', hence William's nickname 'The Sticker'. He too was to return to Scotland in 1582 and play a key role in the early struggles of James VI.

Two other members of the remarkable families of Stewarts of Ochiltree were also to be found in foreign service, both of them brothers-in law of John Knox. John or Hans Stewart of Auchterhouse (1550–1618) was in the Swedish army from 1582 along with his brother Andrew Stewart later 3rd Lord Ochiltree (1560–1632), served as governor of Dorpat in what is now Estonia, then led the 1608 expedition up the west coast of Scotland. He was given an estate at Lagerlund and his three sons all served in the Swedish army. Similarly Sir Robert Stewart of Durisdeer took a regiment of 700 Scots to Danzig in 1571 to help defend it against the King of Poland.

Another veteran of the Dutch wars was Captain William Stewart (1555-1602) from Galston who fought the Spaniards at Zierickzee in 1574 but also moved to Danzig for better pay. He returned to the Dutch service in time for the victory against Spain in 1578 and married a rich Dutch widow but was accused of brutality by his subordinates. After his return to Scotland he was to become captain of the king's guards in 1584 and became involved in some of the Catholic plots that preceded the Armada campaign. He took six ships to Denmark to negotiate the royal wedding and was later in 1596 in charge of the royal troops in the highlands. He was given Houston and the lands of Pittenweem Priory as his reward and his son was made Lord Pittenweem in 1609. Thus overall the experience of a number of Stewarts fighting continental wars in the later sixteenth century enabled them to render useful service to the dynasty.

Chapter Nine

James VI of Scotland

James VI was born in June 1566 in a small, recently refurbished room in Edinburgh Castle where his mother's initials still grace the ceiling. He lost his father when he was still an infant, as had all but one of the first five King Jameses and as of course had his mother. Nor did he ever see his mother again after the age of two, as from then onwards she was in one or another of her various English prisons. The only major difference between his minority and that of his predecessors was that the previous monarch was still alive when he became king – he was on the throne for nineteen years before she was executed. In other respects his minority followed the usual pattern, though if anything the death rate amongst regents was even higher than normal. Three regents, two of them Stewarts, met violent ends in his first four years. The first, his uncle James Earl of Moray, who had helped contrive his mother's abdication and probably connived at the murder of his father was shot at Linlithgow before he was forty. Then his grandfather Matthew Earl of Lennox was shot before his eyes at Stirling along with another Stewart loyal to the young king, Alexander of Garlies, whose son was later made a lord. The next regent, James's guardian, Mar, died in his bed soon after taking over and was replaced at last by the ruthless Douglas, Earl of Morton.

Eight more years passed before James was rescued by his three oddly assorted Stewart allies, Esmé Stuart his French Catholic cousin and Andrew Stewart of Ochiltree with his son Captain James Stewart, both Protestants. It was the latter, newly returned from the Dutch wars in 1578, who boldly confronted the Regent Morton in front of the king in parliament, accusing him of the murder of the king's father Darnley, thus precipitating the trial and execution of the once all-powerful Douglas. Morton became a victim of the prototype guillotine known as the 'Maiden' which he himself had been responsible for importing to Edinburgh as an instrument of intimidation.

Amid all this violence and squabbling the most remarkable fact was that after two abdications and six premature or violent deaths in six generations the Stewart dynasty itself survived without challenge. James VI suffered a more gruelling educational regime than any of his predecessors, for he was brought up by that coldly detached couple the Earl and Countess of Mar and given the irascible, pedantic George Buchanan (1506–82) as his tutor from the age of four. Buchanan was one of his mother's most bitter critics so young James not only had the classics and extreme Protestantism literally beaten into him but also an accentuated hatred for his mother who was by this time a distant prisoner in England. Gossip that his real father had been Riccio (highly improbable as he grew up to look quite like Darnley) could reduce him to uncontrollable fits of anger.

The one subject on which Buchanan failed to convince the boy king was on his radical view of responsible kingship and an independent church, for James stubbornly developed his own view that kings should be above criticism and rule both church and state without hindrance. It was this teenage reaction which was to shape his reign and in turn those of his son and grandsons so that the dynasty was led once more to self-destruction.

The eight impressionable years for James between the age of six and fourteen witnessed the brutal regency of James Douglas Earl of Morton, who James was gradually to realise was one of the principal murderers of his father. In March 1578 John Stewart Earl of Atholl, who had been a loyal supporter of Mary Queen of Scots, led a coup which thrust Morton aside for three months, but Morton was soon back in power and Atholl died under very suspicious circumstances a few months later, probably poisoned. For a boy with very few living relations and no friends it came as a significant excitement when his father's cousin Esmé Stuart (1542–83) appeared in Scotland from his estates at Aubigny in 1579. James developed a huge admiration for this glamorous young man from France and made him first Earl then Duke of Lennox. Esmé who may have been a Jesuit agent and who certainly had a mission to bring Scotland back to the Catholic fold – his sister Henrietta married the leading Catholic Earl of Huntly soon afterwards in 1585 – nevertheless acquired allies like Stewarts of Ochiltree. Of Ochiltree's two sons, Captain James Stewart who had served as a French mercenary and for the Dutch against Spain, helped bring about the dismissal of Morton by falling to his knees in parliament thus creating the dramatic confrontation that led to Morton's conviction for the murder of the king's father, Henry Darnley. James Stewart as his reward was allowed to take the earldom of Arran, by marrying Elizabeth Stewart of Atholl (1554–93), the heiress of the current earl of Arran, who was still alive but had gone mad in 1562 after his stressful attempts to marry two queens. Known, for her loose morals, as Lady Jezebel she had her previous marriage to the feeble Bishop Robert Stewart of Caithness annulled on grounds of impotence.

Arran's brother, William Stewart of Monkton, known as William the Sticker had also served in Holland. Between them the four Stewarts contrived the downfall and execution of Morton in 1582, helped by a fifth Stewart, the rich merchant

Archibald Stewart of Beith (1530–84), an ally of both Knox and Moray who became provost of Edinburgh in 1578. In the background was also a sixth Stewart, William of Houston, an unscrupulous ex-mercenary who became captain of the guard.

James however was still too young to rule in his own right and the replacement regime did not last long as it was suspected of being part of a popish plot. James was trapped in Ruthven Castle and kept a prisoner for ten months by an extreme Protestant group led by the Earl of Angus. William Stewart the Sticker and William Stewart of Houston, who lost two fingers in the attempt, failed to save him. James Stewart, Earl Arran was arrested after allegedly pawning the crown jewels. Esmé Duke of Lennox fled back to France where he died soon afterwards.

In June 1583 James at last escaped and at the age of seventeen claimed the royal authority, with James Stewart Earl of Arran restored as his main adviser. While he was an able and articulate scholar, James was physically somewhat unprepossessing with a tongue too large for his mouth (he may have suffered from cerebral palsy) so that it was hard for him to avoid dribbling, and he had weak, rather bandy legs which made him look ungainly except when on a horse. He thus had a convenient obsession with hunting, but in other aspects of life was timid and awkward. His manners were coarse and his sense of humour crude.

As James became aware of his new regal role there were four objectives uppermost in his mind. The first was to prevent a Catholic uprising and so long as there were fanatical Catholic barons like the Earl of Huntly, that remained a possibility. The second was to prevent the more extreme wing of the Church of Scotland from abolishing bishops, since he realised such a move would take the church completely out of his control. The third was to persuade Queen Elizabeth to acknowledge him as her heir. The fourth was to marry and produce an heir for himself.

Of these four tasks the first was only achieved after several scares when the Catholic earls finally surrendered in 1589. The second caused James considerable difficulty as the anti-Episcopalian wing of the church assembly dominated affairs for some years and he did not have the strength to quash it. By 1600 he had got rid of the ultra-Protestant lords like Gowrie who was accused of attacking him but according to some witnesses had been guilty only of refusing a sexual advance. He had not however rid himself of the fanatical Calvinist ministers. The chances of keeping bishops in Scotland had looked slim until the Presbyterian revolt of 1596 collapsed and he was able to reassert control; consequently there were bishops again by 1599. With his third aim of securing the succession to Elizabeth he resorted to plots with the French when she appeared reluctant, but eventually won her tacit acceptance in 1585 – she was after all by this time in her fifties and he did have a better right than any other possible candidate – but he was to be kept on tenterhooks for the next eighteen years.

The solution to the king's fourth problem, finding a Protestant royal bride was solved when in 1589 he chose Anne, the daughter of Frederick II of Denmark.

Both the Tudor and Stuart dynasties clearly by this time needed a new supply of heirs for despite the prolixity of Henry VIII the Tudors had virtually died out except for the spinster Elizabeth and there were very few remaining royal Stuarts remotely close to the main line. Esmé Duke of Lennox's son Louis or Ludovic was a possible as was Arabella/Arbella Stuart, the niece of Darnley and Mary, but her blood connection was to the English rather than the Scottish crown.

So with the aid of Colonel William Stewart of Houston, who made all the arrangements, James crossed the North Sea to marry the sixteen-year-old Danish princess in Oslo in 1589 and honeymooned at Elsinore where he enjoyed himself but also picked up from the Danes an unhealthy interest in witch-hunting. Anne was the second queen of Scotland to come from the Oldenburg dynasty of Denmark – the previous one to marry a Stewart king had been Margaret, the wife of James III and both their marriages were also useful in cementing Scotland's trading links with the Baltic. Though Anne was blonde, flighty and not very bright she provided him with a level of domestic stability he had never previously enjoyed and was to keep at bay his latent bisexuality for the next two decades. In due course they had seven children of whom four died as infants, so that the combined Tudor-Stuart dynasty had a renewed pool for the succession. However when he decided to send their son Henry away to be educated in the traditional way for Scots kings Anne was furious and never forgave him, so their marital relationship, already endangered by his bouts of misogyny, now deteriorated considerably.

There was one further problem for James which was eliminated at about this time: his mother. He had not seen her since he was two and had been taught to revile her, so since she was to some extent a focus for opposition to his reign (just as she was for that of Elizabeth) he showed no great display of grief when he heard that Elizabeth had reluctantly agreed to her execution, although he gave his envoy, the mysterious Alexander Stewart of Scotstounhill, a very hard time. Yet the progress of his kingship in Scotland was still not smooth. For some years his main adviser had been James Stewart, Earl of Arran but he had been involved in some shady dealings such as the pawning of the crown jewels egged on apparently by his fiery wife Elizabeth, Lady Jezebel, so he had fallen out of favour by 1585 and was murdered ten years later by a Douglas of Parkhead. Elizabeth had taken heed of a prophesy that she would be the greatest woman in Scotland (some have suggested that she may have been the model for Shakespeare's Lady Macbeth) and ironically the prophesy was apparently fulfilled when she swelled up with dropsy and died at the age of forty.

Arran's brother William the Sticker had been murdered in 1588 by the notorious Stewart Earl of Bothwell (see p.137) in Edinburgh's Blackfriar's Wynd for telling the earl to 'kiss his arse'. 'Sir William having his back to ye wall ye earl mad a thrust at him with his rapier and strake him in at the back and out of the belley.'

However, other Stewarts continued amongst the king's aides. Walter Stewart of Minto (1563–1613) a former fellow student under Buchanan was Keeper of the

Privy Seal in 1582, Lord of Session ten years later, and Lord Blantyre seven years after that, despite a short period in gaol for objecting to the king's insistence on bishops. Sir William Stewart of Houston, the ex-Dutch mercenary, Captain of the King's Guard and his minder during the Danish wedding, later led the king's attack on the MacDonalds of Kintyre, tried to colonise Lewis with lowlanders and was made Commendator of Pittenweem as his reward.

It was another Stewart who had now became the chief troublemaker for King James, Francis Stewart (1562–1612) the illegitimate son of Mary Queen of Scots' illegitimate brother John, so the king's half first cousin. He was one of those self-confident, glamorous men who tended to impress James. In 1564 he became Lord Darnley, (Mary's husband no longer needed that title) in 1577 Earl of Bothwell and in 1588 as we have already seen, murdered William the Sticker in the back-streets of Edinburgh. This dysfunctional, near-psychopathic grandson of James V at the age of seventeen had only just been stopped from fighting a duel over a football foul. He met Queen Elizabeth in 1578, oscillated between the Catholics and extreme Protestants, and dabbled in witchcraft. He had been in Italy in 1581 and extravagantly rebuilt Crichton Castle as an Italianate palace. He had been asked to escort the new queen from Denmark but demanded too much money, so the king had to go and fetch his own bride and ironically thus acquired a horror of witchcraft which exacerbated his relationship with Bothwell.

Bothwell who had been left holding the fort during the king's absence in Denmark now terrorised James for several years. By apparently plotting to murder him by supernatural means he succeeded in terrifying the already paranoid king. He contrived extraordinary attacks on James in unexpected places and would then vanish, eluding capture like a latter day Robin Hood. His brother Hercules Stewart of Whitelaw was hanged in 1594 but Bothwell himself kept escaping. It was not until 1595 after a very brief reconciliation during which Bothwell handed his sword to the king and invited decapitation that James finally got rid of him. After a second career as a mercenary and sorcerer in Italy he died in Naples.

One of the by-products of this period of violence which Bothwell abetted was the murder of another Stewart, James of Doune (1560–92), one of the Ochiltree family better known as the Bonny Earl of Moray, a darling of the extreme Presbyterians who was killed by the Catholic Earl of Huntly at Donibristle in 1592 and commemorated with undue veneration by the well-known ballad:

> He was a braw gallant
> And he rid at the ring
> And the bonny Earl of Murray.
> Oh he micht have been a king

The last line seems to suggest something very unlikely but Moray had been involved in Bothwell's plot to kidnap James that year and the song perhaps reflects Protestant bias. Harry Potter in his analysis of the murder refers to him as 'headstrong and irresponsible', a gambler who had been accused of flirting even with the queen.

One of James's more significant achievements before he left Scotland was the further pacification of the west highlands and islands. He supervised a renewed attack on the more recalcitrant clans, employing the Campbells as usual but also relations like his nephew Louis (1574–1624), the son of Esmé Duke of Lennox who was authorised to use any necessary violence to subdue Lewis in 1598. Similarly the ex-mercenary Andrew Stewart, Lord Ochiltree acted as the king's enforcer of peace in the Borders and led a major expedition up the west coast in 1608. He was responsible for the rather sly capture of clan chiefs at Aros which was followed by seventeen of them being imprisoned in three royal castles for ten months to teach them the evils of feuding. Then came the Statutes of Inchcolmkill (Iona) of 1609 by which James made substantial progress in reducing the lawlessness of the more remote clan chiefs after the dreadful series of MacDonald-MacLean feuds in the 1580s and numerous acts of piracy.

Overall therefore the achievement of James as a pacifier was substantial. He kept Scotland out of war for his entire reign, a longer stretch than it is easy to find in any earlier period, and made internal feuding no longer a respectable activity for the Scottish upper class. If his achievements were genuine enough he went out of his way to make sure that the poets of the day trumpeted them in grandiloquent style, cultivating his image as a new King Arthur, a new Solomon , a new Brutus, all rolled into one. As he prepared for his role as the uniter of Britain he also worked on ideas for its new imagery in terms of coins, flags, seals and other artefacts. John Stewart of Baldynneis was one of his tame poets working on propaganda for the new regime.

James also played a remarkably restrained and patient role during the declining years of Queen Elizabeth. He ignored the tempting intrigues of the Earl of Essex who acted prematurely and paid for it with his head. He contented himself with a few vague secret reassurances from the cautious Robert Cecil in London and just waited, avoiding any rash moves or proclamations which might have offended the English.

Part Five

RULERS OF GREAT BRITAIN
AND IRELAND

Chapter One

James I of Great Britain

When Elizabeth died in 1603 the translation of the Stuart dynasty to England went remarkably smoothly except that James had no money and had to send to London for cash as soon as he crossed the border. So after 233 years on the throne of Scotland or 467 years since Walter Fitzalan had left Oswestry the Stewarts achieved their second kingdom. Following a prolonged period of uncertainty the English seemed pleased to be getting an adult Protestant male on their throne and his Scottishness was no immediate impediment. London gave him a remarkably warm welcome.

The nearest thing to a problem, and that a pretty unlikely one, was another Stuart, the bookish Arabella/Arbella, (1575–1615) daughter of Henry Darnley's brother Charles and as King James's own first cousin, the next in line to the English throne apart from his own children. Proficient in six languages she had been made a lady-in-waiting to Queen Elizabeth but was dismissed for chatting to the traitor Essex in 1588, placed in custody and prevented from marrying because of her closeness to the throne. She escaped and was championed by Sir Walter Raleigh in 1603 but seems to have suffered some kind of mental breakdown or anorexia. She was restored to favour by King James but 'a real termagant' according to the Venetian ambassador, she berated both the king and queen for their uncouth behaviour and her passion for diamonds meant that she was always in debt. In 1610 she secretly made a foolish marriage to Edward Seymour who was not only thirteen years her junior but belonged to an unfortunately ambitious family which again drew attention to her closeness to the royal line. After escaping from custody dressed as a man she set sail in the Channel but was captured, placed in the Tower of London and starved herself to death.

Moving to London did not mean that the paranoid James who had survived so many real and perhaps imagined murder or kidnap attempts could dispense with

his stiletto-proof doublet. Within two years of his arrival his ministers' spies had
warning of a Catholic plot and surprised the bomb squad led by Guy Fawkes in
the basement of Westminster. In this situation James postured as something of a
hero, and won a temporary boost to his popularity which had already begun to
erode. The problem was of his own making for he made little effort to adapt to
the different conditions in England. He styled himself 'an old experienced king
needing no lessons' and failed to realise that the House of Commons needed just
as much attention, if not more than the Lords. He made the mistake of promoting
too many favourites, especially Scots, to the Lords, which often meant that he had
no one that he could rely on to give a lead in the Commons. Even his trademark
policy of peace-making, this time with Spain, was remarkably unpopular and
besides removed one good reason for asking the Commons for money.

At thirty-seven James was slightly past his prime and turned out in some ways
to be a less effective king of Great Britain (a name that typically he imposed on his
new joint kingdom without parliamentary consent, just as he did the new combined
flag which was named Union Jack in tribute to his first name) than he had been
of Scotland. But from the English point of view Elizabeth was understandably a
hard act to follow. As we have seen James did continue the work of pacifying the
north-west coast of Scotland and he now made sure that the age-old border clashes
between the Scots and English also came to an abrupt end, so eliminating another
major trouble spot and ending the need for garrisons on the border. The high commissioner he sent to the Scottish parliament was rather tactlessly his French cousin,
Ludovic Stuart Duke of Lennox (1574–1623) son of the beloved Esmé, who received
the English dukedom of Richmond as his reward. At the age of fifteen Ludovic had
been technically in charge of the coastal defence of Scotland against the Armada and
a year later was governor with Bothwell while James was abroad in Denmark for his
wedding. His main function in London as the member of the wider Stuart dynasty
closest to the king was to help orchestrate the elaborate masques which became
the escape mechanism for the queen. She, like James and Arabella, was extremely
extravagant in her taste for such masques, for diamonds, musk and ambergris and the
numerous array of new homes that James gave her – partly to keep her out of his
way – at Oatlands, Pontefract, Greenwich and Denmark House.

James' passion for unity was also true of northern Ireland where he encouraged
large numbers of Scots settlers including Andrew Stewart of Ochiltree, one of the
Morphie descendants of Duke Murdoch Stewart, who left Scotland to found a
new branch of the family at Castle Stewart, Tyrone in 1619. This was a sequel to
James's policy of creating The Ulster Plantations in 1609 though he was not to
foresee the long-term religious divide which would later mean that his efforts
there had unfortunate side-effects. Another Stewart who played a part was Sir
William Stewart one of the survivors of the Orkney branch, and one of James's
Privy Councillors who settled in Ramelton, Donegal in 1623, while his brother
Sir Robert (–1670) after a stint in the Swedish army also settled in Ulster, tried
to marry an eleven-year-old heiress to assuage his financial problems and later

defended Londonderry for Charles I. Sir James Stewart of Blantyre, another of the king's favourites, was made Earl of Roscommon. Within a century the Stewarts were major land-owners in Ulster and in due course held three earldoms there.

The main trouble with James was that after nearly twenty years of power in Scotland he was used to getting his own way and as the scholarly author of *The Trew Law of Free Monarchies* and a fervent believer in his own divinely anointed authority he found it hard to defer to the English parliament, let alone endure criticism or objections to his requests for money. Furthermore, just as James had done his best to thwart the Presbyterians in Scotland he now inherited a similar problem in England, the Puritans. He was determined to retain the episcopacy as an arm of royal government and to steer the church towards high rather than low Christianity. It was this policy in exaggerated form which was to bring about the cataclysmic fall of his dynasty forty years later. The one lasting achievement of his religious policy was the new translation of the Bible, the Authorised Version of 1611, unquestionably a literary masterpiece.

The most notable by-product of James's religious intolerance was the emigration of the Pilgrim Fathers to America in 1620, although in fairness James had made colonies in America more practicable by making peace with Spain in 1604. It was only two years later that the Virginia Company was chartered and the following year in 1607 Jamestown was founded on the James River at Chesapeake Bay by Captain John Smith. The legend of John Rolfe and Pocahontas was to follow as was the first unexpectedly successful planting of tobacco which saved the otherwise doomed colony from extinction, despite its ironic dependency on a plant which James had roundly condemned. The two points on either side of the bay were named after the king's two sons Henry and Charles. Settlements in New Hampshire and Maine came soon afterwards. The wealthy wife of the Stuart Duke of Lennox paid for the recruitment posters for the new colonies.

James was also a coloniser in his own right, at least theoretically, as he instigated the founding of Nova Scotia and awarded a Nova Scotia baronetcy to potential fundraisers for the new colony – eventually ten Stewart families collected these baronetcies between 1627 and 1707. In addition he sent the first official British envoy to India, Sir Thomas Rowe and may have been responsible for sending the present of a sailing dinghy to one of the Romanovs which later inspired Peter the Great to found the Russian navy.

As he approached his forties and he was no longer required to sleep with his queen for reproductive purposes, James once more began to respond to male admirers. The first of these was Robert Kerr who became the first Scots peer in the English House of Lords and was made Earl of Somerset in 1613. Kerr married Frances Howard, reputedly the ex-mistress of the king's son Henry Prince of Wales who died tragically young in 1612. Kerr pursued a life of offensive arrogance and this finally went too far, with the poisoning of one of his young men, Thomas Overbury. James could not altogether save the guilty couple but did commute their death sentence to life imprisonment.

The standards of the court had in some respects declined. James was drinking heavily and once when asked to wave to the London crowds responded by offering to drop his breeches for them. Apart from his continued obsession with hunting, which led to him taking over the Cecil mansion at Theobalds, some of his other activities were bizarre. He kept a zoo of lions and crocodiles in the moat of the Tower of London. The same zoological interest led him to breed the first Arab stallions at his new stables in Newmarket. He persisted as an author in producing poetry, his treatise on the evils of tobacco and more theses on kingship. James could however also appreciate great writing in others, John Donne for example, and was a much more generous patron of William Shakespeare than Elizabeth had been, averaging thirteen royal command performances a year compared with her three. *Macbeth* did contain a small element of Stuart dynastic propaganda and *The Tempest* was performed for his daughter Elizabeth's wedding. However it is doubtful if James should be given any particular credit for the artistic and literary style known as Jacobean which characterised his reign. To some extent it was just to differentiate it from Elizabethan age.

The neglected Queen Anne meanwhile had set up residence in Denmark House and her drift into Roman Catholicism just exacerbated her incompatibility with James. She held lively parties which verged on becoming sleazy orgies and extravagant, beautifully designed masques organised by her favourite architect Inigo Jones and written by Ben Jonson. It was Jones who designed the Queen's House at Greenwich and the new Banqueting Hall at Whitehall which was to be the epicentre of the Stuart monarchy.

Meanwhile as James spent more and more time away hunting he neglected contact with those who mattered. A monster drunken orgy at Theobalds with his brother-in-law the king of Denmark was more to his taste. But while a trade down-turn and a spurt of inflation increased pressure, James had no ministers capable of organising the Commons and his relationship with them deteriorated badly after 1610. Three deaths in the next few years contributed to this decline: that of Henry Cecil, his ablest minister, that of his promising elder son Henry the Prince of Wales and lastly in 1619, that of his wife Anne. With all the talent in the Commons on the other side, its confidence as a voice of opposition increased and after the Commons Protestation of 1621 James took the dangerous step of dissolution.

Meanwhile the disgraced Kerr had been replaced in the king's affections by the dashing young George Villiers who at twenty-four was less than half his age. Villiers' promotion was even faster than Kerr's: knight in 1615, earl in 1617, and Duke of Buckingham in 1623. This affair was more demeaning than its predecessors, reducing James to a whimpering, love-sick old man, gravely impairing his judgement and his relationship with his more serious advisers at court, though it did not apparently disturb his son, Charles.

Buckingham was entrusted with the negotiations for the king's younger son Charles, who had succeeded his dead brother Henry as the Prince of Wales, to marry the Spanish infanta. This mission was doomed to failure since the Spaniards wanted too many pro-Catholic concessions. To make matters worse the Spanish king's Habsburg cousin in Vienna had driven James's daughter Elizabeth (1596–1662 born in Falkland Palace) and son-in-law King Frederick of Bohemia from their capital at Prague. The couple had married in 1613 when James insisted on inspecting the bride-groom's reproductive equipment. At that time Frederick was still just a German princeling, the Elector of the Palatinate based in the lively city of Heidelberg but in 1619 he unwisely accepted the crown of Bohemia as a Protestant champion next to a Catholic superpower, so his reign only lasted a year before he and Elizabeth were deposed by the Austrians. Apart from their actions precipitating the Thirty Years War, their main significance in this narrative is their parenting of the dashing Prince Rupert and their daughter Sophia who was to pass the Stuart genes to the House of Hanover and Windsor. Charles, who had some romantic notion of persuading the Spaniards to help save his sister from Austrian bullying and saw the Spanish marriage as a means to achieve that, was deeply disappointed. After this the ambitious Buckingham began to pursue a more warlike policy, despite the king's wishes to maintain peace. Having failed in Spain he did successfully negotiate Charles's betrothal to an alternative Catholic princess, Henrietta Maria, the youngest daughter of Henri IV of France.

The king's cousin Francis Stewart (1588–1634) the son of the Bonny Earl of Moray and like the queen a patron of Ben Jonson, had been in charge of the fleet which brought Prince Charles back from his failed marriage attempt in Spain, and was now made an admiral, but sadly his career did not work out and he had a spell as a buccaneer in the Caribbean.

One of the king's other cousins was also an occasional pirate, Black Patie or Patrick Stewart (1566–1615), son of his mother's half-brother Robert the Earl of Orkney, who had made himself rich by extortion and allowed his son to grow up with absurd delusions of grandeur. Patrick continued his father's policy of ruthless self-aggrandisement and exploitation backed up by torture or imprisonment in the tiny cells of Kirkwall Castle for those who resisted. He caused substantial misery in his lifetime, particularly in Shetland but left a fine architectural heritage on these remote islands: the completion of his father's palace at Birsay, the Bishop's Palace at Kirkwall and his castle at Scalloway on Shetland. He had a fleet of three ships armed with cannons dredged up from a wrecked Spanish galleon, a permanent bodyguard of fifty musketeers and three trumpeters to play before supper every night. His extravagances brought the islands and himself close to bankruptcy and his schemes fell apart. Eventually after a rebellion by his illegitimate son Robert, who was caught and hanged in Edinburgh, Patrick too was captured, according to legend because smoke from his pipe revealed his hiding place. He nearly escaped from Dumbarton Castle but had a fit of vertigo when provided with a rope to abseil down the rock. He was beheaded in 1615, leaving a clutch of illegitimate brothers and children who soon had to find a living far from the Orkneys. His two legitimate brothers, John and Robert, were professional courtiers, arrogant and inept, who followed the king to London in 1603, one of them being made Lord Kinclaven and later, in Charles I's time, Earl of Carrick.

Another Stewart who became involved in the Orkney piracy scandal was Simon Stewart (–1646) one of the Barscube Stewarts, who captured a Norwegian treasure ship in 1610, was later captured by the Norwegians and put in prison, but escaped to join the Swedish navy. He eventually rose to the rank of vice admiral, led the attack on Reval (now Talinn) in 1618 and guarded the Baltic for King Gustavus Adolphus during the Thirty Years War. Also in Swedish service were a whole group of Stewart mercenary officers many of whom rose to high rank and settled there, ending up with their names corrupted to Styfert, Sztuard or Stiffer. In due course too there were civilian Stewarts who settled around the Baltic, including Poland and Prussia and ran successful businesses, some as travelling salesmen or Kramers, some even farming.

James VI and I died at his favourite hunting lodge of Theobalds aged fifty-nine. At his funeral, which cost £50,000, the sermon was preached by John Donne and the tomb, designed by Inigo Jones, was laid beside that of his great grandfather Henry VII and not far from his mother Mary whose reburial under a fine tomb in Westminster Abbey after many years of neglect at Peterborough he had belatedly organised in 1612. James had only returned to Scotland once since he became king of Great Britain. The painting of his *Apotheosis* in Whitehall was sketched out by Peter Paul Rubens when he came to London as envoy for the king of Spain in 1629 and finished by him later in Antwerp. For a champion of the divine right of kings, *Apotheosis* was perhaps a fitting tribute. His character had shown numerous flaws, yet he had shouldered huge responsibilities for over forty years and made a remarkable success of the tricky situation at the death of Elizabeth. His motto as *Rex Pacificus* was 'Blessed are the peace-makers' and he had adhered to it with admirable consistency until shortly before his death.

Chapter Two

Charles I and the Civil War

Charles I (1600–49) was by any standards a late developer. He was the second son of James VI and his wife Anne of Denmark, born in Dunfermline some seven years after his elder brother Henry Duke of Rothesay, later the Prince of Wales. Charles who was made Duke of Albany at his baptism had one older sister, the very popular Elizabeth, so called as a meaningful compliment to the king's royal English cousin, and there were two other sisters, one older and one younger than himself who both died as infants. Charles was very much overshadowed by the brighter and more attractive Henry until he died in 1612 at the age of nineteen.

In 1603 Charles moved to England where he was made Duke of York at the age of five, by which time he still had not learned to speak properly – he always had a bad stammer. He did not learn to walk until he was nearly seven, perhaps because of rickets. In spite of all this he became an adequate though not brilliant scholar, performed satisfactorily at several sports including tennis, riding, hunting and tilting and was made Prince of Wales when he was sixteen. By adulthood he had grown to 6ft tall, carried himself with arrogant poise but with an almost perpetual air of melancholy.

The year after his brother's death, Charles saw his sister go off as a bride to Heidelberg from which she later moved on to Prague when her husband briefly became king of Bohemia. That same year as a somewhat immature teenager Charles lost his mother Anne, so he was left with his rapidly ageing father and the man who dictated his every move, the charming George Villiers, shortly to become Duke of Buckingham. Hugely lacking in self-confidence Charles fell under the spell of the unctuous Buckingham, surprisingly in some respects as the spectacle of his father slobbering over the Duke with servile kisses can hardly have been edifying. Charles was something of a prude and there was never any hint that like his father he succumbed to male crushes.

To back up his father's policy of peace with Spain at all costs, Charles set off incognito to Madrid in 1623 to seek marriage with the Infanta Maria. He was accompanied by Buckingham but they could not agree to Spain's terms for the wedding, one of which was that Charles should become a Catholic. So six months later they were back in Britain, now desperate to reverse the king's peace policy with Spain. This hatred of the Spanish Habsburgs was exacerbated by the fact that their Austrian cousins had just ejected his sister Elizabeth and her husband from their kingdom of Bohemia. But as plans for war were considered and the old king looked close to death the need for Charles to find a bride became paramount and he was betrothed to his second choice, Henrietta Maria of France (1609–69) a bony little girl of fifteen who apparently on first seeing him burst into tears.

Charles was twenty-five when his father died so he was the first Stewart/Stuart to take over the throne as an adult since Robert III in 1390. He had married his bride by proxy six weeks earlier. Much more of an occasion was made of his coronation some months later when the five hour long ceremony was meticulously organised by Bishop Laud in a way which presaged the obsession with mystical rites of church and state that was in the end to cause both their deaths. As the first British monarch brought up from infancy in the Anglican Church he was all his life devoted to the middle path which it represented between Catholicism and Calvinism.

Meanwhile Maria Henrietta arrived at Dover with thirty priests and four hundred French servants whom it took a year for Charles to pluck up courage enough to send packing. At that time Henrietta was too young, too Catholic and too untouchable for the marriage to be a success, particularly as Charles felt he had missed out on the exotically unseen Infanta. In addition, the influence of the ever-present Duke of Buckingham made the queen jealous. But eventually after the Duke's assassination their relationship was to improve and ripen into an enduring love which produced seven children in ten years. Charles, despite being raised in such a permissive court was one of the very few male Royal Stewarts to have no extramarital affairs. Henrietta's Catholicism was to be a disadvantage, especially as she reserved the right to bring up her children as Catholics until they were thirteen, an act of spiritual inoculation which was to haunt the last years of her eldest son's reign and ruin that of his brother. In her own way, Henrietta became a dominant influence not just in the family circle but in British art, fashion and to some extent, politics.

The Duke of Buckingham meanwhile had led an abortive attack on Cadiz which but for the king's intervention would have led to his impeachment in parliament, for Charles was as incapable of organising pro-government leaders in the Commons as his father had been. Buckingham tried to redeem himself by an expedition to help the French Huguenots in La Rochelle, but they would not let him land and he suffered a defeat on the nearby Ile de Re. To make life even more complicated he used his ambidextrous charms to try an affair with the queen of

France. He was in Portsmouth planning a new attack when he was shot dead by one of his own disgruntled officers, and so at last in 1628 left Charles to go his own way.

Now that Charles had achieved some domestic security he began to show more political initiative, but he remained a rather remote and introverted figure, still retaining a trace of his Scots accent and an almost falsetto voice, still stammering when ill at ease, not mixing readily even with the upper layer of his subjects. As Laud put it he was 'a mild and gracious prince who knew not how to be or be made great'. He never projected any personality other than that of one who regarded his kingship as a mystical but not very desirable duty and expected the same kind of reverence from those whom God had put in his charge. This applied particularly to his dealings with parliament whose right to oppose taxation unless it approved of his policies he found totally unsatisfactory. Thus he called and dissolved three parliaments in his first four years and then did without them altogether for the next eleven.

To make ends meet Charles and his ministers contrived new variations on existing taxes and forced loans. Ship Money was introduced on the basis that coastal towns should pay for defence at sea, but was then extended inland and money was saved by enforced billeting of troops in civilian homes. Those who objected were arrested and punished without proper trial. The Star Chamber Court was used to enforce the new authoritarian government. As Kenyon put it 'it was in Charles's character and in his concept of monarchy to regard those who differed from him as criminals or traitors'.

It was not so much that Charles was a real tyrant, but he was in his own way a perfectionist and idealist who became authoritarian because his religion and temperament dictated it. Even his main hobby, collecting paintings and patronising new artists like Van Dyck and Rubens, seemed extravagant to others and was misunderstood. The country squires fretted that their parliamentary power had vanished and even their economic status was threatened, but the City was doing well enough. In 1640 Britain took over Madras, and the East India Company built Fort St George there to guard its fledgling colony. In 1627 the London shareholders of the Plymouth colony founded seven years earlier by the passengers of the *Mayflower* sold out, but the colony flourished. Charles awarded four Nova Scotia baronetcies to members of his wider family, the Stewarts of Corsewall, Traquair, Tyrone and Ochiltree. In 1629 Sir James Stewart of Killeith, later Lord Ochiltree (1600–53) organised a settlement at Baleine, near Port Royal in Nova Scotia though it was soon overrun by the French. He was consigned to prison in Dieppe and his career ended in ruins (see p.151). Massachussets was founded in 1630 by a much larger group of Puritans, and work began on the site of Boston at the mouth of the Charles River. Maryland was settled in 1634 by Lord Baltimore with Charles's blessing and named after his wife Henrietta Maria. Over the next decade British settlers began sugar plantations in Barbados, St Christopher, Nevis, Montserrat and Antigua. Almost in spite of himself Charles was presiding over a

rapid expansion in the British Empire. The Stuart dynasty was reaching unexpected heights, yet was soon to throw it all away.

Charles's second great area of insensitivity was in religious affairs. Having a
devout Roman Catholic wife did not help and it is not insignificant that both
his surviving sons were eventually to die as Catholics. For the time being he
was himself rigidly high Anglican with a preference for the formality and art-
istry of service which was cultivated by his favourite bishops, particularly William
Laud whom he promoted to Canterbury in 1633. If this was offensive to the still
large number of Puritans in England it was even more so to the Presbyterians of
Scotland. An early sign of the king's remoteness from popular religious feeling was
shown in his belated coronation in Scotland at Holyrood in that same year. He
was anointed with oil and in the service afterwards two English priests in white
gowns officiated in St Giles Cathedral, the occasion before which he famously
lost much of his treasure when a ferry capsized off Burntisland. It was his and
Laud's decision four years later to impose the new prayer book on the Scots without any prior consultation that precipitated the first major crisis. The hurling of
a stool by an Edinburgh vegetable seller, Jenny Geddes, at the Dean or Bishop of
St Giles in 1637 began the whole process by which the royal authority unravelled.
So ironically it was in Scotland, the country where he was born, that Charles first
provoked the opposition which was to bring about his downfall. Yet if he had any
knowledge of history at all he would have been aware that two of his predecessors
had been forced to abdicate for not dissimilar reasons, his grandmother Mary and
his great-great-great-grandfather James III.

Nor was Charles particularly helped in this self-inflicted crisis by the two other
members of his wider family whom he had trusted to look after Scottish affairs.
James Stuart, Duke of Lennox (1612–55) was too anglicised to have any grasp of
Scottish feeling – he had been a grandee of Spain at the age of twenty-one and
charmed the court with his golden moustache and elegant manners. While he
was himself officially a Protestant, his three brothers, all of whom were later killed
in the Civil War, had all been brought up as Catholics so that they would have
good careers in France. He was too fond of the king to be honest with him even
if he had any real grasp of the dangerous situation in Scotland. He was equally
damaging in London where his greed in exacting duty on wool exports made
him unpopular.

The other ineffectual Stewart at this time was John, the newly-made (1633)
Earl of Traquair (1600–59) who had changed sides from the Presbyterians.
He acted as the king's commissioner in Scotland and enriched himself at the
Treasury's expense, but was too weak either to win converts to Charles's policy
or to tell the king to his face that it should be changed. Traquair, a descendant of
the Lorn/Buchan branch of the family, was also responsible for the collection
of Ship Money, as unpopular in Scotland as it was further south. Referred to
by Stevenson as 'quick-tempered, tactless and arrogant' Traquair was the worst
kind of go-between for Charles to have in Scotland, but Charles was anyway too

convinced of his own infallibility to take notice of anyone. Ironically by the time of the Restoration in 1660, Traquair was a bankrupt and reduced to begging in the streets of Edinburgh.

By this time Charles had fallen out with his only other close relative, his sister Elizabeth, whose plight on being forced to leave Bohemia he had done nothing to improve. She refused therefore to come and live in London when he invited her in 1632 after her husband's death.

There was another fringe Stewart who at this time did nothing to enhance the dynastic image. James Stewart, Lord Ochiltree had survived his imprisonment after the failed settlement in Nova Scotia in 1629. After creating riots in the Orkneys by his savage exploitations there he was arrested in 1639 and locked up in Blackness Castle for the next thirteen years until he died, the last of the Avondale-Ochiltree line which had begun with Duke Murdoch's illegitimate grandson, Andrew.

Meanwhile the other main influence on royal policy was Black Tom, Thomas Wentworth, Earl of Strafford who made his name through his ruthless regime in Ireland from 1632–9. When he was brought back to London to stamp out opposition he was seen by the king's opponents as the hated symbol of the new style of absolutism and by the king as the only man capable of imposing discipline on the now actively rebellious Scots. A year after the stool-tossing in St Giles, a General Assembly held in defiance of the king in Glasgow in 1638 abolished bishops and adopted the National Covenant. For once the Scots had more soldiers with recent experience of modern warfare than the English, in particular the two Leslies, Alexander and David, both of whom had served with distinction under Gustavus Adolphus of Sweden during his German campaigns and later in Russia, Alexander rising to Field Marshal. Two of Stewart of Traquair's brothers, William and Andrew had served with Mackay in Denmark in 1626–7. With a substantial pool of experienced ex-mercenary officers the Covenanting army was able to face up to the royal forces in the First Bishop's war and achieve its objectives; increased rights for the Scottish parliament and freedom for the church. It was Colonel William Stewart of the Galloway Foot who guarded the bridge of boats over the Tyne during Leslie's invasion of Northumbria.

Charles had no intention of accepting such humiliation, and initiated the plans that caused the chain reaction leading eventually to his fall. Due to his need for money he had to recall the English parliament in 1640 but the membership was too hostile for his taste, so he dissolved it and called another, but this time he had to listen. His army was defeated by the Covenanters at Newburn, west of Newcastle and he had to come with his cousin Lennox to Edinburgh to accept the humiliating reduction of his royal powers in Scotland. Ironically Charles was so unpopular in England by this time that his army was disgruntled and reluctant to fight the Scots, a mirror image of the problem faced by his ancestors James I, James III and James V, whose difficulties raising Scottish armies to face the English had presaged their downfalls. Charles also aped the classic error of James V in picking generals from among his friends.

The Irish now also rebelled and the English parliament claimed the scalp of Strafford. The leader of the parliamentary opposition John Pym even threatened to impeach the queen and passed several acts to stop the unauthorised raising of taxes. Nor did Charles have any real idea how to cut back on wasteful expenditure: as Wedgewood tartly put it Charles 'made a few personal economies like cutting the painting fees of Van Dyck'.

Then came Charles's botched attempt in 1642 to arrest the five most aggressive Westminster MPs, including John Pym. This merely raised the temperature further and polarised opinions. The intrigues of Queen Henrietta also made things worse rather than better. Charles had to leave his own capital and in August that year declared war on the rebels from his new base at Nottingham.

Even if Charles had won the Civil War, his credibility had already been severely damaged, but he failed to take advantage in the early stages of the war, while he had a professional army and the Parliamentarians were still disorganised. If he had done better at Edgehill where the outcome was inconclusive, he could have marched on London, but he was never to enter his capital again as a free man. As the Roundhead military expertise gradually built up, particularly under Oliver Cromwell, he lost a series of battles which climaxed at Naseby in 1645. Henrietta and his two older sons had to be smuggled out of the country and Charles himself surrendered to the Scots at Newark.

Among the Stuarts or half-Stuarts who had come to Charles's aid in the Civil War the most prominent was his nephew Prince Rupert (1619–82) born in Prague, the third son of his sister Elizabeth and her husband the ex-king of Bohemia. He had served his military apprenticeship on his father's side in the Thirty Years War. Despite being a strict Presbyterian, thus culturally a Roundhead, he came to England in 1642 to help the side of his high Anglican uncle and was made Commander of Horse at the age of twenty-three. For the next three years the brilliant cavalry charges of the 'Mad Cavalier' were a key factor in several Royalist victories, but equally his tendency to disappear in headlong pursuit of the enemy often left his infantry colleagues struggling to the ultimate detriment of his cause. Charles made him Duke of Cumberland in 1644 but fell out with him over the defence of Bristol. He finally surrendered in 1646 and spent two years in French service, then rejoined the Stuart cause in 1648 as an admiral until his fleet was destroyed by Admiral Blake. The following three years he spent alongside his younger brother Maurice as a pirate in the West Indies, preying on British ships. Prince Maurice was killed by a hurricane but Rupert was later to be reemployed in the navy by his cousin Charles II and was a founding member of the Hudson's Bay Company in Canada, where his memory was enshrined in the name Rupertsland. His final years were spent as a keen amateur scientist who achieved three inventions: an improved form of mezzotint, a new alloy known as Prince's Metal and a new recipe for gunpowder. He kept a mistress but died a bachelor in his sixties.

Among Rupert's fellow officers were a number of other Stuarts, particularly from the Darnley-Aubigny branch of the family, the three brothers of the Duke of Lennox who was himself a diehard royalist and had been an unpopular emissary for the king. The dashing young George Stuart, Lord of Aubigny (1618–42) was killed leading three hundred men at Edgehill and his widow Catherine became a spy or recruiter for the royalists until she was sent to the Tower in 1650. His brother Lord Bernard Stuart (1622–45) of Lichfield was killed leading a sally from Chester. He was referred to as 'a very faultless young gentleman whose loss all men exceedingly lamented.' The third brother John Stuart (1621–44) was also killed acting as general of horse at Alvesford. Charles Stewart (1618–51) a grandson of the infamous Francis Stewart of Bothwell died fighting as an ordinary trooper at Worcester. Sir Robert Stewart, one of the survivors of the infamous Orkney branch served in Ireland, captured Sligo in 1645and survived till after the Restoration, settling in Londonderry.

Meanwhile there had been a remarkable campaign in Scotland where the radical ideas of the English parliamentarians had proved too much for some of the Scots Covenanters, particularly the Marquis of Montrose who changed sides and won a succession of remarkable victories against the odds in 1644–5. The backbone of his royalist army were the MacDonalds, just as the backbone of his opponents were the Campbells, but a number of highland Stewarts served in his campaign with varying degrees of success. Colonel Alexander Stewart is mentioned as a drunken royalist plotter in Edinburgh. James Stewart of Ardvorlich was Montrose's adjutant but was disgraced for killing a fellow officer, possibly in a bid to make him change sides, possibly after a lovers' tiff. He reappeared a year later fighting on the other side during the last brutal attack on the MacDonalds at Dunaverty where all the royalists were slaughtered except for James Stewart of Blackhall, whose life Ardvorlich helped to save and who went on to found a new branch of the Stewarts in Kintyre. Another Stewart adjutant, William Stewart of Galloway took the blame for the misunderstood surrender at Philiphaugh, when he thought all prisoners were to be spared, not just himself. Sir John Stewart of Rosyth (d.1660) is referred to as having suffered greatly for his support of the Stuarts. Archibald Stewart of Blackhall had been a prime instigator of the Montrose campaign and was captured by the Campbells. Two less reputable Stewarts were John of Ladywell, Commissary of Dunkeld, who seems to have changed sides and may have been a Campbell spy, but was executed by the Covenanters in 1641; and Walter Stewart of Traquair who was also an ineffectual spy or courier and was captured. The best of the Stewart warriors with Montrose was George Stewart of Baluan who claimed personally to have killed twenty-one Campbells at the Battle of Inverlochy. There was also a John Stewart who fought in all of Montrose's battles and was later transported to America after being captured at Dunbar. He overcame many hardships to become a successful blacksmith near Springfield, Massachussets.

For the last four years of his life King Charles never saw his wife Henrietta though she plotted endlessly to try to save him. In due course he was tried and condemned as 'the tyrant, traitor and murderer Charles Stuart'. In many respects his death was one of his greatest accomplishments for he went to the scaffold with courage, dignity, self-control and a display of faith that made him an iconic martyr. He was convinced that the arrogance of his opponents would in due course destroy them and that his dynasty would be restored. And surprisingly he was right.

Queen Henrietta survived him by twenty years and spent most of them vainly trying to manage their two surviving sons, the future kings Charles II and James II. Their daughter Elizabeth saw Charles shortly before his execution but herself died soon afterwards at the age of fifteen, reputedly of grief. Of their two other daughters, Mary (1631–60) had married William, the stadholder of the Netherlands in 1641, a union which nine years later produced a posthumous grandson for Charles, William, who blended the genes of the Stuarts with the House of Orange and was to be the next nemesis of his dynasty. Charles's other daughter Henrietta Anne or Minette (1644–70) had been born ten weeks after her parents' final parting, smuggled out of Oxford in rags and had a loveless marriage with the misogynist Duke of Orléans. It did surprisingly produce a daughter Anne Marie who went on to become Queen of Sardinia, thus further spreading the Stuart genes. But genetically most important of all was the birth in 1660 of a son, George to Charles's niece Sophia, the wife of the Elector of Hanover.

From the dynastic point of view the most dangerous thing Charles I had done apart from losing his throne was to choose a Bourbon wife, for this connection with Europe's most powerful Catholic dynasty was to shape the spiritual and political attitudes of both his sons and created the atmosphere which led the Stuarts to their penultimate disaster.

Chapter Three

Charles II and the Second Chance

So far, of nine Stewart monarchs three had been deposed by force, two executed, two killed in acts of military bravado and two murdered, but of all the dynastic disasters the fall of Charles I had been the most drastic and in 1649 restoration looked a most unlikely prospect. Charles II (1630–85) the first Stuart monarch born outside Scotland – at St James's Palace – was genetically quarter French Bourbon, quarter Medici Italian, quarter Oldenburg German-Danish and quarter Stuart Anglo-Scot. Perhaps the high proportion of Mediterranean genes accounted for his dark complexion, hence his family nickname, Blackboy. His first decade was spent pleasantly at Windsor, Greenwich, Theobalds, Whitehall and Hampton Court, the five royal residences in England. He was only twelve when the Civil War began and though he was at the Battle of Edgehill he was too young to play much of a part.

As things grew worse he was sent for safety first to the west of England where at fifteen he was nominally the Captain General, then to the Scilly Isles and Jersey where he learned to sail, then Amsterdam where he met his first mistress Lucy Walter who in 1649, the year of the king's execution, gave birth to a bastard son, James, later Duke of Monmouth. Charles had a spell serving briefly with the rump of his father's navy, but in the end that came to nothing and he reluctantly completed his education at St Germain in France where he had as his maths tutor the hugely erudite Thomas Hobbes. Academic diligence was not really for him and surprisingly he had an inhibition about learning French, his mother's tongue. Charles assumed the title of king immediately on his father's death and in Scotland at least his accession was proclaimed. So he headed there in June 1649 and, for the sake of Scots help, signed up to the Covenant. This meant that he had to promise to abolish bishops in England and disown one of his father's most successful commanders, the Marquis of Montrose. Despite the defeat of the Scots army of 16,000 at Dunbar by Cromwell he was still crowned at Scone in January 1651 and all four highland branches of the Stewart family came forward to support him. He headed south with a Scots army, remarkably covering ten miles a day right down to the Midlands. There, despite a personal display of courage, he was badly defeated at Worcester and escaped only with difficulty via the legendary hollow oak tree of Boscobel and a chain of royalist safe houses including Moseley Hall, Whitelady Priory, and Trent Manor. Posing as a Will Jackson he was on the run for six weeks, an experience which clearly helped to broaden his outlook. Then came a ship which he helped to sail from the mouth of the Adur near Brighton to France. A reward of £1,000 had been offered for the finding of 'Charles Stuart a long dark man above two yards high.' But no one claimed it. Three thousand Scots had died in this premature attempt to put him on the throne and many more were condemned to the plantations in the West Indies and America.

The next nine years were to be spent as a somewhat impoverished exile mainly in the Louvre, the Palais Royal or St Germain-en-Laye outside Paris with his mother and sister, the two Henriettas. He also spent time in Holland with his now widowed sister, Mary of Orange until she also moved to St Germain and began an unfortunate affair with one of the other exiled royalists.

Charles was a much more relaxed, easy-going personality than his father and for the next sixteen years was to allow his mind to be shaped by his chief adviser Edward Hyde (1609–74) later the Earl of Clarendon and later still grandfather of the last two Stuart monarchs. Charles had endured many dangers and privations, enjoyed many kindnesses from ordinary people when he was in the depths of despair, yet he was not the sort of person to work conscientiously for his restoration. Instead he escaped into a succession of affairs with Lady Shannon, Lady Byron and Isabelle Angelique, Duchess of Chatillon. In the words of Macaulay, albeit with some acerbic Whig bias, he was 'addicted beyond measure to sensual indulgence, fond of sauntering and of frivolous amusements, incapable of self-denial and of exertion, without faith in human virtue or in human attachment, without desire of renown and without sensibility to reproach. According to him every person was to be bought, but some people haggled more about the price than others.' The only subjects which seemed to interest him apart from his sporting and leisure pursuits were the techniques of ship-building and sea warfare. It was he who first called the British fleet the Royal Navy and his interest in it remained passionate.

In the end therefore the resurrection of the Stuart dynasty resulted not from any concerted effort by its surviving members but from the total collapse of its opponents. After Oliver Cromwell died in 1658 – Charles was hawking at Hoogstraten on the Dutch border when he heard the news – the idea of continuing a Cromwell dynasty under his son Richard appealed neither to the moderate Roundheads who should have been his supporters nor naturally to the royalists. Just as the Great Rebellion had been started in Scotland so it was from Scotland that the force came to bring it to an end. In 1660 General George Monk who had been one of Cromwell's most successful commanders used his troops to oust young Cromwell, took control of the country and handed it over almost bloodlessly to Charles II. As Charles set sail from St Malo on his way home it was a coincidence that he was just a few miles away from the long-forgotten family home at Dol-de-Bretagne.

Given that the Stewart/Stuart dynasty had already suffered several cataclysmic failures the Restoration of Charles II was a remarkable event. Yet it would be wrong to suggest that after this miraculous change of fortune Charles made any serious effort to avoid further disaster. For the next seven years he left Clarendon to do most of the work of government and allowed the blatantly biased Cavalier Parliament to pass acts making life difficult for Catholics and Puritans.

If Charles had any further ambitions it was simply for his monarchy to be more like that of his cousin Louis XIV, absolute rather than constitutional. He also had his own agenda for an aggressive naval war against the Dutch who had given him shelter. One of his favourite pastimes was to sail in the dinghy which he kept on the jetty near his Whitehall apartments and he soon replaced this with a larger yacht – it took ten tons of ballast – which he could race down to Greenwich or the Nore to see how his fleet was progressing. Michael Lewis describes him as 'the father of yachting' as well as a major reformer of the navy. He amazed many of his fellow courtiers by his energy – up early for a hard game of tennis in the Pall Mall court, a sociable walk in St James's Park, a session of cockfighting then skulling or a swim in the Thames at Battersea with his brother the Duke of York, followed by a late night with his friends of both sexes. He was also an accomplished fencer and horseman, a keen patron of Newmarket, a huntsman and sometimes in winter drove a sleigh on the iced ponds of St James's, yet by contrast like his uncle Prince Rupert he had an avid curiosity for scientific novelty. He would often adjourn to his private laboratory or to Gresham College and the room of Christopher Wren, at this point in his career a professor of astronomy, who was gathering the group which shortly was blessed by Charles as the Royal Society. They even discussed the reduction of smoke pollution in London. So enthusiastic were they that when Rupert was sent with the fleet to harass the Dutch on the west Africa coast he was told to collect soil samples from the bottom of the sea.

To the horror of Macaulay the Restoration coincided with one of the most marked changes of mood ever to occur in British history, a dramatic reaction to the prudishness and restraint of the Roundhead period that saw the theatres and the racecourses reopen, the fashions change, the moral climate defrost. So it was a change of mood very much in tune with the new king's own personality. He was a 'known enemy to chastity'.

Charles was by this time thirty and in the prime of life but it is fairly typical of him that despite fathering numerous bastards he was the first Royal Stuart in twelve generations who made no particular effort to produce a legitimate heir. Just before the Restoration he had forced his reluctant brother James to marry Clarendon's pregnant daughter Anne Hyde (1638–71), a shotgun wedding before which James had ungallantly accused his bride of having had other lovers. The baby died, but two years later the couple produced a daughter Mary and three years after that another one, Anne, both of them destined to be queens.

Charles himself denied the rumours that he had ever married Lucy Walter, the mother of his favourite son James, but in 1662, the year that his niece Mary was born, he martyred himself somewhat by marrying the unattractive Catherine of Braganza in return for the naval bases of Tangier and Bombay, a useful addition to his burgeoning empire that appealed to his nautical interests. The marriage produced no signs of children, and Charles continued with a succession of mistresses such as Barbara Villiers Lady Castlemaine and Louise de Kerouaille and at variance with his normal charm he treated poor Catherine with considerable mental cruelty. Yet he made no effort to replace her with someone more fertile, nor did he take the opportunity offered to him later to legitimise his favourite bastard, James Duke of Monmouth, who as a Protestant might if he had succeeded have kept the Stuart dynasty going a bit longer. Certainly Monmouth was treated as a favoured son in a way that later gave him delusions of grandeur which ultimately led him to his death. As well as Monmouth, four of Charles's other bastards were also given dukedoms, three of them; Grafton (1663), Southampton (1662) and Northumberland (1665) born by Barbara Villiers and Richmond (1673) by Louise de Kerouaille. He also had five or six acknowledged daughters, of whom one significantly became a Benedictine nun and two borne by Barbara Villiers became Countesses of Lichfield (1664) and Suffolk (1661).

Among the ladies who are believed to have succumbed to the king's charms there was one member of his own family, the famous beauty Frances Teresa Stuart (maiden name Stewart 1647–1702), the English-born daughter of one of the Blantyre Stewarts known as 'la belle Stuart' and 'the prettiest girl in the world' who became the star attraction of the court when she returned from France at the age of fourteen. According to Samuel Pepys she had amongst other assets an 'excellent taille'. In 1667 she posed for Roettier's image of *Britannia* which was adopted for the coinage. At the age of fifteen she almost displaced Castlemaine as chief mistress but managed to fend off the king. The politicians rejected her as a potential lobbyist when they found she was more interested in playing blind man's buff. Pepys put it well again: 'The king is now besotted with Mrs Steward (*sic*) that new wench is so subtle that she lets him not do anything more than is safe to her.' She fell out with Charles for a couple of years when in 1667 she eloped with Charles Stuart Duke of Lennox and Richmond (1639–72), the latest representative of the French-Darnley branch of the family. He drank, was already disliked by the king and had done homage to Louis XIV for the Aubigny estates. He was always short of money to sustain his expensive lifestyle which included Cobham Court in Rutland and the purchase for Frances of the house she renamed Lennoxlove in East Lothian. He was involved in a murder in 1671 and left Frances once more at the mercy of the infatuated king when he set off to be ambassador in Denmark where he found Copenhagen boring and a year later drowned as a result of missing his footing after dinner aboard a warship off Elsinore. Charles was the last – he and Frances had no children – of the Stuart Dukes of Lennox, so the dukedom was transferred to one of Charles II's bastards Charles Lennox (1672–1723)

In one respect Charles pursued the same policy as Cromwell, that of making war with the Dutch, who had become Britain's aggravatingly successful commercial rivals. With his brother James acting as high admiral and Prince Rupert assisting, the war produced mixed results and was very expensive but in the end it did bring about the acquisition of New Amsterdam, the colony on the River Hudson which in deference to the Stuart admiral was renamed New York. It was one of the more enlightened aspects of Charles's reign that Britain was able to absorb the east coast colonies with their Dutch, German, Swedish, Irish and French settlers with a policy tolerating religious and ethnic diversity. The same thinking applied when the Tory backlash was at its height in 1681 and Charles was persuaded by his brother James who had been a naval colleague of Admiral Penn's, to let the Quakers found their new colony of Pennsylvania.

When taken alongside Cromwell's conquest of Jamaica and the Portuguese dowry of Tangier and Bombay this was an encouragement to those who saw the expansion of Britain in terms of overseas colonies and trade rather than fruitless efforts to acquire bits of France. Charles also gave his name to the new colony of Carolina in 1663 with its capital Charlestown, while New Jersey and Delaware were both founded the year after. Charles admittedly gave back to the French the part of Canada known as Acadia which had been acquired from them by Cromwell but encouraged his cousin Rupert to back the expansion of British fur trappers behind the French towards Hudson's Bay, the area called Rupert's Land. This the enterprising Rupert was happy to organise from his bachelor apartments in Windsor. As part of the general expansionist policy Charles authorised the naval attack on the Dutch in west Africa which provoked the Dutch in turn to attack Britain's east coast in 1665, the war that ended with the acquisition of New York.

Meanwhile Charles gave out another three Nova Scotia baronetcies to his relations: the Stewarts of Blackhall, in 1667, of Castlemilk in 1668 and of Moray in 1681.

It was in this context that Charles let Clarendon sell Dunkirk (another of Cromwell's captures) back to the French. The apparent shame of this sale and the image of venality which it conveyed were among the factors which led to the fall of Clarendon and his replacement by the cabinet of five whose initials made up the punning acronym CABAL: Clifford, Arlington, Buckingham, Ashley and Lauderdale (two of them Catholics, two adventurers and a time-server). Other factors had included the humiliating Dutch naval attack on Charles's beloved Chatham dockyard – even the flagship *Royal Charles* was captured – followed by the Plague of 1665 and the Great Fire of London in 1666 all combining to reduce morale.

It was during the Cabal regime that Charles was secretly approached by his favourite sister Minette, Duchess of Orleans and sister-in-law therefore of

Louis XIV of France. Not only was France a significantly larger and wealthier country than Britain at this time with about four times its population, but the French king did not have to put up with parliamentary interference in his power. Louis, who was eight years younger than Charles but much more ambitious and politically energetic, now saw the possibilities of serious expansion for France and saw the opportunity to buy Charles's help. Charles, who simply wanted to keep his crown and his life of pleasure without the nagging of parliament succumbed readily to this bribery and agreed in return for cash to renew his war when required against the Dutch and secretly to convert to Catholicism. The Treaty of Dover represented the peak of Stewart power and the nadir of the dynasty rolled into one. At least the anti-Dutch policy had a small element of moral credibility for Charles, as in an oblique way he was helping his nephew, the half-Stuart, half-Orange William who had still not been given the hereditary position of his ancestors as Stadholder of Holland. But in fact the treaty would have resulted in the dismemberment of Holland, most of it taken by France and only a small puppet regime left for William, who as it turned out would have been far from satisfied.

In the event there was a rebellion in Holland which unexpectedly brought young William to the position he wanted in 1672, so that he then organised the famous 'last ditch' defence against Louis' invasion. Charles on the other hand, despite French gold, had come close to bankruptcy as a result of his war effort and had to get rid of the Cabal. Parliament, which held the purse strings and thus had the whip hand had begun perhaps rightly to see the Anglo-French attack on Holland as some kind of Catholic master-plan so it would only raise money for Charles if he agreed to measures which kept Catholics and other Nonconformists out of office, the Test Act of 1673. Even the king's brother James, Duke of York was forced to resign as High Admiral, an event that drew attention to the fact that the heir to the throne was a Catholic – Charles had by this time been married to Catherine of Braganza for eleven years with no sign of a family. Moreover, James, who seemed oblivious to his unpopularity, compounded his difficulties by taking a new Catholic wife, Mary of Modena, showing quite openly that he at least still intended to try for a male heir and that the boy would be a Catholic. Even his late wife Anne had in her final years surprisingly converted to Catholicism, perhaps to try to squeeze some fidelity out of her errant husband – his most famous bastard James Fitzjames, later Duke of Berwick and Marshal of France had only been born in 1670.

The Cabal was replaced in government by the parliamentary majority leader Thomas Osborne Earl of Danby who presided over a pro-Dutch policy which saw the marriage of the king's niece Mary (daughter of James Duke of York) to the king's nephew William of Orange, son of his elder sister Mary. As both the bride and groom were Protestant and in their own right second and fourth in line respectively to the throne, it offered a political life-line to the majority in parliament who were still petrified of a Catholic coup by the king and his brother. It was politically, though perhaps not genetically, very sound. Danby was however as tainted with French bribery as the king and fell after only two years in power.

As the British obsession with avoiding a Catholic takeover became more febrile and as the king grew middle-aged a plan was hatched to prevent his brother James from succeeding him. The Earl of Shaftesbury (previously as Ashley, the second A in Cabal), now a prototype Whig, orchestrated a brilliant campaign against Stuart absolutism, directed in particular against the succession of James, Duke of York who was forced into exile. The atmosphere of paranoia was helped considerably by the phoney conspiracy dreamed up in 1678 by Titus Oates which involved a massacre of Protestants, the murder of Charles and his replacement by James. But perhaps Shaftesbury's choice of Monmouth as the successor rather than William and Mary was not the wisest. In the end he was shown to have used the fake evidence of Titus Oates to push his cause and he was disgraced. The Exclusion Crisis was over and the Duke of York's inheritance secure, even if he was a Catholic. It was in this tense atmosphere that the paranoid Sir George Maxwell of Pollok accused one of his servants, John Stewart, of being a warlock and using spells to make him ill. The wretched Stewart and three companions were burned at the stake in Paisley in 1677.

As the tide turned in favour of the king the Tories' comeback was transformed into a total triumph as a result of another, probably genuine plot, this time by the die-hard Whigs. It would have led to the murder of Charles and James at the Rye House as they came back from the races at Newmarket and the reaction to it was sufficient to make Charles much more popular in the last few years of his reign. It also helped him very nearly to achieve his ambition of becoming an absolute monarch, a success which perhaps led both Charles and his brother to overestimate the power of their dynasty.

James Duke of Monmouth (1649–85) meanwhile had been given a brief taste of power in Scotland. Having arrived in England as Mr James Crofts though a Stuart in all but name, he was the ward of Lord Crofts, he had been made a duke by his father in 1663 and married a rich heiress, Anne Countess of Buccleugh. At the age of twenty-one in 1670 the pampered youngster, whom Pepys noticed was as hyperactive as his father, had been made Captain General in succession to Monk and two years later led 6,000 men to help the French army against Holland, the country of his birth. In 1679 he was sent up as commander-in-chief to Scotland where there had been another serious revolt by the Covenanters. He led his troops to an easy victory against them at Bothwell Brig and earned general popularity by killing so few of the rebels – many of the prisoners were sent to the plantations instead. It was perhaps a mixture of his minor military successes and the level of popularity he achieved as a potential Protestant heir to the throne that gave him the delusions of grandeur which later led to his fall. He was implicated in the Rye House Plot and the Shaftesbury scandal so it was his turn to face exile.

Now Monmouth's resurgent uncle James Duke of York was sent by Charles to deal with Scotland and he did so with a mixture of repression and leniency which in particular saw him standing up for the underdog clan chiefs of the west coast. Undoubtedly he was looking for allies and he was successful, for the highlanders whom he supported were later to be the backbone of Jacobitism.

Charles II died in 1685 at the age of fifty-five of apoplexy exacerbated by mercury poisoning perhaps attributable to the hours he spent in his private laboratory. He was at the peak of his political power, but surely aware that his brother's Catholicism might well lead the dynasty into trouble. He had presided over a period of reasonable prosperity and imperialist expansion and a post-war political climate which had seen the polarisation of attitudes between the two forces in parliament, the Whigs and Tories. If remembered as a king who rode two winners at Newmarket and had affairs with mistresses as different as Nell Gwynn and Honore Mancini, he was also the man who briefed Wren to build the new St Paul's Cathedral, Greenwich Hospital and numerous other fine buildings which left London a much more impressive city than it had been before the Great Fire. There had also been the foundation of the Royal Academy with a new flourish in scientific creativity. Much of the drama known as Restoration did not appear until after his death, but there were exciting developments in the comedy of manners and a general revival in the arts which had been stifled by Cromwellian censorship.

The building in London most associated with Charles II is his Chelsea Royal Hospital, one of Wren's masterpieces, where by tradition the old soldiers still celebrate his restoration on Oak Apple Day, 29 May, his birthday and the anniversary of his return in 1660 with its homage also to the oak tree which saved him from capture at Boscobel back in 1651.

It is not insignificant at this juncture where the future of the Stuart dynasty had been narrowly saved that in the previous few years three members of the immediate family had died from small pox: Charles's older sister Mary of Orange, his younger brother Henry and his brother's first child the baby James. Had the last of these three in particular survived history might have been very different. So too if Charles had died earlier – he was once severely ill after an excessively hot game of tennis and perhaps had a mild dose of the plague after visiting Salisbury in 1666. As it was he passed over the throne in what appeared superficially to be a strong position for the dynasty, yet the reality was different.

Chapter Four

James II, Dismal Jimmy

James II or VII (1633–1701) was, like his brother, over six feet tall but far more relaxed and sociable, harder working but less intelligent. He was also the better looking and their mother's favourite. In Macaulay's words, as ever tinged with a touch of bias but still very much to the point, 'Though a libertine James was diligent, methodical and fond of authority and business. His understanding was singularly slow and narrow and his temper obstinate, harsh and unforgiving.' Like Charles who was only three years his senior he had rebelled against their widowed mother's dictatorship and nurtured a strange posthumous reverence for their father.

James had only been eight when the Civil War broke out and saw everything in terms of black and white; parliament as the source of all his ills, the cavalier army, warts and all as the image of perfection. Captured at the end of the war he had managed to escape two years later in girl's clothes on a barge heading for Middelburg. He arrived at St Germain aged fourteen, a fair-haired, fine looking youth doted on by his mother but already with a strong streak of arrogant obstinacy. The next few years were ones of bitter frustration because he was not allowed to take part in either the naval or Scottish campaigns for his brother after their father's death in 1649, but he was determined to be a soldier and wore down the resistance of Charles and his mother.

During the early 1650s he served first in the French army as a captain in the *Gendarmes Ecossais* under Turenne (a descendant as it happened of the Albany Stuarts of Auvergne) during the campaign against the Fronde and was rapidly promoted to Lieutenant General. He had to change sides to fight in the Spanish army under Condé against Turenne and Cromwell's Ironsides when the French began the conquest of the Spanish Netherlands. This climaxed in 1658 at the Battle of the Dunes where both he and his younger brother Henry fought with distinction, though on the losing side. A year later his émigré career climaxed when he was made Lord High Admiral of Spain until he was forced to resign that position when his brother became king of Great Britain.

Thus James's independent career came to an end when he was twenty-seven. Yet he had no real expectations of becoming king even after his brother's restoration, nor until quite late in his life when it became clear that Charles was not going to father any legitimate children. Up to that point he had seen it as his duty simply to make his living as a mercenary officer, and then help his brother's route back to power.

Meanwhile James had undergone a personal crisis in 1659 when one of his mistresses, Anne Hyde, the daughter of Clarendon, became pregnant and much against his own will – his friends all volunteered that the child was theirs – he was ordered by his brother to do the decent thing. In the end their baby son died and it was two subsequent pregnancies that were to produce the two Protestant daughters, Mary (b.1662 at St James Palace) and Anne (b.1665 also at St James), who were to be the penultimate and last of the royal Stuarts.

The next twenty-five years were spent by James as heir apparent but at least for the first part of it he was kept busy. As Lord High Admiral he commanded the new Royal Navy at the Battle of Lowestoft in 1665 where he scored a difficult victory against the formidable Dutch fleet, sinking twelve and capturing fourteen ships, a result which would have been even more decisive if the victory had been followed up, but the legend is that Duchess Anne was so concerned about her husband's safety that she had him recalled. James was also in command seven years later at the Battle of Solebay in 1672 when a third of his fleet was French and disappeared at the start of the battle, blaming a misunderstood signal. James had two ships burned from under him as the Dutch made ingenious use of fire-ships, but in the end he managed a creditable draw. Meanwhile he had overseen the beginnings of reform of the navy with men like the efficiency-minded Samuel Pepys streamlining the administration. Michael Lewis refers to James as 'an administrator who deserves a high place in our naval history and a commander by no means negligible' and Pepys himself spoke out in his favour 'There has never been a greater Lord High Admiral nor one better fitted to name a naval officer.'

Soon after Solebay James had to resign his position as the Test Act forbad any Catholics to hold such posts, and the king himself took over most of the functions as the work of Pepys proceeded. He did have one further nautical escapade in 1682 when on the *Gloucester* and despite his protests an overenthusiastic pilot ran them onto a rock, breaking the ship's back. At least two hundred seamen were drowned, but James and his dog Mumper were rescued.

Throughout his naval career, James had pursued his other interests. He was an active chairman of the Royal Africa Society during the setting up of the first British trading stations on the west coast of Africa to service the slave trade. He was also a shareholder in the British East India Company which was obtaining its first footholds on mainland India and he had not only won the key victory which resulted in Britain's acquisition of New York but also done most of the parliamentary lobbying which preceded it. As the first proprietor of New York he gave some plots to his old friends from Jersey, so that the area became New Jersey.

Like all the Stuarts James was passionate about hunting and a trend-setting pioneer of the fox hunt. He played the guitar and like his brother was an adulterous husband: his favourite mistress was Arabella Churchill, the career of whose cousin John Churchill (later Duke of Marlborough) he did so much to accelerate. It was she who in 1670 at Moulins bore the ablest of his bastard sons, James Fitzjames, Duke of Berwick. Their three other children were Henry Fitzjames (1673–1702) Duke of Albermarle, Henrietta, later Lady Waldegrave and Arabella, the nun (d. 1762). In all James like his brother produced around twenty children including two Dukes of Cambridge and a Duke of Kendal but in his case fifteen were legitimate. As to James's religious beliefs it is hard to reconcile the belligerent, womanising huntsman with a man of deep religious sensitivity, but there is no doubt that his final conversion to Catholicism in about 1668 was deep-felt and genuine, even though it was to be a severe handicap for the rest of his career. His first wife Anne for some strange reason, perhaps to please her husband, also became Catholic at about this time but died soon afterwards. They made little attempt to hide their conversion but the king sensibly forbade them to meddle with the religious views of their two daughters who at the time were nine and six.

After his resignation from the navy, James's career went for a while from bad to worse. Duchess Anne had died in 1671 and his second marriage to the obviously Catholic Italian, the teenage Mary of Modena, combined with making his conversion public at the Test Act, created a major panic about his possible succession to the throne. The image of Monmouth as a potential Protestant alternative heir was enhanced by his military promotion and the propaganda campaigns of Shaftesbury. By this time James was forty, while his brother at forty-three had been married to Catherine of Braganza for eleven years without any sign of an heir. Monmouth on the other hand was in his mid-twenties, attractive and popular.

James in 1677 had virtually no say in the marriage of his elder daughter Mary to the Protestant champion William of Orange – she was fifteen and William at twenty-seven was on the verge of extracting a favourable peace from the French. The Exclusion Bill designed by Shaftesbury to deprive James of his right to inherit the crown backed up by hysteria over popish plots made life so uncomfortable for him that the king sent him into temporary exile in Brussels.

After Shaftesbury's fall in 1679 James was able to return and was sent soon afterwards as the king's commissioner to Scotland, replacing both Lauderdale and his own nephew Monmouth, whose turn it was now to go into exile as he paid for his possible connection with the Rye House Plot to murder the two royal brothers. Just as Monmouth had won friends in Scotland by his relative leniency to the Covenanters, so now James tried to court popularity at the other end of the spectrum by favouring the clans whom his predecessors had done their best to suppress. In particular he showed his partiality by imprisoning and condemning to death the chief of the Campbells who had so often been the instruments of repression – as it happened Argyll escaped from prison dressed as his step-daughter's page and lived to fight James another day. Amongst the Stewarts who backed James in this period was Alexander Stewart, (1634-1701) 5th Earl of Moray who converted to Catholicism and was made one of the first Knights of the Thistle in 1686.

James thus laid the foundations for the movement to which he unwittingly gave his name, Jacobitism. He shot a lot of grouse, played golf, hunted foxes and Covenanters. At the same time he seems to have been a generally effective governor of Scotland which was beginning to show some signs of increasing prosperity: Edinburgh was offering hints of its future as the Athens of the North.

It was the period of pressure on the Scottish Covenanters first by Monmouth and James Graham (later known as Bonnie Dundee), then by James that led to one of the first major migrations of Stewarts and other Scots families to America. There had been a John Stewart in the Albany garrison killed by Indians in 1671. Now there were a whole group transported out, some like Isabel Stewart as indentured servants in 1684–5, others like James and Alexander Stewart as religious refugees to the new settlement at East New Jersey.

There was another mini-colony founded in 1684 called Stewart's Town beside Port Royal and Charleston on the Ashleigh River, Carolina, but sadly within two years it was overrun by the Spaniards. Further south there were also Stewart settlers in Barbados – Agnes Stewart had gone there from Leith in 1663 and at least a dozen others had gone either as sugar planters or with the army. Thomas Stewart born in Galloway in 1666 became a rich Bridgeton merchant before returning to die in London in 1722. In addition the new colony of Pennsylvania that owed much to James championing the rights of his fellow admiral Sir William Penn and his rebellious Quaker son of the same name was later given a boost when James in 1686 had all Quakers released from prison. An Alexander Stewart was sent to Philadelphia as an indentured servant for eight years in 1697 and became a converted Quaker. One of James's illegitimate daughters Jane (1654–1742) became a Quaker, gave her life to helping the poor and lived in a Wisbeach cellar. Though she worked as a farm labourer she could read the New Testament in Greek.

On his return to London James was able to ignore the Test Act, resume control of naval affairs and became once more the heir apparent. In 1683 his second daughter married George Prince of Denmark, a Protestant, but that did not pose any particular threat. In fact James seems to have been almost too sure of himself with the fall from favour of Shaftesbury, his own military prowess and the continuing problems of his other son-in-law William of Orange who was still trying to consolidate Holland against renewed French pressure.

James was fifty-two when his brother died in February 1685 and he at last became king. His wife, the new Queen Mary, though none of her pregnancies to date had been successful, was a mature and beautiful twenty-five, although this did not persuade James to give up his latest mistress, Catherine Sedley.

James had perhaps been lulled into a sense of false security by the success of Charles in his final years in suppressing parliamentary opposition. He immediately did three things likely to cause offence: without parliamentary approval he began levying all the customs and excise duties which had been granted to Charles for his own life only; he openly attended mass; and he accepted the same kind of bribery arrangement from France that had propped up his brother's regime.

In June 1685 James was faced with his first crisis which should have been a warning, but in the end was not grave enough to make him change direction. James Duke of Monmouth at thirty-five made his rather disorganised landing at Lyme Regis with only eighty men, announced that James was a Catholic usurper and that he himself was the true King James II. He gathered a poorly equipped army of around 2,700 which was mown down by the king's artillery at Sedgemoor in July, followed by ruthless reprisals including James's ordering of the execution of his own nephew, Monmouth. Most frightening for the middle-ground Tories was the use of Colonel Percy Kirk's old Tangier garrison to finish off the stragglers and the merciless punishments meted out by Judge Jeffreys. With almost equal inevitability the Scottish end of this attempted coup collapsed with the capture of James's old Campbell adversary, Archibald Marquis of Argyll. Here too there were savage reprisals as James let the western clans plunder the Campbell domains unmolested. And this time there was no mistake about Argyll's execution.

One rebel however was spared, James Stewart of Goodtrees (1635–1713 – pronounced 'Gutters', now Moredun in Edinburgh) referred to at the time as 'a damn Macgregor' who had been plotting in Holland, changed sides several times and rose to be a legally creative but obese Lord Advocate who spent hours meditating in the Meadows. He later helped exonerate William III for his share in the massacre at Glencoe in 1692 and drafted objections to the Act of Union in 1707. Amongst other anti-Jacobite Stewarts was Goodtrees' brother Sir Thomas Stewart of Coltness, an ardent Presbyterian who after the fall of James II pushed the Westminster Confession through the Scottish parliament in 1690.

Instead of being made more cautious by the Monmouth rebellion James simply became more arrogant. He turned the long-dreaded Catholic plot into a reality by suspending the Test Act and rapidly replacing senior officials in the government, army and church with Catholics. He even planned to introduce more Catholics into parliament. His execution of his nephew had simply served to drive Monmouth's supporters into the camp of William and Mary, now the sole hope of the Protestants if James should die. His amassing of a huge standing army of 30,000 men and posting it threateningly on Hounslow Heath added to the sense of outrage, particularly when Catholic officers began to take over and Irish Catholic peasants were brought across to help fill the ranks. As if aware from which direction his enemy would come James had Portsmouth fortified on the landward side.

In reality the removal or disillusionment of the experienced Protestant officers for the time being merely demoralised the army and made it less efficient, so it motivated William of Orange to act sooner rather than later. It was in this atmosphere that James's supposedly loyal generals like his mistress's cousin Marlborough were to change sides when the confrontation came in earnest.

Meanwhile events in France served to enhance the worries of the Anglican Tory majority. There Louis XIV had just abolished the Edict of Nantes and was persecuting all non-Catholics, driving many of France's most skilled artisans to seek asylum in Britain and spread more rumours about papist persecution. James compounded this by accepting French subsidies to help create the same kind of one-sect state in Britain. Once more for the sake of religion the Stuart dynasty was self-destructing. Not even the British Catholics found the king's policies realistic.

Against this background, when all but a tenth of the population were Protestants of one kind or another and united against a forcible return of Catholicism, James made his most serious error. He rashly had seven English bishops including the Archbishop of Canterbury charged with seditious libel for refusing to act as propaganda spokesmen for him in their churches. Even if he had made sure that the juries were packed with his supporters it would still have caused outrage, but the bishops were acquitted in June 1688 and this exacerbated the crisis. To add to the urgency for action there was another event that same month, the birth of an apparently healthy baby son to his wife Mary of Modena. No aspersions on the legitimacy of the baby James, even the assertion that he had been smuggled into her bed in a warming pan, a future symbol for anti-Jacobite propaganda, made the news any less terrifying. Princess Anne, whose babies so far had all died young, hated her stepmother and contributed to the rumours helped by the fact that there had been no disinterested witness at the lying-in.

Soon afterwards the secret letter signed by the 'Immortal Seven' (three Tories and four Whigs) was sent to William of Orange the king's nephew and son-in-law, inviting him and his wife to seize the British throne. At the same time the Dutch printing presses were churning out anti-James propaganda to circulate in London and the sound of *Lilliburlero* was driving crowds to hysteria.

William made his landing at Torbay in November 1688, a rash undertaking because he was leaving his own country exposed to attack by the French and his army was only half the size of James's. But wisely he took his time, waiting for the king's nerve to crack and for his supporters to drift away. The strategy worked, for in this crisis James, once such a highly successful commander, was much less decisive than usual. He was often confined to his room with a bleeding nose and it has been argued that he may have been suffering from premature senility brought on by venereal disease.

James was at Salisbury within a fortnight of the landing and had a large army which should have been able to defeat William. But no great battle took place and the king dithered, apparently playing for time so that his wife and child could escape into exile – even if he went down himself, he wanted the dynasty which he had done so much to weaken to survive. The royal army simply began to disintegrate. The turning point was when one of James's longest-serving and ablest protégées John Churchill deserted, arranging at the same time for his wife Sarah to take with her their friend Princess Anne, the king's daughter.

Inexplicably the king ordered his illegitimate son the Duke of Berwick, still a teenager but one of his ablest officers, to surrender Portsmouth to William. He himself headed for Rochester. William who was under strict instructions from his wife not to hurt her father and who anyway dreaded the implications of parricide did his best to make James's escape route simple. Even then on its first attempt the king's ship went aground. Soon, after a twenty-eight year interval, James was back in St Germain, where the courtiers who listened to him said out of earshot that they could understand why he had lost his throne.

The only spontaneous effort to save James came from Scotland. There his kindness to the clan chiefs paid off and they fought hard for him under James Graham, Bonnie Dundee, who as it happened was proud of an inheritance of royal Stewart blood going back to Margaret, the daughter of Robert III who had married Graham of Fintry. Quite a number of homeland Stewarts rallied to the cause, particularly those less prosperous branches of the family left stranded in the highlands, the Stewarts of Atholl and Balquidder, many of whom were descended from the bastard brood of the Wolf of Badenoch, and the Stewarts of Appin, who had struggled on the west coast after their main legitimate line had died out as Lords of Lorn. Also with Dundee was his friend Sir Thomas Steuart of Grandtully and Patrick Steuart of Ballechin, the Atholl bailie who held Blair Castle. The brilliant victory at Killiecrankie however achieved no lasting result as Dundee was killed in his moment of triumph and there was no adequate replacement.

James himself did not take long to recover from his apparent breakdown in 1688. He was goaded partly by his wife Mary of Modena who had gained new enthusiasm for the cause after the birth of her son. Early in 1689 James was provided with an army of 20,000 men by the French and set sail from Brest for Ireland for his last campaign. In January he made his state entry to Dublin accompanied by his bastard son the Duke of Berwick who was now in his twenties, an experienced soldier and appointed as a major general. But James wasted too much time enjoying the social life of Dublin where one of his other bastards Henry Fitzjames, Duke of Albermarle and Grand Prior was rarely sober enough to mount his horse.

There is no need to recapitulate the narrative of the next eighteen months, which climaxed in the battle at the River Boyne where the two rival kings of Great Britain confronted each other. James had an early advantage there and could have won, for William was injured and had an asthmatic attack, but James failed to stop the Dutch mercenaries crossing the river and had few able generals. His son the Duke of Berwick was in charge of the cavalry but at barely twenty was still too inexperienced to make an impression. One of his bastard nephews Henry Fitzroy Duke of Grafton was killed at Cork. In the end William won the battle, but James was fighting in the wrong place anyway, for the French had just defeated the Anglo–Dutch navy off Beachy Head and James should have used this opportunity to invade England, rather than wasting it in Ireland. It was too late. A year later when James had an army ready to invade his old kingdom from La Hogue, the Royal Navy reversed their previous defeat by the French and the invasion plan had to be scrapped.

That was the last chance for James to be restored. He was already a fairly pathetic old man devoting himself to his tiny new daughter Louise Mary and to thoughts of life after death. He was a regular visitor for silent meditation at the convent of La Trappe yet he was still hunting in his mid-sixties and died at sixty-eight in 1701, surviving his own elder daughter, Queen Mary. Mary of Modena lasted another seventeen years and died in 1718, a couple of years after her son's abortive attempt to regain his father's crown. Of James's two surviving illegitimate sons the elder James Duke of Berwick went on to have a spectacular military career (see pp. 178–9) while even the younger and less stable Henry Duke of Albermarle and Grand Prior reached the rank of vice admiral in the French navy, serving at the Battle of Lagos Bay in 1693 and in charge of a squadron off Toulon three years later, but he drank himself to an early grave in 1702.

Chapter Five

William, Mary and the Orange Afterglow

Both Queen Mary II (1662–94) and William III (1650–1702), the first royal Stuarts never to visit Scotland, were grandchildren of Charles I, Mary the daughter of his son James and William the son of his daughter Mary, so they were first cousins. It was Mary, on the basis of the male line who had the greater right to inherit the throne of Britain but it was her husband William who had acquired an international reputation by his stubborn, 'last ditch' defence of Holland against the French and in real terms was the stronger candidate. Besides he had to be included in the package because without him there was no military force to stand up against the royal troops – few at this point expected such a rapid rate of desertion. In fact when the 'Immortal Seven' wrote to him they probably had no expectation that the couple would be anything other than joint regents. But James II in effect forced their hands by absconding from London with his wife and son, thus leaving a vacuum which had to be filled.

William refused to take the role of Mary's consort but insisted on becoming joint monarch, which meant that if she died first he would still be on the throne, and as it happened this was to prove the case. Mary as a dutiful and not personally ambitious wife backed up his demand, so it became law.

Neither of them had had an easy childhood. Mary was born in St James' Palace soon after the Restoration. Her mother died when she was nine and her father James Duke of York spent most of his time away at the wars or with his mistresses and was not allowed to see much of her once he came out as a Catholic. Thus she was brought up at Twickenham along with her sister Anne under the supervision of an Anglican bishop who focussed on their religious education at the expense of most other subjects. Mary was the prettier of the two girls and a good dancer who won plaudits as the star of several court masques.

The two princesses saw even less of their father when he married Mary of Modena who was only five years older then Mary and of course a Catholic. The relationship was naturally difficult and James was soon afterwards sent into exile.

It was therefore not he who organised her engagement at the age of fifteen to her Dutch cousin William who was twelve years her senior. Even her wedding was ruined by a scandal over her French-made wedding dress and a very stormy passage back to Holland afterwards. It was said that when she first saw William she burst into tears (the same story as Henrietta with Charles I) but in due course became an adoring and submissive wife. Sadly she suffered two miscarriages in 1678 when still only seventeen and after that there was no possibility of her producing an heir. Two years later she was severely ill and her busy husband totally ignored her plight.

Mary was too valuable to William's career for him to dispense with her entirely, but he felt able to humiliate her in public and spend more time with his mistress. Mary lived for the next decade in Holland, mostly at Houslardyke and at House in the Wood near The Hague. She was visited by her extrovert cousin Monmouth and by her step-mother, Mary of Modena with whom she seems to have briefly become friendly again. It did not last long however for when her sister sent the catty gossip about her new half-brother's birth in 1688 she was furious at the idea of losing her British inheritance. Meanwhile she learned to speak Dutch and achieved considerable popularity in a country where her husband was respected rather than liked. But he was away fighting so much that she saw little of him and turned half their dining room into a chapel. Thus when she returned to London as a potential queen she was a lonely woman in her mid-twenties with only six more years to live. Nevertheless despite William's bouts of mental cruelty he clearly had a deep underlying respect for her honesty and warmth which sustained him at times of crisis.

William III had been born in The Hague several months after the death of his father, William II of Orange, from smallpox. William senior had been stadholder and captain general of the Netherlands for only three years and since his office was part elective, part hereditary his early death meant that not only was his son deprived of a father, but the Orange dynasty had no one in a position to claim its rights in the new republic of Holland. The boy's mother Mary (1631–60), daughter of Charles I was barely twenty when he was born and also died from smallpox when he was still only ten. Anyway she had already left him to fend for himself as she joined her exiled Stuart siblings in the fleshpots of Paris and had a scandalous affair with Henry Jermyn.

The young Prince of Orange grew up a thin, sharp-nosed, deeply repressed and asthmatic child, scarred by an early attack of smallpox. He lived quietly under the republican regime of Jan De Witt without much expectation that he and his dynasty would ever regain power, particularly after Oliver Cromwell predictably interfered to help the anti-Stuart/Orange cause. Ironically it was his country's greatest enemy, Louis XIV who did him a favour by invading Holland in 1672 and exposing the military incompetence of Jan De Witt. De Witt was murdered and William at the age of twenty-two with virtually no military experience was elected as the new stadholder. He then waged a remarkable six year campaign in which he opened the flood gates on the dykes and against all the odds was able to embarrass the French sufficiently for them to make peace in 1678, the year after his marriage to Mary.

The next decade saw William consolidate his power in Holland and continue defying the French. It also saw him neglecting his wife for his vivacious mistress Elizabeth Villiers who had been one of Mary's ladies-in-waiting. Despite his military successes it was nevertheless a huge risk when he undertook the invasion of England in 1688. He was faced by an army much larger than his own and under determined leadership it should have been able to defeat him. If so he would not only have failed to win the crown of Britain but also lost his position as stadholder in Holland which he had left almost defenceless against French invasion. He was also living dangerously when he insisted on equal rights with his wife to the British crown and again when he fought his father-in-law James II for the last time at the Battle of the Boyne, because if defeated he could have been cut off in Ireland by the French fleet.

Mary's support for William's claim to an equal share of the British crown earned her a promise of conjugal fidelity but by this time William seemed to be more interested in male companions than female. Hans Willem Bentinck had been his closest friend and assistant from childhood onwards. Besides William was becoming increasingly asthmatic and drinking heavily after 1688. Mary's relations with her father went from bad to worse for despite the fact that she had insisted that William should let him escape unharmed, he still disowned her and made her miserable with a father's curse. Partially as atonement she encouraged less rakish habits in the London court and organised communal fasts. She had sadly also fallen out with her sister Anne who disliked William intensely and resented very much the fact that he now stood between her and the throne should Mary die, a throne that now meant much more to her as she had just produced an apparently healthy son, the Duke of Gloucester.

William was constantly aware that the support of the British political classes depended very much on his performance and that many of them, including a number of Stewart branches like those in Galloway and Blantyre who had supported his takeover, were at the same time keeping on good terms with James II in case the climate should change. In addition the fringe Stewarts of Appin, Atholl and Balquidder had all fought against his troops at Killiecrankie, and those of Appin, in particular, refused to take the oath of allegiance, even after their unfortunate tenants, the MacDonalds of Glencoe, were so severely punished on the king's orders in 1692. It was the irrepressible turncoat James Steuart of Goodtrees, nicknamed 'Jamie Wilie' who as one of the commissioners helped whitewash the king's role in ordering the massacre.

William naturally became quite paranoid about Jacobite plots and did not trust generals like Marlborough who had so easily deserted James II when he had the most need of him. Hence his natural preference for Dutch generals and Dutch friends. Indeed he spent about six months of each year campaigning in Holland, the homeland which he blatantly preferred to his new kingdom. It was suggested that he allowed his Dutch commanders to use their British troops as cannon fodder at battles like Steinkirk, an idea which made him even less popular (ironically his cousin James Duke of Berwick was a captain with the French royal guard there and had his revenge for his part in the defeat at the River Boyne). Much of William's time was spent with his male cronies at Het Loo. It was only due to the natural charm of his British-born wife that his relationship with senior politicians was no worse, as one minister after another was dismissed. Luckily by the time Mary died of smallpox in 1694 his position had been secured and three years later he was even recognised as King of Great Britain by the French. Surprisingly he was deeply shattered by Mary's death and soon afterwards got rid of his mistress, as if in an act of posthumous atonement.

Meanwhile the huge cost of William's wars had led to the founding of the Bank of England in 1694 and four years later to his disgust he had lost control of the British standing army to parliament – he still of course had separate control of his well-trained Dutch troops.

At this time William began to fall out with his oldest friend and supporter Hans Willem Bentinck, now Earl of Portland, who was jealous of the new Dutch favourite Arnoud van Keppel, Earl of Albermarle. It was a disagreement that embittered the last few years of William's reign and gave plenty of scope for the Jacobite scandal sheets to portray it, almost certainly unfairly at least in the physical sense, as a lovers' tiff. In 1700 came a dynastic crisis when William's nephew, Anne's only surviving child, the Duke of Gloucester died at the age of twelve. It was bad enough in Holland where William's only heir was a cousin and where there was anyway only a vague tradition that the House of Orange should provide hereditary stadholders. But if Britain reverted to James II and his family then Holland would be endangered, so William set his mind to secure the Protestant succession by the Act of Settlement which made Sophia of Hanover the next heir after his own and his sister-in-law's deaths.

At the same time William was reconciled with Marlborough who was made commander in chief as war once again threatened with France. This new war which centred on the problems of the Spanish succession was made more aggravating by the death at long last of James II at St Germain at the age of sixty-eight and the outrageous French recognition of his son as James III of Great Britain. It was William's great triumph that he was able to form the Grand Alliance against his old enemy Louis XIV in 1701, but his tragedy that almost immediately afterwards his horse stumbled on a mole hill and threw him. The only damage was a broken collar bone, but William's stressful life, his asthmatic chest and excessive drinking left him too weak to survive and he died a fortnight later. He was only fifty-two. He still had a lock of his wife's hair and her wedding ring in a casket round his neck.

Meanwhile the former royal family was not the only branch of the Stewarts to have found a new home in Europe. A year after William's death the family of Frederick Stewart, who had done well in Sweden and settled in Swedish Livonia, had to change allegiance when this area was conquered by Peter the Great of Russia, as they remained there as his subjects. It is typical of the Stewart diaspora that a few generations later there was a Baron Dimitri and a Baron Alexei Stuart (1838–1902) who died shortly before the first Russian Revolution. They were not the only Stewarts in Russia for a John Stewart had become a colonel in the Russian army in 1671, an Albert Stewart fought at Chigirin in the Ukraine while Robert Stewart had transferred from the Swedish to the Russian army in 1661. In addition, several Stewart stonemasons including a Peter and Neil Stewart worked on the buildings of St Petersburg from about 1730 and later the exotic palaces of Catherine the Great at Tsarskoe Tselo.

Yet of the Stewarts still in Scotland several branches had fallen on very hard times. After the massacre of Glencoe the Stewarts of Appin were regarded as just as recalcitrant as the unfortunate MacDonalds, their neighbours, and held out against accepting the London olive branch. They along with the similarly impoverished Stewarts of Atholl and Balquidder were to join in the rebellions of 1715 and 1745. They still had their lands, even if they needed to indulge in cattle raids to keep up their pretensions of grandeur. Much worse was the fate of Alexander Stewart of Perth who was charged with theft in 1701 and fitted with an iron collar to mark his life sentence in the dripping coal mines of Alva.

Chapter Six

Anne and Mrs Freeman

Queen Anne (1665–1714) the last of the royal Stuarts, was born like her sister Mary in St James' Palace and was only seven years old when her mother died. Her education followed exactly the same lines as Mary's and she grew into a tolerably attractive teenager, but less so than Mary in whose shadow she had to spend the first thirty years of her life. When her father remarried she was still only eight and she took a hearty dislike to her step-mother Mary of Modena, not least because she was a Catholic. Similarly when her sister Mary married their cousin William of Orange she took an instant dislike to him too. She mellowed somewhat after her own marriage in 1683 to the handsome but somewhat empty-headed George Prince of Denmark (1653–1708) most often remembered for his March, whom she married in the Chapel Royal at St James' Palace, Venus and Mars as it was portrayed, the third marriage between a royal Stewart/Stuart and the Danish dynasty of Oldenburg. She was utterly devoted to him for the next twenty-five years and he to her, but with seventeen pregnancies, twelve miscarriages and six infant deaths from hydrocephalus – two within one week in 1686 – and only one semi-healthy child to show for it, their marriage must have been most often a very miserable affair. The dropsical infection which made her pregnancies so unsuccessful also gradually made her puffy and obese.

Five years after her marriage she stirred up trouble for her father when he and Mary of Modena after fifteen years of trying, produced a son, James. She wrote scurrilous stories about her new step-brother to her sister Mary in Holland, backed up the warming pan scandal because neither she nor any high-ranking Protestant had been at the birth, and she was furious that a Catholic boy could now stand between Mary's and her own expectations of inheriting the throne. Her excitement was all the more because she and George also managed to produce a son that year who given Mary's gynaecological problems had been potentially the next king until the baby James appeared.

In this atmosphere she deserted her father's cause in 1688, as did her husband George who dined with the king in Andover one evening and the next morning stole out of the camp to join William. Anne, who slipped out of London with her friend Sarah Churchill (née Jennings), felt parricidal pangs of guilt afterwards, particularly when like Mary she received a father's curse for her disloyalty. She and Sarah wore Orange ribbons in the theatre to catch the mood, but her inner feelings belied appearances.

Anne soon also fell out again with her brother-in-law whose insistence on an equal right to the throne with her sister she deeply resented. Mr Caliban or the Dutch Monster was how she would refer to him in letters to her friend Sarah, blaming him for forcing her to desert her father. She also soon came to blame him for not giving an exalted military post to her husband Prince George, who was not without courage but showed very few signs of initiative. William claimed to have tried him sober and tried him drunk with equally little evidence of ability. George doggedly turned up during the Irish campaign at his own expense. Perhaps William also resented the couple's amazing fecundity.

Anne's friendship with Sarah Churchill, later Sarah Duchess of Marlborough (–1744) or 'Mrs Freeman' to her 'Mrs Morley', began when they were both children and lasted over thirty years. In 1682 Sarah had married the promising army officer Sir John Churchill, cousin of James II's mistress Arabella. Anne was much quieter in company than her sister Mary and tended to give vent to her feelings, which at times must have been overwhelming, in intense conversations first with Sarah and later Abigail Hill. Her husband after all was not very bright and never bothered to learn English properly.

Having fallen out with her father and brother-in-law the next victim was her sister, Queen Mary. Not only had the royal couple continued to neglect Prince George but in 1692 William dismissed John Churchill, by this time Earl of Marlborough, despite exceptional service during the Irish campaign. The problem was that as Marlborough had deserted James II in 1688 there was always the suspicion, not entirely unjustified, that he would change back to the Jacobite side. Anne and George were forbidden to see the Marlboroughs, a hurt made the more offensive by the fact that William had been so mean in his financial arrangements for them that they were in danger of losing their London home. Mary sided with her husband and the two sisters never spoke to each other again, even cutting each other dead in Hyde Park. When Mary was dying of smallpox Anne did offer to visit her, but the suggestion was politely refused. By that time George and Anne were no longer even entitled to a guard of honour.

Despite all her problems the last few years of the century were relatively happy for Anne because her only surviving child William Duke of Gloucester appeared to be growing up normally and on his birthday marched out his troop of small soldiers into the park. Prince George was happy enough attending the races at

Newmarket and Anne who often joined him there gave him a horse costing 1,000 guineas. She herself enjoyed playing cards, held regular Monday balls, drove her single-handed chariot to the hunt and conscientiously attended the Anglican Church. Then two deaths hit her badly: first that of her beloved son in 1700 at the age of twelve, which was a shattering blow and ruined her hopes for the future. It was this death which caused William, now king on his own after Mary's death, to agree to the Act of Settlement which after his own and Anne's death would pass the crown of Britain to Sophia of Hanover (1630–1714), daughter of Elizabeth the Winter Queen of Bohemia and the nearest Protestant descendant of the main Stuart dynasty other than Anne and William. Yet as she was of the same generation as themselves this effectively meant that the next king would be her son George (1660–1720) who had just become Elector of Hanover on his father's death.

The other death that hit Anne the following year was that of her estranged father James II with whom she had just begun a postal reconciliation and whose betrayal by her had left such feelings of guilt. However this was soon followed by a third death, that of William III, so at last at the age of thirty seven she became queen. Thus, the last of the Stuarts to reign made a speech in parliament boasting that 'she knew herself to be entirely English' (she was genetically at least fifty per cent English, thirty per cent French and twelve per cent Germano-Danish) and promised an Act of Union between England and Scotland. Prince George was at last made a general with the compliant Marlborough as the real commander-in-chief by his side. Anne herself was by this time suffering from gout though she believed in her power to cure other people for she was the last British monarch to practice the Royal Touch and even put a hand on the infant Dr Samuel Johnson.

The other branches of the Stewart family were mixed in their reaction to the Act of Union: James 5th Earl of Galloway whose uncle David had died in the ill-fated Scots colony of Darien was an opponent as were Walter Stewart of Blantyre and the inevitable Sir James Steuart of Goodtrees whilst others such as Robert Stewart of Tillicoultry who was made a Nova Scotia baronet in 1707, were in favour. Other Stewarts to die in Darien had included army Lieutenant James Stewart of Kincarrochie, Captain Andrew Stewart of the ship *Adventurer* and a John Stewart, gentleman. A lieutenant in the navy, John Stewart, spent his time on Darien trying to use the *Hugo of Boness* as a fireship against the Spaniards, but on the whole the Stewarts suffered fewer losses in Darien than many of Scotland's great families.

There had been a period of remarkable military success in which the Anne-Sarah Marlborough relationship reached its apogee. In 1704 they drove in a coach with eight horses to St Paul's to join in the thanksgiving for Marlborough's massive victory at Blenheim. Yet ironically this War of Spanish Succession in which the British scored so many prestigious victories was largely settled by the skill of her illegitimate half-brother, James Duke of Berwick, who also since his mother was Arabella Churchill, was Marlborough's nephew. It was he as a marshal in the French army who defeated the British in the crucial but less publicised Battle of Almansa, west of Alicante. It was this victory won by an illegitimate Stuart which effectively consolidated the Bourbons as kings of Spain, the prevention of which had been the sole official objective of all Marlborough's wars. Berwick was still only thirty-seven and by his own efforts had worked his way to the top in the demanding service of Louis XIV. For this he was now created Duke of Liria, a title which he immediately passed to his eldest son. With his first wife, the Countess of Lucan he had two children, one of them the new Duke of Liria (1696–) and with his second, Anne Bukley, another ten including Charles, Duke of Fitzjames (1712–87) Francis, Bishop of Soissons (1709–64) and Henry Abbot of Berwick (1711–31). Thus ironically this bastard line of the Stuarts was far more fertile than the royal family. Berwick's career had blossomed since he became a general despite losing to William III at Landen in 1693 after which he was briefly a prisoner of war. Apart from Almansa, his siege of Gibraltar, his capture of Nice in 1706 and his role as the final defender of France after Marlborough's victory at Oudenarde marked him out as France's most trusted commander and his career was to extend into the next reign (see p.184).

By 1710 Anne was an obese, childless widow in her mid-fifties, for her oldest surviving child had died ten years earlier and her beloved but corpulent Prince George at the age of fifty-five in 1708. She now spurned her old friend Sarah Duchess of Marlborough and turned instead to a new confidante, Abigail Hill or Mrs Masham, Sarah's cousin. Sarah's fall from favour was soon followed by that of her husband whose expensive wars and grandiose ideas had been sufficient motivation to reinvigorate the Tories who used talented writers such as Jonathan Swift to mount a campaign against him. So with some help from Mrs Masham they swept to power and charged him with embezzlement in 1711.

Thus Anne's last four years on the throne were shared with a Tory administration and despite declining health she continued to attend cabinet meetings. Her dismissal of both the Marlboroughs and of her long-serving minister Sidney Godolphin showed the same streak of pettiness that had led to her falling out with her sister. So did her last letter to her cousin Sophia of Hanover who was made so miserable by it that it was said to have contributed to her death soon afterwards, two months before Anne's. However Sophia was by this time eighty-four so had she outlived Anne and become Queen Sophia of Great Britain her reign would certainly not have been a long one.

Having won the election of 1710 the Tory ministers made peace with France on terms which were overtly unacceptable to Hanover, so as the queen grew steadily less healthy they realised that they had little to look forward to when she was replaced by the Elector George. There was therefore still a real possibility at this point that the Stuart dynasty could have survived, for Anne could well have been willing to back the Tories in cancelling the Act of Settlement and letting her half-brother James succeed her on the throne as James III. But the one basic requirement for this to happen was that James should switch from the Catholic to the Anglican Church and this he was unwilling to do.

Even then there was a remote possibility that the dying queen had such feelings of guilt about disloyalty to her father that she might still have backed a Jacobite succession plan. After all at this stage a Lutheran German king seemed almost as unattractive as a half-Italian Catholic. But as the privy councillors haggled over the queen's deathbed at Kensington Palace they made their decision to send for George of Hanover and as Anne's heart finally gave out, the Stuart dynasty after 344 years in power at last came to an end.

Meanwhile one of the less grand descendants of the Steward had also made his mark in the world. The almost illiterate fur trapper William Stewart based at the York Factory of the Hudson's Bay Company had learned to speak the Cree language, so he was chosen in 1714 to lead an expedition to explore the regions west of the bay. Taking a party of a hundred Cree he set off up the massive Athabaska valley which stretched 700 miles through the Rockies and he is reputed to have reached the Great Slave Lake, a return journey of some 1,600 miles. He was helped in this extraordinary journey by a half-Cree serving woman called Thanadelthur who seems to have had great skills of diplomacy and guided them successfully through hostile territory.

Part Six

THE PRETENDERS AND THE DIASPORA

Chapter One

James the Old Pretender

.

In 1688 the birth of James Francis Steuart, (1688–1766) the Old Pretender or the Chevalier St George, had caused a great deal of controversy because of his father's age and the long gap between his second marriage and the first signs of an heir. The doubts about the baby's parentage had not been helped by the failure to invite any reliable non-Catholic witnesses to the lying-in at St James's Palace, hence the stories about warming pans. Yet by 1714, when he might have become the fifteenth Stuart to wear a royal crown he was showing signs of stubbornness that should have removed all doubts about his parentage.

As a tiny baby he had been smuggled out of London in a pile of rags along with his mother disguised as a washerwoman and spent the next thirteen years at St Germain outside Paris. His father James II was away a lot in the early days trying to win back his kingdom and when he did reappear was increasingly morose, so much of the boy's upbringing was in the hands of his Italian mother, Mary of Modena. When the embittered James II died at the age of sixty-eight in 1701 young James was declared James III (VIII of Scotland) by the French who believed in doing anything that would irritate William III, but some pursuivants who dared to make the same announcements in London were pelted by the mob.

The awesome figure in the background of the young prince's boyhood was his grand-uncle King Louis XIV, *Le Roi Soleil*, who by this time was sixty-three and at the height of his powers. The exiled Stuarts were just poor cousins who might be useful pawns in the game of power-politics by which Louis was making France the dominant power in Europe with Spain now included in the Bourbon empire.

Louis was seventy and James nineteen when the French king made his first attempt to place him as a French puppet on the British throne in 1708. By this time the boy's much older half-sister Anne was queen and Marlborough, her favourite general, had been scoring significant victories against the French. This was offset by the French victory at Almansa however where one of James's illegitimate half-brothers James Duke of Berwick, fifteen years his senior, was the commander of the French army. A force of twenty-seven ships and four thousand men sailed from Brest after a delay because James had measles. It reached the Firth of Forth but there met a British fleet under Admiral Byng which prevented landing. So the invasion force had to retreat to France without James having set foot on Scottish soil though he begged impetuously to be allowed to do so alone.

The following year James gained some military experience fighting in the French cavalry against Marlborough at Malplaquet. It was a defeat but James took part in twelve risky charges and came away with an enhanced reputation. The Treaty of Utrecht in 1713 put an end to the war and James was forced to leave Paris, settling at Plombières-les-Bains in Lorraine. The next year, James at the age of twenty-six made the most important decision of his career: he refused to give up his Catholic faith when potentially offered the crown of Britain if he would become an Anglican. This effectively put an end to the hopes of Queen Anne and her Tory ministers who were looking at the possibilities of changing the Act of Settlement to let James succeed her instead of George of Hanover. So when Anne died it was George who took over. Though his accession was far from popular the alternative of the Catholic James did not look any more satisfactory.

With the failure to secure a legal succession for James in 1714 the only other possibility was by armed rebellion or invasion. Any hopes of this were dealt a severe blow by the death of Louis XIV in 1715. Nevertheless despite the prospect of little French help and the lack of initiative being shown by James himself there was such a rebellion in 1715. The main instigator was a disillusioned politician, John Erskine Earl of Mar who had been passed over for promotion by George I and turned Jacobite. James himself wanted the rising postponed until foreign troops could be enlisted to help, but Mar went ahead without his initial blessing. The news was enough to persuade James to move from Lorraine to St Malo where, coincidently, he was very close to the original Stewart home town of Dol-de-Bretagne. He was there when news arrived of two battles, one a Jacobite defeat at Preston, the other an indecisive encounter at Sheriffmuir which showed that success might still be possible. Meanwhile he had appointed his half-brother the Duke of Berwick as his commander in chief in Scotland – a post which Berwick as a French citizen and marshal of the French army felt obliged to refuse. The Stuart cause was therefore deprived of the services of its ablest general though he would have been too late anyway due to Mar's impetuosity. Besides, his continental style of generalship might not have suited the Scottish situation.

By this time in his late twenties, James no longer had the excuse of immaturity yet he had not developed any outgoing charisma which would have won over devoted supporters. He had physical courage, he showed that he could on occasion be decisive and by refusing to turn Anglican for the sake of a crown he had shown that he was not a hypocrite, but he never shared his father's commitment to turning the British back to the old faith and lacked the ruthlessness to do so. He was instead rather reserved and sometimes moody. He showed lack of commitment to the continuance of the dynasty by making no effort to marry but had mistresses based at Barr and Luneville whom Bolingbroke cattily described as his female ministers.

Despite the setbacks James still felt obliged to support Mar but was very slow to move, partly because the French regent refused to let him leave, partly because he hoped in vain for French help. Eventually disguised as a sailor he evaded the French guards and embarked at Dunkirk for Scotland in December 1715 with five companions including Berwick's son James Duke of Liria at his side and at least some moral support from Berwick, who stayed behind but did what he could on the diplomatic front, though he had very little faith in Mar. In all his correspondence he always referred to his half-brother James as 'the King'.

James landed at Peterhead and headed for Scone where early in the new year he was to be crowned James III and VIII supposedly with a makeshift crown made from the melted-down jewellery of his followers' wives. Yet there is no evidence that the coronation ever went ahead and for a week he was laid up with flu at Fetteresso. He made a poor impression on Mar and his other followers with his lack of friendliness, his vacuous processions through empty towns and his requests to all the churches to pray for him rather than his hard-pressed followers. Besides this, it was a bad winter, food was short and the highlanders were beginning to head for home. By the end of the month James had to start moving northwards as Argyll approached. His callous orders to burn Auchterarder and other nearby towns to deny shelter for Argyll's approaching army won him no friends. Crossing the frozen Tay he headed for Montrose and his advisers were already warning him that to save bloodshed he should make his escape. Nevertheless the letter he sent to his followers after he had gone, saying that he had done so in order to spare lives was received with derision. From Montrose he sailed for Holland having been in Scotland for six weeks, and he never returned.

Many had died or been wounded and captured in this attempt to put him on the throne, including Stewarts. At least a dozen Stewarts were transported to Carolina after the first Battle of Preston, some on the *Wakefield* and some on the *Susannah*. Another Preston prisoner, William Stewart was transported to Williamsburg for seven years. The punishments meted out to senior Stewarts on the Jacobite side were less severe. Francis Stewart had been the treasurer and was not treated harshly. On the government side there had been a number of Stewarts including Sir James of Goodtrees, the solicitor general. Charles Lennox, Duke of Lennox (1672–1723) the Pretender's cousin and one of Charles II's bastards lived comfortably at Goodwood and was not interested. His son, the next duke, fought at Dettingen and became a redcoat major general.

As James crossed back to France he stopped off at Luneville and Barr for consolation from his two mistresses before heading south to his mother's old home at Modena. She died of breast cancer two years after his return and at some point he moved to Urbino, then Rome, where he was given the Palazzo Muti by the Pope.

Meanwhile, his courtiers were trying to find him a suitable bride and suggested Clementina Sobieski (1702–35), grand-daughter of the Polish hero, John III, fighter of the Turks. Her journey from Poland to Italy was made extremely hazardous by the efforts of English agents sent out to prevent the Stuarts from producing an heir who could claim the throne. She had to be rescued at Innsbruck by the Irish mercenary Charles Wogan, later suspected of some romantic attachment to her, and by the Scotsman John Walkinshaw. James was away working on another would-be invasion plot at Las Rosas in Spain when she arrived, so the marriage took place by proxy. Yet James was no more than an observer of the Spanish-backed expedition which set sail under James Butler, Duke of Ormonde with 5,000 Spaniards and arms for 30,000 Jacobites. A separate smaller fleet with Scottish Jacobites and a few hundred Spaniards made a landing in Kintail, but Ormonde's fleet was smashed by a gale and had to return to Cadiz. The joint Jacobite-Spanish force garrisoned Eilean Donan castle but it was pulverised by the Royal Navy. Soon afterwards the remainder of the invading force was beaten at Shiel Bridge and the last semi-serious attempt to make James a king was finished. Ironically the atmosphere in London was at this time distinctly anti-Hanoverian and the city shortly had a series of Jacobite Lord Mayors including Sir William Stewart in 1721.

So James returned to his new wife. Clementina was seventeen and James thirty one. Their first brief marital home was in the village of Montefiascone sixty miles from Rome, then they returned to the Palazzo Muti where their first son Charles Edward Casimir was born in 1720, followed two years later by their second, Henry. But after five years the marriage began to show signs of strain, for Clementina had competition in the shape of the ebullient wife of James Hay, James's new secretary of state. Besides she found it hard to cope with her husband's dark moods, so she shut herself in a nunnery and died in her early thirties when her elder son was only fifteen.

James by this time in his late forties was an increasingly morose figure who discouraged his son's dream of still pursuing the British crown. He outlived his wife by thirty years, a lonely figure haunting the Rome opera house, sometimes seen vainly calling for encores.

James also outlived his half-brother James Duke of Berwick with whom twelve years after the '15 he was eventually reconciled. Berwick's remarkable career as a French general had continued when he was made commander-in-chief in France's war against Spain in 1720, a war in which his son James Duke of Liria fought equally hard but with no ill-feelings as a brigadier on the other side – the boy had decided on a career in Spain instead of France. Berwick's abilities as a civilian organiser were also demonstrated when the Regent gave him the job of halting the plague pandemic which hit France in 1721 and he had the task after that of reforming the French army. There then followed a few years of retirement which he spent expanding his ornamental gardens at Fitzjames, his estate near Clermont or attending the Parlement of Paris where he was noted by St Simon as 'one of the big bastards' or 'that great dry devil of an Englishman'. His last command came in the War of Polish Succession when in his early sixties he led the French troops over a pontoon bridge across the Rhine into Germany and was decapitated by a cannon ball while inspecting the front lines at the siege of Philippsburg. With him at the time was his younger son Charles Duke of Fitzjames who survived and was succeeded at Warties by a series of French Dukes of Fitzjames right up to the Revolution – there was a Duke of Fitzjames Regiment of Foot fighting for the British in 1794. His eldest son James Duke of Liria who was later the Spanish ambassador in St Petersburg became Duke of Berwick and Liria, and began a new Spanish mini-dynasty which included the later Dukes of Alba. Among his descendants were two notable Spanish sailors (see p.200) and Don Jacobo Fitzjames Stuart (d. 1947) who was sent to London by Franco as Spanish ambassador during World War II.

Chapter Two

Charles the Young Pretender and Culloden

Charles Edward Louis Philip Casimir Stuart, the elder son of the Old Pretender and his wife Clementina Sobieski was born in Rome in 1720 and inevitably had an unusual childhood. Relations between his morose father and his romantic-minded but disillusioned mother worsened rapidly and when the boy was five she shut herself in the San Clemente Convent, dying some ten years later. His father, burdened with an ever-increasing sense of failure, was to live for another thirty years and it was almost in reaction to his pessimism that Charles developed such an unhealthy and extravagant optimism. He was surrounded by those whom it suited to fill the boy's head with dreams of his illusory kingdom which even his father had only visited for six weeks and both his grandfather and great-grandfather had lost in humiliating circumstances.

Charles proved to be an outward-looking all-rounder. He learned French, Italian and English, coped with Latin and even a little Greek. He was fond of music and played the violin quite well, enjoyed tennis, golf, shooting and riding. He grew into a tall, thin young man of confident posture with dark impressive eyes set in a pale face. This was normally surmounted by a light bag wig which covered his own dark reddish hair. Ethnically speaking this supposedly iconic figure of Scottish history was twenty-five per cent Polish, twenty-five per cent German, twenty-five per cent Italian, fourteen per cent French, seven per cent Germano-Danish and the remainder Anglo-Scots, yet at an early stage he came to think that Scotland would be the place in which his hopes of a crown might take root. And when someone sent him a kilt he tried it on.

In 1734 Charles was given his first taste of warfare in his early teens by his cousin James Duke of Liria who at the time was helping his Spanish masters to reconquer Naples. According to some Charles was just an observer at the siege of Gaeta; according to others he took a courageous part in the action. Whatever the truth of that it is certain that he was on the winning side and perhaps acquired a rather rosy view of the ease of military operations, particularly of the way the Spanish Bourbons had conquered a new kingdom for themselves. He was perhaps also led to underestimate the British army when he was given a small role on the French side at Dettingen nine years later, the last battle in British history where a king, George II was allowed nominal control of the troops, and nearly lost.

By this time Charles was mixing with a group of Irish mercenaries and other Jacobite hangers-on who spent their lives making plots against the Hanoverians. The next year he won his father's reluctant blessing to try to regain the Stuart kingdoms and set off in disguise from Rome. He seems to have lodged for a while at his cousin's castle of Fitzjames. At this point the French army under Marshal Saxe was seriously planning an expedition with 15,000 men to invade England.

There are shelves full of books about the '45 so this is not the place to try to summarise them, only perhaps to point out some of those features which relate to the overall history of the dynasty. Certainly in 1744 there was the genuine prospect of French assistance and even the Old Pretender was ordering new uniforms for his guards in the expectation of success. But as on previous occasions the prospect of French help suddenly disappeared – a combination of British naval dominance in the Channel and a succession of gales was enough to end the whole project. Despite numerous warnings that his situation was now hopeless, Charles impetuously decided to go it alone. Some of the less responsible of his advisers believed that 20,000 armchair Tories would turn into fighting Jacobites the moment Charles stepped onto Scottish or English soil. This was what Charles wanted to hear. Under his current alias of the Chevalier Douglas he talked to as many exiles as he could, mixed at the opera and in French diplomatic circles learning and preparing. He paid heed to the Jacobite nostalgia of men like Stewart of Traquair who 'drank enough loyal toasts to float a ship' but in the end made no useful contribution.

When he at last boarded the frigate *Doutelle* at Nantes he was disguised as a student and had grown a beard, for security was one of his specialities. He still had no promise of serious French support, only seven hundred men, two ships and some arms. In the end even that reinforcement was to be denied him. He anchored for a while off Belle Ile and corresponded with his father. The response to his famous promise 'to bring back three crowns or die in the attempt' was the affectionate but realistic plea that James would prefer his 'dearest Carluccio' to come back alive.

Things started badly when the larger of his two ships, the *Elizabeth*, carrying the seven hundred troops and their arms, was severely damaged by the British ship *Lion* and had to limp back to France. Charles went on his way with only the 'seven men of Moidart' apart from the smaller ship's crew. His decision was to cost more than five thousand British lives and ruin many more.

So in July 1745 Charles made his famous landing on Eriskay disguised as a priest, later transferring to the mainland at Loch nan Uamh in Moidart.

Significantly of his seven followers three were Irish, one was English and of the three Scots, two were MacDonalds. Not surprisingly, even in the west highlands the response to his arrival was lukewarm. It is a tribute to his undoubted charisma that he converted so many waverers and within a month, sporting a highland broadsword and targe, he was raising his red and white standard at Glenfinnan. A month after that he had an army of six hundred men capable of capturing Edinburgh though he was probably helped by the fact that the Lord Provost was an Archibald Stewart who went out of his way to mismanage the defences. Charles, wearing his red breeches and blue bonnet had turned out a brilliant and unexpectedly successful leader who marched on foot all day at the head of his troops, refusing to ride a horse except in battle and was first to leap into the water when crossing rivers even though it is said that he could not swim. While success lasted he was energetic, decisive, inspiring, a tireless yet thoughtful general. As he marched past Bannockburn just out of range of the redcoat artillery in Stirling Castle he showed the right kind of bravado and appreciation of history. His good treatment of redcoat prisoners and refusal to let his troops do as much looting as was normal in such circumstances was sensible and impressive.

The first four months of his campaign took Charles so close to an extraordinary triumph that they totally amazed both the fringe Jacobites who had foretold disaster and the Whigs and Hanoverians who had grossly underestimated the danger. Charles was helped by the military experience of Lord George Murray (1700–60), a man twice his age who had served in both the 1715 and 1718 rebellions and whom he made joint Lieutenant General with the less able Duke of Perth. Their outmanoeuvring of General John Cope, the experienced Hanoverian general was extremely skilful and both Cope's earlier reluctance to fight using his poorly-trained troops and his subsequent heavy defeat at Prestonpans were immensely important for Jacobite morale. Captain James Stewart of Perth's regiment was one of the scouts and crawled amongst the coal pits at Prestonpans with a blunderbuss and four pistols. Given Cope's numerical superiority the impact of the highland charge on untried redcoats was a triumph. For some Stewarts in the Prince's army however Prestonpans was not a happy experience: Dugald and John Stewart, both from Appin were severely wounded there and took no further part in the '45.

The Prince's army now rose to around 8,000 which meant it was large enough to be credible and a major short term threat until the Hanoverians could recall more of their regular troops from the continent. So Charles had the huge satisfaction of relaxing briefly in Holyrood, the palace of his ancestors, and enjoying the acclaim of his new subjects. Colonel John Roy Stewart (1700–52) a Gaelic poet, an inveterate Jacobite plotter and experienced mercenary soldier who after deserting from the Scots Greys had been with the French army at Fontenoy, was able to take out his press gangs and mop up recruits from the streets of Perth and Edinburgh to form a new regiment of some five hundred men. His main motivation like that of most of the west highland Stewarts was obsessive hatred of the Campbells. The same applied to the Appin Stewart contingent whose chief was an infant but who were led by the fanatical Charles Stewart of Ardshiel, another inveterate plotter and brilliant swordsman who led some three hundred men throughout the campaign. But this was the poor wing of the Stewart dynasty. The wealthy ones like Alexander Stewart Earl of Galloway (1694–1773) who was a redcoat general at Fontenoy and his brother William, also a redcoat, stayed away. The same was true of the Prince's cousin Charles Lennox, son of one of Charles II's bastards who was a major general at Dettingen.

One of the few lowland Stewarts to come over to the prince at this time was Sir James Steuart of Coltness (1713–80) referred to as 'the prettiest little cur' who had gone to Rome to drink in Jacobitism in 1739 and joined the Young Gentlemens' Travellers Club, a euphemism for aspiring Jacobites. He was sent to Paris to chase up French help, but though he failed to do so he was to spend the next twenty years in exile. He was regarded as a traitor both by the British and by the French for he was arrested while in possession of the British plans for the capture of San Domingo and spent three years in a French prison. The one benefit of this was that he did a lot of thinking and drafted his highly innovative *Inquiry into the Principles of Political Economy* which was published many years later.

After Prestonpans there followed one of the first major disagreements on strategy in which Charles allowed himself to be overruled by Murray. Whereas Charles wanted to attack the aged General Wade and his army of 10,000 based in Newcastle as the beginning of a slow move southwards, Murray was worried about numbers, knew Wade's troops were better than Cope's had been and wanted to bypass Wade by invading down the west coast. Murray's advice was accepted and ten weeks after Glenfinnan the Jacobite army was heading over the border past Carlisle at a speed that would have done credit to Montrose. Given that Murray's strategy was to avoid a pitched battle he was adhering to the maxims of Robert the Bruce and had learned the lesson of Mar's loss of momentum at Sheriffmuir. He was also aware that given the vastly superior numbers of George II's army, the Jacobites' one real chance was to create a panic in London sufficient to demoralise the English Whigs and win active support from the still chair-bound English Tories.

The plan was remarkably successful. Within four weeks they had passed Preston and outmanoeuvred Wade. They then managed by a feinting movement westwards to wrong-foot the Duke of Cumberland, George II's younger son and main royal general who had at last arrived back from Flanders. So unhindered the Jacobite army reached Derby, 130 miles or about ten days march from London. There the desired panic was produced with a run on the banks, the shops shut and George II ready to head off for Hanover. However Jacobite recruitment in the north of England had been extremely disappointing and the supposedly keen Jacobites of Lancashire and north Wales had failed to materialise. Murray knew that he would almost certainly have to face a pitched battle before he got to London and was worried not just by lack of numbers but by the weather, for December did not suit a fast-moving army that needed to pick up food as it went along. In addition the French diversionary force supposedly being organised by the Prince's brother Henry was not ready. The force led by William Stuart of Blantyre gathered in Gothenburg to head for Scotland at the expense of Louis XV, never appeared.

For a second time Charles allowed himself to be overruled by Murray on a major decision. In realistic military terms Murray was right, yet Charles had been successful so far by ignoring realities and William III's invasion of 1688 had shown that psychology could be more important than troop movements. Certainly from the moment of the turn-around at Derby the dream was shattered and the prince's character changed completely. The infectious confidence and camaraderie with his men were gone. His troops endured appalling weather as they dragged his artillery back over Shap. He ruthlessly abandoned his garrison in Carlisle to its fate.

By Boxing Day of 1745 the Jacobites were in Glasgow where they were far from popular and stayed for the last week of the year. Some of the troops slept in the half-finished St Andrew's Church while Charles used Shawfield Mansion by the Trongate and held one of the first ever public reviews of what was left of his army on Glasgow Green. Here Charles met for the first time Clementina Walkinshaw, daughter of John Walkinshaw of Barrowfield in Renfrewshire, the man who had helped rescue his mother Clementina Sobieski from Innsbruck, hence the choice of his daughter's christian name. Like Charles Clementina had been born in Rome, so they had much in common, but there was to be some suspicion that her motives included espionage, for one of her sisters became a Hanoverian chamber-maid. However at this stage Charles was too busy for their affair to ripen and it was some six years before he met her again.

A few weeks after leaving Glasgow some of Charles's confidence had returned and he rejected Murray's advice to carry on the retreat north of Stirling. He was determined at least to hold on to the highlands. On his own initiative Charles set about a siege of Stirling Castle which allowed the first of the English armies under General Henry Hawley to catch up with him. So the first pitched battle since Prestonpans took place at Falkirk in January 1746 and lasted barely half an hour. For the second time the impact of the highland charge unsettled a redcoat army and although losses were small on both sides Hawley admitted defeat and withdrew.

Meanwhile William Duke of Cumberland, resolute, slow-moving but efficient, the same age as his distant cousin Charles (they each had about the same amount of Stuart DNA), had recaptured Edinburgh and was only a few days away from the Jacobites if he chose to hurry. Once more Murray advised retreat and this time Charles reluctantly agreed. By February the Jacobite army was in Inverness and Charles who was becoming increasingly depressed was ill for several weeks at Elgin. Inexorably the cautious Cumberland edged closer. He arrived at Nairn while the Jacobites were at Culloden. There then followed a tragic error of judgement and a show of logistic incompetence by the Jacobite generals. They decided on a bold night attack on Cumberland at Nairn, but miscalculated badly the distance and roughness of the ground and ran out of food. The result was that instead of a night attack which could conceivably have been successful, they exhausted themselves with a fruitless night march and then, without much food or rest, had to trudge back to their old positions and wait for Cumberland to attack at Culloden.

The odds against even the so-far invincible highland charge being effective against properly organised artillery were very slight and at Culloden the Jacobite command structure lost control. The Stewart of Appin contingent who threw their muskets aside for the charge collided with Clan Chattan and had ninety-two men killed including eight Stewart officers. Of the eighty-six men in the regiment bearing the name Stewart, fourteen were killed at Culloden and twenty wounded. Similarly of the fifty-two Stewarts in the Atholl regiment, at least thirteen were killed at Culloden and the same again wounded. The remains of John Roy Stewart's Edinburgh Regiment were in the front line and suffered badly. The battle turned into a massacre and Charles, who had earlier declared his intention to win or die on the battlefield was persuaded to leave the field to try again somewhere else. Between 1,200 and 2,000 Scots were killed and the many who were wounded and not finished off by Cumberland's men had to lie on the battlefield for two days before they were given help. Major Stewart of Kynachan was wounded and then burned to death in a barn after the battle. Thomas Stewart, a Hanoverian and secretary to the Lord President took some food and water to one group, but they were slaughtered soon afterwards. Another Hanoverian Stewart present at the battle was Captain Alexander Stewart of Dunearn of Kerr's regiment.

In the aftermath of the battle 120 Jacobites were executed, over nine hundred transported to the colonies and nearly a hundred died in prison. Stewart of Ardshiel escaped to hide under a waterfall in Duror but his wife was harassed in his stead. His colleague Captain James Stewart of the Glens (1700–52) an Appin shopkeeper and smuggler also survived only to be executed, almost certainly undeservedly, for the murder of the Red Fox Campbell six years later. Another survivor was Alexander Stewart of Invernahyle (1709–95) who had done well at Prestonpans, was wounded at Culloden and was the inspiration for Walter Scott's *Waverley*. Similarly Allan Breac Stewart (–1789) who became a courier between France and the Appin Jacobites and may have been the real murderer of the Red Fox, was certainly the basis for Robert Louis Stevenson's *Kidnapped*. Major James Stewart of Perth's regiment was kept handcuffed for ten days. Even Alexander Stewart, the Prince's footman was condemned to transportation. Orkney Jacobites like Sir James Stewart of Burray who had murdered a naval captain in 1728 died in one of the Southwark prison ships as did a David Stewart, though Archibald Stewart of Brugh was never caught. John Stewart (1689–1776), the builder of Dalguise spent some time in prison but lived a long time afterwards as did the mysterious James Stewart (1728–1844) allegedly born in Carolina, who fought as a teenager at Prestonpans and died at Tweedmouth aged 116 having had five wives and twenty-seven children of whom ten sons were killed fighting in the British army.

It is estimated that around five hundred Stewarts were either killed or trans-
ported and of those few survived for long. Among them were John and Thomas
Stewart, both deserters from the Black Watch who after a spell in the Tower of
London were transported to the Leewards. John and Henry Stewart from Fort
Augustus who had been in the Glengarry regiment were both transported to
Barbados and Duncan Stewart of Ardshiel to Jamaica. Private D. Stewart was in
Carlisle prison for two years, as was John Stewart of Glencoe. In the end Culloden
was not a battle between Scots and English for there were Scots on both sides and
even a few English among the Jacobites. Nor even were the Stewarts all on the
same side. It was the last bloody effort of a failing dynasty to regain power after
losing it several times as a result of poor judgement and incompetence. The more
successful of the Stewart landed families were largely on the Hanoverian side and
only the disaffected highland Stewarts who had not made careers as mercenaries,
ministers or lawyers were on the Prince's side.

There could have been one last stand at Ruthven where nearly 5,000 survivors
had gathered but Charles regarded further fighting as useless. He had no desire
for a guerrilla war, only to reach London, and that was now out of the question.
So the troops dispersed, many of them to be hunted down over the next year
by Cumberland's men. Charles himself famously took five months to make his
escape. Having evaded capture by many different ruses and through the help of
many who risked their lives to save him, including Flora MacDonald, he at last
found *L'Heureux* anchored in Loch nan Uamh and sailed away from virtually the
same spot as where he had landed fifteen months earlier.

His ship took him to Morvaix on the Breton coast from which on his way
to Paris he must have passed close again without knowing of it to the ancestral
family home at Dol-de-Bretagne. In Paris he met his brother Henry whom he
blamed for the slowness and ultimate non-appearance of the French reinforcements he had been trying to organise. Henry who had tried his hardest but had
been ill in Avignon on his way from Rome was disgusted by the ingratitude and
decided soon afterwards to abandon any political ambitions to pursue his career
in the church. At least given his misogynistic tendencies his vows of celibacy in
that direction were easy for him to keep and there was no question of his fathering a new heir for the dynasty, an objective in which Charles also showed no
interest. The following year at the age of twenty-two, Henry Stuart was made
Cardinal Deacon of Santa Maria in Campitello.

Charles spent the next two years in Paris begging for help, quarrelling and
drinking. His relationships and attitude to women are clouded in obscurity. There
is some evidence to suggest that his prime obsession with regaining a crown pre-
cluded any other attachments. In this first period of exile however he developed
a friendship with a woman fifteen years older than himself, Marie-Louise de
Talmond, a Paris sophisticate, and they lived together in the Convent of St Joseph.
There were also other ladies of the demimonde who consoled him intellectually
as much as physically. Plots were still being hatched on his behalf by die-hard

Jacobites and in 1750 he seems to have made an incognito visit to London, where he saw little evidence of support.

Soon after this Clementina Walkinshaw reappeared in his life, possibly hired as a Hanoverian spy: at least given their previous brief acquaintance followed by a six year gap, it did not suggest any urgent passion. The couple lived together in Ghent as Charles had been declared undesirable in Paris – he had once been arrested just outside the opera. In 1753 their daughter Charlotte was born in Liège. Clementina sometimes used the name Countess d'Albestroff, sometimes the couple were called Mr and Mrs Johnson or Thompson. They moved to Basel then back to France. Both were now drinking heavily and Charles had taken to beating her quite regularly. In 1760 when Charles was a prematurely middle-aged man of forty and Clementina six years younger, she left him with the sympathetic help of the Old Pretender and Cardinal Henry, who now had the income from two rich French abbeys and a Spanish pension. She settled with Charlotte in the Abbey of Meraux outside Paris. She was to live into her mid-seventies and die in Freiburg, Germany leaving £12. Shortly before her death she was visited by John Stuart, Earl of Bute who took a kindly interest in her welfare.

Charles was forty-six when his father died in 1766 and to an uninterested world he proclaimed himself King Charles III of England, Scotland and Ireland, yet still had no heir, nor had he made any effort to produce one for his phantom kingdom. Yet the French still thought there was some value in the Stuarts as an irritant to the British, so it was their initiative which led to the finding of an obscure young German princess, Louisa, daughter of the impoverished Count of Stolberg, a small town only sixty miles from Hanover. Charles had by this time moved to Florence and this was where they married in 1772. The age difference between the fifty-year-old prince and the convent-educated Louisa, now made Countess of Albany and promised wealth and a crown, was thirty-four years. Charles made an effort initially to please her but soon reverted to the bottle and physical abuse, so no legitimate heir was forthcoming.

Cardinal Henry, now Bishop of Frascati tried to patch things up for them but while she was in his care he condoned the visits of the philandering poet Vittorio Alfieri whom she had met in Florence in 1777. She became his mistress 'La mia Donna'. When she died many years later in 1826 having meantime taken a French painter called Fabre to be her replacement paramour their ashes were buried together in the Santa Croce.

Meanwhile after the failure of his marriage Charles thought once more about his daughter Charlotte (1753–89) whom he had last seen when she was seven and who was the same age as Louisa. In 1784 he persuaded her to come to Rome to share the last four years of his life. By this time Charlotte was in her early thirties and had three children from a relationship with Ferdinand de Rohan, the Archbishop of Bordeaux. Charles with his usual vanity had forbidden her to marry anyone but a royal, so even if she could have been legitimised, her children could not. Charles gave her the title Duchess of Albany which inspired Robert

Burns to write one of his less successful songs *The Bonnie Lass of Albanie*. She turned out to be a kindly, loving daughter who persuaded Charles to drink less and helped nurse him for the last four years of his life. Thus Charles died in his late sixties in the Palazzo Muti in Rome in the same room where he had been born and was buried initially in his brother Henry's cathedral at Frascati before being moved to the fine tomb of the Stuarts in St Peter's. He left his Florentine palace to Charlotte.

So Cardinal Henry Duke of York (1725–1807) announced himself to the dedicated few as King Henry IX of England, Scotland and Ireland. He had shown kindness to the three women maltreated by Charles: his mistress Clementina, his daughter Charlotte and his wife Louisa. He did many other good works perhaps as compensation for his alleged predilection for young boys. He had been at one time one of the wealthiest prelates in Italy, but a year after his brother's death he lost nearly all of his income as a result of the French revolution and was to lose the rest when Napoleon invaded Italy. So in his final years he was sent a pension by George III and reciprocated by leaving the surviving crown jewels, removed from London by James II, to his successor the Prince Regent.

Charlotte only survived her father by a year and fell ill after a riding accident near Bologna. She was thirty-six and her teenage children with one possible exception (see p.205) vanished from history. Their father Ferdinand de Rohan survived the French revolution and went on to become the confessor to the Empress Josephine.

A rather more successful contemporary of Prince Charles was Major General Stuart who in 1735 was serving in the Russian army but later transferred to help the Duke of Holstein conquer Sweden for himself. There he might have come across Colonel Sir John Steuart of Grandtully who had joined the Swedish army after fighting with the Atholl Stewarts at Sheriffmuir. After the '45 he returned to Edinburgh an allegedly penniless widower and paid court to the most eligible spinster in Scotland, Jane Douglas, sister of the childless old bachelor Duke of Douglas. Their subsequent surprise elopement to France when she was forty-eight and her even more surprising production a year later in 1749 of twin boys created one of the greatest scandals and one of the most protracted legal disputes of the eighteenth century. In the end their surviving son Archibald Steuart Douglas was declared genuine and allowed to inherit the vast Douglas estates.

Both the '15 and the '45 accelerated the drift of Stewarts and other Scots across the Atlantic whether as transported criminals or voluntary emigrants. Alexander Stewart had moved to Philadelphia while Charles Stewart from Orkney was a successful merchant in Virginia by 1750 and another Charles Stewart was a Royal Navy admiral patrolling the West Indies station in the 1730s. John Stewart of Dalguise was a prosperous Charleston shipwright at about the same time and there was still a band of Stewarts at the little enclave of Stewart Town founded in 1684. James Stewart from Islay settled on the Hudson River in 1738, and another James Stewart followed in 1776. Another Alexander Stewart served as a lieutenant under Oglethorpe in the Georgia frontier post of Frederica during the Florida War of 1739 when he held out valiantly against the Spaniards aided by a Sergeant John Stewart

What was remarkable was the way that so soon after the '45 numerous highlanders including Stewarts were fighting in the Hanoverian British army. A number including Charles Swede Stewart fought with Wolfe at Quebec in 1756 and settled in Canada afterwards where several Stewarts also fought and died, as did Peter, George and Patrick Stewart at Ticonderoga a year later. More Stewarts were killed fighting for the 42nd in New York that same year and several discharged soon afterwards.

Chapter Three

John Stuart and the American Wars

Remarkably within fifteen years of Culloden a Hanoverian king appointed a Stuart as his chief minister.

John Stuart, Earl of Bute (1713–92) who for two years was effectively prime minister of Britain was descended many years back from John the Black Stewart, an illegitimate son of King Robert II, whose family in 1385 were given the hereditary sheriffdom of Bute and usually also the custody of Rothesay Castle. This was not necessarily the easiest of tasks as it was twice besieged and badly damaged by the MacDonalds in 1453 and 1648. The family plodded on without any significant achievements, until the tenth Stewart sheriff was made (or paid to become) a baron of Nova Scotia. His obese son James changed sides three times in the Civil War and again Rothesay Castle was all but destroyed in 1685. It was his grandson, another James, the thirteenth hereditary sheriff in the family, who was at last made an earl by Queen Anne for helping to push through the Act of Union in 1707, though his brother Dougal turned out to be a Jacobite. He moved the family from its Old Mansion House in Rothesay to a new one a few miles away at Mount Stuart.

John Stuart, the third earl was born in Edinburgh in 1713 and seems like his predecessors to have had no desperate ambitions. After studying at Leiden University where he was attracted by the latest developments in botany he spent his early years cultivating trees and studying the flora and fauna on his own island. Then in 1737 at the age of twenty-four he was chosen a representative peer and appeared occasionally at Westminster. Soon afterwards his career suddenly accelerated. In 1750 he was picked as a Lord of the Bedchamber for the eccentric Prince of Wales, Frederick, and when the prince died only a year later continued as a close friend of Augusta, Princess of Wales. He won the post of Groom of the Stole for the new heir to the British throne, her son the future George III who at the time was only twelve.

Bute was thus a formative influence on the young prince's development and gathered influential friends like the Elder Pitt. When the boy, Bute's 'dearest friend' became king in 1760 it was not long before he was made a secretary of state alongside Pitt, then a year later First Lord of the Treasury, this despite the fact that as Dorothy Marshall perhaps rather harshly puts it 'he was unfitted for the task in that not only did he lack political experience and any gift for leadership but he also lacked nerve and a grasp of realities.' Furthermore he had never sat in the Commons and had no power base there. It was even then straining the unwritten British constitution for the king to appoint a personal friend as chief minister. For all these reasons he had a poor press in his own lifetime and has done ever since, exaggerated by the fact that the Whig interpretation of history cast him as a villain impeding the progress of democracy while the Tory interpretation equally vilified him for damping down the aggressive expansion of the empire.

Bute and the new king shared a dislike for using British troops to fight in Hanover and in this they fell out with Pitt. Bute's mission, pushed in his own propaganda sheet, the *Auditor*, was to cleanse the government of corruption and restore the king's role as the head of state.

Meanwhile the government was attempting to make peace with France and Spain after the spectacular victories of the Seven Years War, but Pitt still wanted a further naval attack on Spain. Bute and the king manoeuvred the popular war minister into resignation. Even after he had gone the war continued successfully but expensively under Bute with the capture of Havana from Spain and an attack on Manila. Then as Bute drastically cut the army expenditure for the continental part of the war he also forced out the Earl of Newcastle so that 'the dearest friend' could be First Lord of the Treasury. He now pushed hard to end the war and made a treaty which gave Britain all of Canada, the hinterland of the American colonies, Grenada, Dominica, St Vincent, Tobago, Florida and Senegal. In addition, Britain regained Minorca and had control of Bengal. The king's electorate of Hanover had its borders restored. Yet by the treaty Bute gave back to France a number of captured territories such as Martinique and St Lucia, as well as the fishing areas off Newfoundland. All this added to the unpopularity he had already engendered by his aloofness from ordinary political life and his reputation as 'the minister behind the curtain'. Bute had secured a peace which in many ways was a remarkable and sensible achievement but Pitt in opposition poured scorn on it and Bute paid the penalty for appearing less than imperialist, for being a Scot and for being the king's friend. It was now his turn to resign.

As it happened the attack on Havana had been led by James Stuart (d.1797) from Torrance at East Kilbride, who had served as a captain in Holland, was at the siege of Louisburg in 1758, and was the general who captured Martinique in 1762.

He later served in India in 1775 where he lost a leg at Pollilore in 1781 and fought a one-legged duel back in London using a tree to keep himself upright. He is easily confused with another General James Stuart (1741–1815) from Blairhall who fought at Seringapatam and helped conquer Ceylon in 1796.

Bute's later years were spent harmlessly as President of the Society of Antiquaries of Scotland and he played a major part in the development of Kew Gardens, also amassing a huge collection of paintings at his new Bedfordshire home, Luton Park, where he had a laboratory for examining his even larger collection of minerals and fossils. In science as in politics he was not the mere amateur that his great wealth suggested.

John, the eldest son from among his eleven children married a rich Welsh heiress and then after her another rich heiress from the Coutts banking family, thus substantially increasing the family's wealth. He became Baron Cardiff, ambassador to Spain and was made 1st Marquis in 1776. His fourth son Charles was a general (1753–1801) in the Cameronians who served in the American wars and after capturing Minorca was made its governor. Admiral Vincent commented about him that 'his troops would follow him to hell.' Charles's son, another Charles Stuart, Baron Rothesay (1779–1845) acted as Wellington's contact in Portugal during the Peninsula Wars and built the romantic Highcliffe Castle near Christchurch. Later he became ambassador in Russia where he was so ill that he was referred to by colleagues as '*le cadavre ambulant.*'

General James Stuart was another Bute Stuart who fought with Nelson and like him lost an eye. He was credited with saving Portugal in 1798, was popular with his troops but not with politicians whose orders he ignored, for instance refusing to hand over Malta to Tsar Paul of Russia. He became ill, resigned and died soon afterwards in 1801.

The Bute family added the Crichton to their surname when the 2nd Marquis inherited the earldom of Dumfries from his mother and he made them even richer by his astute development of Cardiff harbour. It was his great grandson, John Crichton Stuart (1847–1900) an archaeologist and mystic who thanks to his ownership of Cardiff docks and some coal mines became allegedly the richest man in the world of his day and left an extraordinary architectural heritage. He rebuilt Cardiff Castle and Castell Coch in Wales, built the exotic Mount Stuart on Bute with its amazing chapel, restored amongst others Rothesay Castle, Falkland Palace, Dunblane Cathedral, the north side of Charlotte Square including Bute House in Edinburgh and gave the Bute Hall to Glasgow University. He died at Dumfries House and having converted late in life to Catholicism had his heart buried in Jerusalem.

One of the stranger Stuart contemporaries of Bute was Don Pedro Stuart, a son of James Duke of Liria, described as a lieutenant general in the Spanish navy who was in charge of a fleet of sixteen ships which sailed in 1759 from Cartagena to collect the King of Spain. The man believed to have been his son Don Jacobo Stuart was captain of the *Santa Sabina* and put up such a heroic fight against Nelson in 1796 – he lost a mast and 164 men before surrendering – that even Nelson was moved to admire his conduct.

One of Bute's protégées was an even stranger member of the family, John 'Walker' Stewart (1749–1822) born in London the son of a Scottish cloth merchant. Bute helped him get a post with the East India Company and after a brief career in the army of Hyder Ali when he acquired a deep cleft in the head, he became chief minister of Arcot. He learned to speak Persian, studied the Abyssinians and became known in London for walking the streets in faded Armenian costume.

Another Stewart who literally made his name in India was the eccentric Major General Charles 'Hindu' Stuart (1757–1828) from Galway who joined the East India Company in 1777 and worked his way up from quartermaster in Bengal to major general by 1814. He kept an Indian concubine and learned a number of native languages but offended many by converting to the Hindu religion and regularly worshipping on the banks of the sacred river Ganges. He disapproved strongly of Christian missionaries whom he regarded as upsetting the status quo in India and did his best to improve the lot of the sepoys in a way that might have avoided the later Indian Mutiny. He died in Calcutta and left his huge art collection to the British Museum.

Meanwhile as George III presided over the loss of the American colonies, several Stewart settlers had surprisingly chosen to fight against independence and keep their Hanoverian overlord. Alan Stewart of Invernahyle, son of the Appin hero was a colonel in the North Carolina Highlanders. Alexander and Robert Stewart had both joined the Virginia Regiment in 1756. John Stewart was a volunteer in the Royal Highland Emigrants in New York in 1778. A Colonel Stuart commanded the Guards at the hard-fought Battle of Eutaw Springs near Charleston and was killed at Guildford in 1781 while capturing Washington's guns. Captain Patrick Stewart was briefly in command of the Tories at Savannah. Charles 'Swede' Stewart/Stuart who had fought at Quebec and been a superintendent of Indian affairs died as a prisoner of war at Mobile in 1780.

Another expert on Indian affairs was John Stuart/Stewart (1718–79) from Inverness who won riches when as a young seaman he shared in the prize money from Captain Anson's epic voyage round the world in 1744. He emigrated to Charleston in 1748 where he joined the local militia to fight the Cherokee. After a heroic defence of Fort Loudoun he was captured by the Cherokee but won the friendship of his captors and became a peace negotiator for various tribes of native Americans, paying off their debts and organising their frontiers, even seeking their help against Washington, but also preventing white settlers from impinging on their territories. He even took a Cherokee mistress in addition to his Scots-born wife and had a large second family which took the name Bushyhead. His legitimate son John (1759–1815) fought with the Buffs during the American wars later becoming a general and Count of Maida.

Anthony Stewart (1738–91) son of an Aberdeen merchant who had emigrated to Annapolis in 1753 owned a ship called the *Peggy Stewart*. He was unfortunate enough to bring back a cargo of tea to Boston at the height of the patriot riots when the duty on tea was a serious issue and chose to burn his own ship to placate the mob, then fled back to London.

Among the Stewarts who did fight for American independence was Major John Stewart of Maryland who led the 'forlorn hope' at Stony Point in 1791 and was given a silver medal by Congress. Another was Colonel Walter Stewart of the Pennsylvania Regiment who fought at Brandywine and was badly wounded at Monmouth when ordered to cover Washington's retreat in 1781. William Stewart served as navigating officer on the privateer *Guildford* which harassed British shipping in 1776. Captain Charles Stewart (1778–1819) 'Old Ironsides' commanded the USS *Constellation* in the war of 1812, famously captured two Royal Navy ships off Madeira in 1815 and rose to the rank of admiral. His grandson was Charles Stewart Parnell (1846–91) the charismatic Irish politician who nearly won home rule for Ireland in the 1880s. Another Stewart who fought the British was the lawyer Archibald Stuart (1757–1832) from the North Carolina militia who ended up with a plantation in Augusta and twelve slaves.

One of the chief iconographers of the new United States was the painter Gilbert Stuart (1755–1828) born on Rhode Island, who as an apprentice of Benjamin West had painted the ceilings of Somerset House and produced numerous portraits of Washington including the favourite one painted at the Atheneum.

Many Stewart Loyalists lost their properties and were compensated by the British with small estates in Canada – two John Stewarts from the New York area, both with large families were among those who made this move. Other Stewarts were to make their mark in Canada and the Western United States, particularly as explorers. David Stuart (1765–1853), from Callander, son of one of the Appin Stewarts who challenged Rob Roy, joined his cousin John Stewart in the North West Company in 1812 to help found the Astoria fur trading post now in Oregon. He also founded Fort Okanogan and explored the Kamloops area while his cousin John founded Fort Estekadine on the upper Columbia. Another John Stewart (1779–1847) from Strathspey and also with the North West Company accompanied Fraser in his first descent of the Fraser River – both the Stuart Lake and Stuart River were named in his honour.

David Stuart's nephew Robert Stuart (1785–1848) from Balquidder sailed from New York via the Falklands and Cape Horn with his uncle to make a dangerous landing at the mouth of the Columbia River where he helped found Astoria as a fur collection depot. He then went on several epic overland journeys to find the eastward route from Astoria to St Louis, particularly the South Pass through the Rockies which provided a crucial link in the Oregon Trail. He later became involved in helping escaped slaves and as superintendent of Indian affairs in Michigan he defended the rights of Native Americans, though he had a quick temper and once killed a disobedient voyageur. His grandson was a brigadier general in the Union Army under Sherman (see p.208). James G. Stewart was an assistant to Robert Campbell in 1850 and his name survives in the Stewart River which was navigable, apart from the Fraser Rapids. Andrew Stewart (1789–1822) from Glasgow was with the Hudson's Bay Company and chief trader at Moose Factory in 1821. Alexander Stewart (d. 1840) managed the Lesser Slave Lake and Athabaska area for the North West Company and was at the capture of Fort Astoria before becoming chief factor for the Hudson's Bay Company at Fort William. The town of Stewart at the mouth of the Bear River owes its name to R.M. Stewart its first postmaster who organised the miners' claims during the gold rush of 1898.

Rather more sedentary were Charles James Stewart (1775–1837) who came out as a missionary then became Anglican bishop of Quebec, and another missionary, John Stuart, who helped translate the gospels into the Mohawk language in 1763. Sir William Drummond Stewart from Murthly in Perthshire had fought at Waterloo but led several plant-collecting expeditions high into the Rockies during the 1830s, sleeping at nights in a crimson tent. He escaped scalping by pretending that the Indians who were attacking his encampment simply were not there and brought back plant specimens and buffalo to his estate at Murthly in 1843. The lawyer Sir James Stuart (1780–1853) drafted the Canadian Act of Union in 1840. Finally there was Harriet Stewart (1862–1931) who claimed to be the first female arts graduate in the British Empire.

Meanwhile back in Edinburgh the elegant and immaculately dressed mathematician Dugald Stewart (1753–1828) from the Bute branch of the family succeeded the great Adam Ferguson as professor of moral philosophy in Edinburgh. This key figure of the Edinburgh enlightenment befriended Robert Burns, was both a friend and supporter of his Glasgow counterpart Adam Smith and co-founded what became known as Common Sense Philosophy. As Henry Cockburn wrote 'To me his lectures were like the opening of the heavens. I felt I had a soul. His noble views, unfolded in glorious sentences, elevated me to a higher world.' That other remarkable Steuart, Sir James of Goodtrees and Coltness (1713–80) a lawyer and grandson of the covenanting banker and lord provost of Edinburgh of the same name, who had done some Jacobite scheming in his day produced a book *The Dissertation on Money* which laid many of the foundations for the new subject of economics which Adam Smith was to take on to a wider stage two decades later. Equally ahead of his time was the ex-ships doctor Alexander Stewart (1673–1742) who helped pioneer inoculation for smallpox in 1720 and did other useful medical research. Later Alexander Patrick Stewart (1813–83) was to do pioneering work on the treatment of typhoid, while Peter Stewart did the same for cholera.

Chapter Four

Robert Stewart, Viscount Castlereagh, Beauty Stuart and the Rest

Robert Stewart, Viscount Castlereagh (1769–1822) born in Dublin was undoubtedly one of the ablest of all the Stewarts. His family were Ulster Presbyterians of fairly humble origins who by a mixture of hard work and some good marriages clawed their way up the social scale at Ballylawn Castle, Donegal from 1640, until Alexander, the first Castlereagh of Mount Stewart, County Down, was sent to France to help dissuade James II from trying to make a comeback in Ireland. He failed and was thrown into the Bastille for his trouble, but the family had made its mark. Alexander's grandson, Robert's father, became an MP in the Dublin parliament the very year his son was born. Twenty years later he was made Baron Londonderry, then Viscount Castlereagh in 1795 and after the Irish Union of 1801, organised by his son, became an Irish peer at Westminster. He also remodelled the family home at Mount Stewart in County Down.

Young Robert himself studied at Cambridge in 1788 without waiting for a degree and was then chosen as a Whig MP for County Down in the Irish parliament in 1790. He spent some time in France where he sympathised with the early aims of the revolution but was alarmed by how far it had gone and five years later he switched sides to become a Tory. Thus in 1797 as a supporter of the Younger Pitt he was made Chief Secretary of Ireland at the age of thirty-one to push through Pitt's Act of Union. This abolished the Dublin parliament and moved the MPs to Westminster. As envisaged by Pitt, it was a radical move which if carried through completely might have solved the Irish problem, but the element of Catholic emancipation that would have allowed Irish Catholic MPs to come to Westminster was vetoed by King George III, so Pitt along with Castlereagh, resigned.

By the middle of 1802, the crisis of Napoleon's possible invasion of Britain was such that Pitt was called back as prime minister. This time Castlereagh was put in charge of India, where he had to cope with the mercurial Lord Wellesley, the governor general who was a fellow Irishman and elder brother of Arthur, the future Duke of Wellington. After this Castlereagh served twice in the arduous position of war minister in 1806–7 and in 1807–9 under a new prime minister. As such he took the blame for the disastrous Walcheren expedition. Tempers were so raw that he fought a duel with fellow cabinet member George Canning who was an opponent of the expedition. He was slightly wounded.

From 1812 until 1822 Castlereagh served as foreign secretary under Lord Liverpool during a period when alliances were critical and the task of peace-making after the fall of Napoleon extremely demanding. Never a charismatic crowd-puller, he was an extremely able parliamentarian and a consummate diplomat whose crowning achievement was his reorganisation of Europe at the Congress of Vienna after the fall of Napoleon. He was associated with policies of repression at home which led to him being hissed in the streets, yet though he failed to court popularity he was referred to as a 'gentleman who could be trusted'. After twenty years of virtually continuous high office he began to show signs of mental disturbance. There is some suggestion that he was the victim of entrapment by a transvestite prostitute and in a fit of deep depression at the age of fifty-three he cut his own throat.

While Stewarts like Castlereagh wielded the real power there were still those who occasionally dreamed of reviving the old dynasty and its claims to the throne of the fast expanding British Empire. One of the strangest of these was General Charles Edward Stuart, Count Rohenstart (c.1780–1854) who was probably the son of Charlotte Duchess of Albany and thus illegitimate grandson of Bonnie Prince Charlie. His Christian names, his date of birth and the fact that his title was a strange concoction of Rohan from his father and Stuart from his mother, all give some credence to the idea. He was in the Austrian army with the Stuart Regiment defending Vienna in 1799, possibly also served with the Russians and died in Dunkeld in 1854 after being involved in a coach crash on his way southwards from a visit to Inverness. He had been married to Anna von Leiner Negelfurst.

If he was a descendant of the Stuart kings, Rohenstart was much more discrete about it than the two Allen brothers who changed their name to John and Charles Sobieski Stuart Stolberg in what seems to have been an elaborate piece of self-delusion. John Allen (1795–1872) learned Gaelic, convinced many that he was genuine, reinvented the Scottish tartan industry and lived in royal grandeur in London and at an elaborate hunting lodge at Ailean Aigas on the Beauly River.

Serious neo-Jacobites preferred the claims of the legitimate descendants of Charles I's daughter Henrietta whose daughter became Queen of Sardinia. From her came three generations of Sardinian kings, the third of whom had a daughter, the Duchess of Modena. Her granddaughter Maria Theresa (1849–1919) was put forward by hopeful Jacobites as Mary III of Scotland and IV of England.

She married Ludwig III who was very briefly king of Bavaria and their son Ruprecht or Rupert (1869–1955) who was thus ninth in descent from Charles I, represented Bavaria at Queen Victoria's jubilee in 1897.

Sadly as a potential candidate for the British throne Rupert suffered from the double disadvantage of being both a Catholic and a German, in fact in the early part of the First World War he commanded a German army group in France. His son Duke Albert of Bavaria (1905–96) opposed the Nazis and was interned with his wife and four children in a concentration camp. Reputedly he decorated his Schloss Berg on Starnberg Lake with tartan, but even if he was less overtly Germanic than his father he was still a Catholic. With his death in 1996 at the Nymphenburg Palace in Munich the illusory succession went to his son Prince Franz of Bavaria (1931–) an elderly art expert and confirmed bachelor so on his death the ever more tortuous trail of royal Stewart ancestry would, for anyone who still cared, lead via his niece to the Prince of Liechtenstein.

Such has become the eccentricity of the nearest legal claimants to the doubtful honour of heading the powerless dynasty that it has been fertile soil for new impostors like the Allen brothers. One of the most recent, a Brussels retailer who called himself Michael Stewart (b. Michael Roger Lafosse in 1958), claimed descent from Bonnie Prince Charlie's alleged marriage to Marguerite O'Dea d'Audibert de Lussan, Comtesse de Massillan (1749–1820) and their almost certainly non-existent son Edward James. Nevertheless he had sufficient credibility to be considered for the throne of Estonia in 1994, but the Estonian electorate perhaps wisely thought better of the idea. He returned to live with his mother in Belgium.

Almost as unlikely was the American Prince James Edward Stuart of Greenwich, Connecticut who founded a new Jacobite party in 1982. Born in Italy, he claimed to be a descendant of Cardinal Henry Stuart and promised if enthroned to reduce income tax to two per cent.

The tradition of Stewarts as fighting men continued. Among other Stewart generals during the Napoleonic wars was Castlereagh's half-brother Charles William Stewart (1778–1854) who as 'Fighting Charlie,' a dashing cavalry officer, was so short-sighted that he sometimes failed to see the enemy but rose to be a Lieutenant General under Wellington whose criticism was enough to reduce him to tears. Later, after helping his brother at the Congress of Vienna as Earl Vane he was ambassador to Prussia and Russia. He had married an extremely wealthy coal heiress from Durham and built Seaham harbour. General Charles Stewart (1775–1812) from Banff served in St Lucia in 1791, fought at Seringapatam in 1792 and at Walcheren where he covered the retreat but was killed at Corunna having thus waged war in three continents, a not unusual feat in this period. Charles Lennox, descended from Charles II, and 4th Duke of Lennox was a general in the West Indies, then Governor General of Canada in 1818 where he died from the bite of a rabid fox.

Colonel William Stewart (1774–1827) from the Galloway branch led the Grenadiers in St Martinique in 1793, then served in the Russian and Austrian armies where he became a great admirer of Tyrolean marksmen and brought the idea of specialist riflemen back to the British army. He fought as a marine with Nelson at Copenhagen and again in Egypt as a general after which he was known as Auld Grog Willie because he gave his men extra rum rations at his own expense. Commanding the Highland Division in 1811 he all but lost the Battle of Albuera in the Peninsula War, ordering his pipers to play *Hey Johnnie Cope* as his fellow officers were decimated. Described as 'incapable of obeying orders' he commented with fashionable sangfroid as a shell exploded at his feet 'A shell, sir. Very animating.' Wellington however thought him indecisive for 'his boiling courage reclaimed his judgement.' In seventeen campaigns he was seriously wounded six times. His brother Charles, Earl of Galloway was an admiral as was George Stewart (1768–1834) from the same family who served in the West Indies under Hood.

General Sir John Stewart/Stuart (1725–1815) born in Georgia, the son of the round-the-world sailor (see p.201) fought at Alexandria and was the ambitious but self-opinionated commander in Sicily in 1806 who attacked southern Italy without orders and was made Count of Maida for defeating the French there in 1806. He regularly fell out with the navy and as a result took some of the blame for failing to stop Napoleon capturing Vienna. He was described as so vain that he spent most of his time writing his own eulogies rather than actually preparing for battle.

Robert Stewart, 3rd Lord Blantyre (1775–1830) served throughout the Peninsula campaign but was then accidentally shot while leaning out of a hotel window during the Brussels revolution. General David Stewart of Garth (1772–1829), descended from the Wolf of Badenoch had joined the Black Watch in 1787 and was a reluctantly obedient young officer when he had to do his duty keeping order during the early clearances in Sutherland. He later saw service in America, Egypt, Guadeloupe and Minorca before retiring due to the after-effects of his wounds to the family seat at Garth when he championed the Highlands in his seminal *Sketches of the Character, Manners and Present State of the Highlanders of Scotland* (1822) and earned the friendship of Sir Walter Scott. Then in 1825 he served as governor of St Lucia.

Among naval Stewarts of this period, apart from Auld Grog's brothers, there was Sir Houston Stewart (1791–1875) of the Blackhall Shaw-Stewart branch who served with Cochrane on the *Imperieuse* in the amazing defence of Rosas before becoming an Admiral and being second in command of the navy during the Crimean War. His son, Vice Admiral Sir William Houston Stewart (1823–1901) displayed gallantry as a midshipman during the Syrian War of 1840 before attending a course on steam power after which he captained the paddle sloop *Virago* in the Pacific. Famously he recaptured Punta Arenas from the rebels along the coast of southern Chile where an island is named after him. He captained a paddle frigate at the siege of Sebastopol and later sailed the Tsar of Russia's new yacht *Livadiya* from the Clyde to St Petersburg. Less respectable was his racist grand-nephew Houston Stewart Chamberlain (1855–1927) who switched sides to the Germans in 1916 after taking Richard Wagner's daughter as his second wife and became an early advocate of Aryan supremacy.

Two later Victorian era generals from the Stewart family stand out. Patrick or Peter Stewart (1832–65) from Kirkcudbright organised the telegraph in Persia and India, then served in the Indian Mutiny at the relief of Lucknow and helped tackle an outbreak of cholera. Also in India was Sir Donald Martin Stewart (1824–1900) from Forres who helped suppress the Indian mutiny, fought in two Afghan wars and in Abyssinia before becoming commander in chief in India in 1880 and a field marshal in 1894 by which time he was seventy.

Sir Herbert Stewart from the Galloway branch (1843–85) first came to prominence by his quick action in preventing the spread of cholera in Bengal, then explored areas of the North-West Frontier. He commanded the Dongola Camel Corps, took part in the Zulu War of 1878, and led a brigade at the defeat of Majuba Hill where he accepted his share of the blame, saying his men were too exhausted to dig trenches. He was briefly a prisoner of war of the Boers, then led the desert column in the Sudan to rescue Gordon of Khartoum and won the Victoria Cross in the Mahdi campaign. Two other Stewarts won the Victoria Cross: William of Grandtully, a captain in the 93rd won it for charging two sepoy cannons in the Indian Mutiny of 1857 but sadly died ten years later when attempting a sword-swallowing trick. Captain Ronald N. Stuart R.N.R. won it in 1917 for sinking a German submarine from his mystery ship *Pargurst* despite having been hit by a torpedo.

In Africa, the missionary James Stewart (1831–1905) of Lovedale learned the Xhosa language, published the *Kaffir Express* and in 1881 became almost scandalously over-friendly with David Livingstone's neglected wife. He did pioneering work in education and had a penchant for roast sirloin of hippopotamus.

Perhaps the most brilliant of the Stewart generals in the nineteenth century was General James Ewell Brown Stuart (1833–64), known as Jeb or Beauty Stuart or the Cavalier of Dixie, the charismatic Confederate cavalry commander under General Lee in the American Civil War. Grandson of a fur trader (see p.208) he was tall and fair-haired and renowned as a lady's man. He kept an Irish banjo player at his side and was first heard of during the attack on the abolitionist John Brown in 1856, before fighting the Cheyenne at Solomon's Fork in 1857. He was aide to General Lee during the storming of Harper's Ferry which resulted in the capture of John Brown, then led a series of dashing cavalry raids against the Union armies in 1862. This often involved blowing up railway lines within enemy territory and he scored a notable victory against General Hooker at Fredericksburg. Known as 'Lee's Eyes' he was perhaps unfairly blamed for poor scouting before Gettysberg, and in 1864 made a stand against one of Sheridan's forces at the Yellow Tavern Crossroads just north of Richmond. Outnumbered by two to one and outgunned as the Union soldiers had quick-firing carbines he still held up their advance, but he was killed muttering 'I had rather die than be whipped.' This was described as 'a blow to the Confederate leadership next only to the death of Jackson a year earlier.'

Other Confederate generals included General Alexander P. Stewart (1835–1911) a West Point graduate who before the war had been a mathematics professor but had a successful career under Lee in the Tennessee campaign. The other was Brigadier General George Stewart who was captured by his friend General Hancock at Spottsylvania in 1864 but refused to shake hands. There was also a rebel Colonel Stewart at Bull Run.

Perhaps just as significant as any of these was John Tod Stuart (1807–85) an Irish lawyer in Sangamo who was Abraham Lincoln's senior officer in the Black Hawk war of 1832 and then made him a partner in his legal firm five years later, thus helping him considerably towards a political career. Another lawyer Alvan Stewart (1790–1849) was a pioneering abolitionist orator in New York while Charles Stuart (1781-1868) born in Bermuda fought in the Indian army before becoming a missionary and an eccentrically kilt-wearing campaigner against slavery.

One of the more picturesque of the American Stewarts in the nineteenth century was Granville Stuart (1834–1918) who joined the California Gold Rush at the age of fifteen with his father Robert and brother James. They did not do particularly well though they successfully prospected Gold Creek in Montana but left others to take the pickings. Granville became a pioneering rancher in Montana, married a twelve-year-old Shoshone girl who bore him nine children and when cattle rustlers attacked his stock he gathered together a posse which was known as Stuart's Stranglers. When he retired in 1886 after organising over a hundred lynchings he recommended the traditional rancher's diet of beans, bacon, coffee, bread and beef.

Among Stewart intellectuals the Edinburgh physicist Balfour Stewart (1828–87) stands out for his studies of radiant heat, the earth's magnetism, sunspots and spectrum analysis. The same can be said for Sir Henry Steuart of Allanton (1759–1836) one of the great pioneers of tree-planting who ultimately did much to change the British landscape. Among Stewart engineers, one of the most energetic was Francis Lee Stuart (1866–1935) from South Carolina who did much of the early work for the Panama Canal, for the New York Docks and the port railway network.

Among the first Stewarts to settle in Australia was John Stewart, a rioter from Castle Menzies who was transported in 1798. Helen Stewart, an alleged child-murderer was transported for fourteen years in 1803; Ann Stewart a thief from Banff for a mere seven years in 1811; another Ann Stewart a tinker and David Stewart a thief, both from Perth for fourteen years each in 1829.

John McDowall Stuart (1815–66) from Fife joined Charles Sturt's expedition into the Australian interior in 1845, then made six expeditions of his own round Lake Torrens and across the Australian outback, crossing Australia from south to north in 1860. He gave his name to Mount Stuart. Only a decade younger was Sir Alexander Stewart (1825–86) an immigrant from Edinburgh who rose to be prime minister of New South Wales in 1883. Among New Zealand Stewarts the best known was probably William Downie Stewart (1878-1949) a lawyer from Dunedin who fought with ANZAC in France, was a pioneer of trade development and eventually acting prime minister of New Zealand in 1927.

Of the more philanthropic modern Stewarts Miss Jane Shaw Stewart, sister of Sir Michael Shaw Stewart who had trained in Germany was one of the key pioneers of improved nursing in the Crimea where she became a major supporter of Florence Nightingale. Woodham Smith describes her as 'the prop and mainstay of Crimean nursing,' but sadly she had a thin-skinned approach to criticism and failed to win the credit her work deserved. Isla Stewart (1855–1910) made a name for herself as a nurse in the smallpox epidemic of 1868 and became a pioneer of nursing education, noted for her long lace cap. May Stewart (1862–1925), a London almoner became a pioneer of social work. Alexander Turney Stewart (1803–76), a Belfast-born American millionaire founded the Garden City, Long Island as a model middle class township.

The number of Stewarts who had run sugar or cotton plantations in the south and in the West Indies is attested by the number of black Stewarts. Alvan Stewart was a prominent New York abolitionist and Maria Stewart (1803–79) was a leading black activist in Hartford. Bennet McVey Stewart (1912–88) a Chicago city alderman opposed the somewhat racist stance of Mayor Daley and became a champion of the poor when elected to Congress. Rex W Stewart (1907–67 was a brilliant jazz cornetist and Stan Stewart (1914–87) an equally talented bassist.

The most politically influential Stewart in the twentieth century was probably Michael Maitland Stewart (1906–90) the British Labour politician born in London who, after studying at Oxford University, became a pre-war school teacher but in 1945 was elected MP for Fulham in the Labour landslide. Within two years he was Secretary of State for War and helped involve Britain in the Korean War before the Conservatives took over in 1951. After thirteen years in opposition he spent a year as Minister for Education and Science under Harold Wilson before being moved to the Foreign Office in 1965, then Economic Affairs, finally succeeding George Brown as Foreign Secretary for two years in 1968. He led the Labour delegation to the European parliament 1975–6 and then transferred to the House of Lords in 1979.

On the Conservative side there was James Stuart who acted as Churchill's chief whip during the war and subsequently served as Secretary of State for Scotland in 1951. He had a less controversial career than Charles Henry Vane Tempest Stewart (1878–1949) from the Castlereagh family who became an MP in 1906, served on the Western Front, became Northern Ireland Minister and hung on to various offices in the National Government. He at first encouraged rearmament when at the Air Ministry until 1935 and helped push the Spitfire forward but then began to show an unhealthy admiration for Hitler and was nicknamed 'the Londonderry Herr'. It was believed that he had owed his promotion to the excellent cuisine organised by his wife Elizabeth who 'catered his way into the cabinet' despite his string of extra-marital affairs and her reputation as an almost scandalously close friend of Prime Minister Ramsay Macdonald whose Labour colleagues were shocked by his partiality for a Marchioness. She surprisingly had been a suffragette and was a pioneering founder of the A.T.S in 1938.

Slightly more conventional was the political career of Donald Stewart (1920–92) the much respected Stornoway MP who became leader of the Scottish National Party in 1974.

Famed for his exceptional reflexes was Jackie Stewart (1939–) from Dumbarton who raced in his first Grand Prix in 1965 and won the World Driver Championship three times between 1969–73.

Among many successful Stewart lawyers on both sides of the Atlantic was Potter Stewart (1915–85) the Supreme Court justice who forced President Nixon to hand over the White House tapes in the case of Nixon v the U.S. in 1974.

It could be argued that the Stewarts were no longer producing quite such distinctive leaders as they had in the past, certainly no monarchs, though each decade turned up its own eccentric claimant to the throne, but in sheer numbers they were widely scattered over the English-speaking world and beyond. In some cases perhaps a residual pride drove them harder, in others the loss of bygone wealth or the inherited energy of having for generations had to live by their wits in an often hostile environment. In the nine hundred years since leaving Dol-de-Bretagne they had played a remarkable role in the history of the world.

It would be unfair to suggest that they had gone from clogs to clogs in two dozen generations, but we could leave the last words to John Alexander Stuart (1866–1929) a New South Wales trade unionist amongst the Clermont sheep shearers:

I am deformed by labour
I am the working man
Cursing the fate that holds me
A dull-browed Caliban.

Gazetteer of Main Surviving Stewart Monuments

1. Breton Period

Dol-de-Bretagne, original home of the Stewards, still has its cathedral (although rebuilt in the thirteenth century), its La Grande Rue des Stuarts and La Maison des Plaids, a medieval house attributed to the Dapiferi. Other nearby sites relevant to the Stewarts include Mont Dol, Château Combourg, the old walled town of Dinan, the port of St Malo and Mont St Michel.

2. English Period

The ruins of Oswestry Castle can still be seen on its motte above the town. Some parts of Wenlock Abbey survive as do the ruins the later Fitzalan castle at Clun.

The later home of the Fitzalans, at Arundel Castle in Sussex, is a major site. The family's now ruined Fotheringhay Castle in Northants was visited by the first Steward and also the last prison of Mary Queen of Scots.

3. Period as Royal Stewards

Sadly only the sites of the first and second castles remain at Renfrew, King's Inch, the family's first base in Scotland. Their hunting lodge at Blackhall has survived although frequently rebuilt. Between them is the monument marking the spot where Marjorie Bruce fell off her horse and gave birth to Robert II, also the site coincidentally of the defeat of Somerled in 1164. Paisley Abbey still retains parts built in this period by the Stewards and also a number of important Stewart tombs.

The place names survive of the numerous estates held round Glasgow by Steward vassal knights: Houston, Symington, Ralston, Ingleston, La Muerne or Mearns, Talahret or The Hurlet, La Drep or Drip by Carmunnock and Partick though there are surviving structures at Cathcart, Crookston, Pollok, Polnoon and Duchall. Archaeologists have also confirmed a Wallace castle at Elderslie, and a plaque marks another at Riccarton near Ayr.

Substantial remains of Dundonald Castle in Ayrshire survive and it was a major Steward residence up to the time of Robert II who refurbished it. It along with Symington and Riccarton are close to Largs where a monument marks the site of the other early Stewart victory. Spittalhill recalls the crusading Stewards.

Rothesay Castle was another early acquisition and one of the few kept by the family after it became royal. The Stewards also rebuilt St Blane's Monastery on Bute and St Mary's Chapel.

The dramatic ruins survive of the Stewards' first castle on the east coast at Innerwick near Dunbar, but little or nothing at Stenton, Legertwood, Hassendean or Tranent. The first major offshoot of the Steward family, the Menteith Stewarts, have left a fine heritage including the superb tomb of their founder at Inchmahome Priory on the Lake of Menteith, the ruined nearby Inchtulla castle, their two major castles in Kintyre, Castle Sween and Skipness, the meager ruins of Dunoon and Eilean Dearg on its island in Cowal, and three castles on Arran; Brodick, Loch Ranza and probably Kildonan although all substantially altered.

The second major offshoot were the Stewarts of Bunkle of which meagre ruins remain near Preston/Pearston. Other mainly ruinous castles owned by this family include Garlies, Glasserton, Cally, Cruggleton and Corsewall, all in Galloway. A sub-branch was given the tower of Innermeath/Invermay south of Perth, added Red Castle near Montrose and built Rosyth Castle then later married its way into Dunstaffnage with the Lordship of Lorn. Another sub-branch built Darnley whose ruins are now part of an Indian restaurant and Crookston whose impressive keep survives. They also had two Lennox Castles, one at Balerno and one in Glasgow, now vanished.

Walter the penultimate Steward was given Dalswinton, Bathgate and Bridge Castle at Armadale, of which some remains survive, but also Farme and Riccarton which have vanished.

4. The Period of Stewart Kings in Scotland.

As kings, the Stewarts naturally took over the three main royal castles of Scotland: Edinburgh, Stirling and Dumbarton, the first two of which they substantially rebuilt, with Stirling as the most lavish of their creations. They also built four new royal palaces all of which survive to varying degrees: Holyrood which had been a monastery, Linlithgow which had been a castle, Dunfermline, an earlier royal residence and Falkland, a hunting lodge.

Other surviving royal castles include Blackness, refortified by James V.

The vast family of Robert II resulted in a flurry of new castles being built; including the impressive Doune Castle built by Robert of Albany, plus Inchmurrin, and Dundochill which belonged to his son Murdoch. Loch Leven, Braal and Urquhart were held by Albany's brother David, but the most dramatic ruins come from another brother, the Wolf of Badenoch, who had the two island castles of Loch an Eilean and Lochindorb as well as Drumin, Kilnmaichlie, Garth and Ruthven – now replaced by a Hanoverian barracks. The Wolf's illegitimate son, the victor of Harlaw, had Kildrummy and Kindrochit. Other Wolf progeny held Grandtully, Careston and Ardvorlich. The most devious of Robert II's sons, Walter of Atholl, had Blair and Methven. One of Robert II's illegitimate children had Cardney, Murthly and Meggernie, another was given Bute. The Bute Stewarts were custodians of Rothesay Castle, had Ascog for their home, later the Old Mansion House in Rothesay followed by the first Mount Stuart which burned down in 1877 and was exotically rebuilt by the ultra-rich 3rd Marquis. He also had Dumfries House near Cumnock, Old Place of Mochrum, and West Kames Castle on Bute as well as building Bute House, now the residence of Scotland's first minister in Edinburgh, and the Bute Hall of Glasgow University.

Robert III gave Blackhall to his illegitimate son John, who rebuilt Ardgowan and his descendants took over Kildonan, Castle Levan and Newark.

James II's half brothers had Balvenie, Auchterhouse and Traquair. His cousin Andrew of Morphie got Strathaven, Ochiltree and the family later gained Kinneil.

James III's brother built the recently restored Auchindoun.

John Stuart, Duke of Albany rebuilt Dunbar.

Mary Queen of Scots gave Castle Stewart in Inverness to her half-brother Moray.

Her other half brother Robert and his son Black Patie between them constructed the remarkable group of buildings in Orkney: Birsay Palace, the Earl's Palace, Jarlshof and in Shetland Scalloway Castle.

Of surviving churches built or rebuilt by the Stewarts apart from their own Paisley Abbey there is Melrose Abbey, rebuilt in 1389, Elgin, new naves at Glasgow and Dunkeld Cathedrals, St Giles in Edinburgh built mainly by Robert III, St Michael's in Linlithgow and the Holy Rude at Stirling by James III, Kings College Chapel, Aberdeen and Ladykirk on the Tweed by James IV and Grandtully by the local Steuarts.

James IV's bastard son Alexander began St Leonard's College, St Andrews.

Francis Stewart Earl of Bothwell, the tormentor of James VI, spectacularly rebuilt Crichton Castle outside Edinburgh.

5. The Stuart Monarchs of Great Britain.

The main additions in London by James VI and I include the Banqueting House of Whitehall with its Rubens ceilings extolling the dynasty while both Denmark House (Somerset) and the Queen's House Greenwich were built for his wife by Inigo Jones. He also had a zoo in the Tower of London and built a tomb for his mother and himself in Westminster Abbey. Ashdown House was built for his daughter and Theobalds rebuilt as his own favourite hunting lodge.

Charles I was responsible for Hyde Park and Covent Garden. He remodelled St James's Palace, adding the Queen's Chapel and also began the Pantiles Gallery at Tunbridge Wells to please his wife Henrietta Maria. Clarence House also came from this period.

Charles II had the courage to let Wren build St Paul's Cathedral, commissioned the Monument for the fire of London and Chelsea Hospital with a statue of himself outside. He also remodelled Windsor and built the Church of King Charles the Martyr at Tunbridge.

William and Mary bought Kensington Palace which Wren refurbished for them and Queen Anne added the Orangery and Gardens. William also had Hampton Court rebuilt with Thornhill's paintings celebrating the demise of the Stuarts. Mary converted Greenwich Palace into a Royal Hospital.

Of the other Stuarts in England Matthew Earl of Lennox had Temple Newsham outside Leeds where his son Darnley was born.

John Stuart the Earl of Bute, who helped found Kew Gardens, used Adam to rebuild Luton Hoo and Capability Brown to design the gardens. One of his grandsons, Baron Rothesay, built the romantic Highcliffe Castle by Christchurch. The Bute Stuarts also built extensively in Wales including the romanticised Cardiff Castle, the Bute Docks Company Offices and the exotic Castell Coch.

In Wales the Londonderry Stewarts built Plas Machynlleth and its clock tower.

The migration of Stewarts to Ireland accelerated in 1609 though there were earlier examples like the Bute Stewarts at Dunseverich Castle in 1540. Castle Stewart in Tyrone went to the Ochiltree branch. The best known were the Stewarts who came to Ballylawn, then moved to Mount Stewart in Down and produced the Londonderry/Castlereagh family. Other Stewart outposts included Athenree, Lochmacrory, Roughan, Aghantie, Killymoon, and the Ramelton Stewarts who became Viscounts Montjoy.

6. The Diaspora

France

The first substantial group of Stewarts came to La Rochelle to fight the English in 1422. They won at Baugé but lost badly at Verneuil and Rouvray St Denis, the Battle of the Herrings. Prominent Stewarts/Stuarts who died in the battles are buried in both Tours and Orleans Cathedrals. Three châteaux given to Stuarts of the Garde Ecossaise survive, Aubigny , now the Hotel de Ville at Aubigny-sur-Nère , nearby La Verrerie, built by the marshal Berault Stuart and ruins at Concressault. Alexander Stuart, duke of Albany had Château Mirefleurs by Clermont Ferrand and parts of the Vic-le-Comte castle survive.

Thouars has the tomb of the unfortunate Margaret Stewart, daughter of James I who married Louis XI.

St Germain-en-Laye was a palace lived in by young Mary Queen of Scots as dauphine and later regularly used by exiled members of the Stuart dynasty.

James II's illegitimate son the Duke of Berwick had his chateau at Fitz-James near Clermont.

Italy

Berault Stuart was made Duke of Terranuova after his famous victory there in
1502. Stuarts were involved in other battles such as Marignano and Pavia. Later,
General John Stuart was made Count of Maida in Sicily for his victory there in
1806. The Palazzo Muti in Rome was the main home of the Old Pretender while
the citadel at Gaeta was the scene of Bonnie Prince Charlie's first military experience along with his cousin the Duke of Liria.

Holland

There are a number of palaces and lodges associated with the two Mary Stuarts
who both married a William of Orange: Huis ten Bosch, the first Mary's favourite,
Houslardyke, the Mauritzhuis and Het Loo. Veere, the married home of James I's
daughter Mary had Kastel Sandenburch and its Schotse Huizen for the Scots merchants. Arnhem in Gelderland was the home of Mary of Guelders, wife of James II.

Germany

The castle at Heidelberg still has the Elizabethpforte built in 1615 by the Elector
for his wife Elizabeth Stuart and its Englischer bau Juttenbuhl built in imitation
of Linlithgow.

United States

Jamestown, Virginia was founded in 1607 and named after James I: the original
fort has been reconstructed. Maryland was called after Henrietta Maria, wife of
Charles I, whose friend Lord Baltimore was encouraged to found the colony in
1634. Charlestown was founded in 1670 and named after Charles II as were the
two Carolinas. Stewart's Town followed in 1684.

New York got its new name in 1687 as a result of the naval victory of James
Stuart Duke of York which led to its handing over by the Dutch. Philadelphia
owed its foundation to James's encouragement of the Penns.

Laurel Park Virginia was the birthplace of the Confederate general J.E.B. Stuart
who was killed at Yellow Tavern. Astoria and Fort Okanogan were mainly founded
by Stewart pioneers exploring the Oregon Trail.

Canada

The Port Royal National Historic Site recalls the landing of James Stewart at
Baleine, Nova Scotia in 1629. Rupertsland is called after the half-Stuart Prince
Rupert, founding director of the Hudson's Bay Company. Several lakes and
rivers in British Columbia and the Yukon commemorate the pioneers James and
John Stewart.

Australia

Mount Stuart, Stuart Creek and the Stuart Highway commemorate the achievements of the explorer John McDouall Stuart.

Bibliography

Alexander, D., and Steel, Alan, Wallace, *Renfrewshire and the Wars of Independence*, Renfrew, 1997.

Anderson, Peter, *Black Patie: the Life and Times of Patrick Stewart Earl of Orkney, Lord of Shetland*, Edinburgh ,1992

Anderson, Peter, *Robert Stewart: Earl of Orkney, Lord of Shetland*, Edinburgh, 1992.

Barrol, J. Leeds, *Anna of Denmark Queen of England*, Philadelphia, 2001

Barrow, G.W.S, *The Anglo Norman Era in Scottish History*, Edinburgh, 1980

Barrow, G.W.S, *Robert Bruce: the Community and Realm of Scotland*, Edinburgh, 1988

Black, C. Stewart, *The Story of Paisley*, Paisley, 1953.

Boardman, Stephen, *The Early Stewarts: Robert II and Robert III*, Edinburgh, 1996.

Bower, Walter, *Scotichronicon*, ed. D.E.R. Watt, Aberdeen, 1987–99.

Bridge, John, *History of France from the Reign of Louis XI*, Oxford, 1924.

Brown, Michael, *James I*, Edinburgh 1994.

Buchan, John, *Montrose*, London, 1928.

Bumsted, J.M., *The Scots in Canada*, Toronto, 1982

Cameron, Jamie, *James V*, Edinburgh, 1998.

Cowan, I.B., *Medieval Church in Scotland*, Edinburgh, 1998.

Dobson, David, *Original Scots Colonists*, Baltimore, 1989

Donald, Peter, *An Uncounselled King: Charles I and the Scottish Troubles*, Cambridge, 1990

Donaldson, Gordon, *Scots Overseas*, London, 1966.

Douglas, H.O., *Jacobite Spy Wars*, Stroud, 1999.

Dunbar, John *Scottish Royal Palaces*, East Linton, 1999.

Duncan, A.A. M., *Scotland, the Making of the Kingdom*, Edinburgh, 1975.

Coventry, Martin, *The Castles of Scotland*, Musselburgh, 2001.

Fischer T.A., *The Scots in Sweden*, Edinburgh, 1907.

Foot, Shelby, *Civil War*, New York, 1980.

Forbes-Leith, W., *Scots Men at Arms*, Edinburgh, 1852.

Fradenburg, Louise O., *City, Marriage, Tournament,* Wisconsin, 1991.

Fraser, Antonia, *Mary Queen of Scots,* London, 1971

Fraser, William, *The Red Book of Menteith,* Edinburgh, 1880.

Fraser, William *The Red Book of Lennox,* Edinburgh, 1874.

Glassey, Lionel J.K., *Charles II and James VII &II,* Basingstoke, 1997.

Haswell, Jock, *James II: Soldier and Sailor,* London, 1972.

Hewson, J., *Bute in Olden Times,* Edinburgh 1895.

Historic Scotland, Guides to Stirling Castle, Edinburgh, Falkland, etc.

Holmes, F., *The Sickly Stuarts,* Stroud, 2003.

Hutton, R., *Charles II,* Oxford, 1991.

Lenman, Bruce, *The Jacobite Risings in Britain,* London, 1980.

Linklater, Magnus and Hesketh, Christian, *Bonnie Dundee,* Edinburgh, 1992.

Livingston, A., Aikman, C., and Hall, B., *No Quarter Given: Muster Roll of Prince Charles Edward Stuart's Army,* Aberdeen, 1984.

McCartney, Laton, *Across the Great Divide: Robert Stuart and the Oregon Trail,* Stroud, 2003.

McCulloch, Andrew, *Galloway,* Edinburgh, 2000

Macdougall, Norman, *James III,* Edinburgh, 1982.

Macdougall, Norman, *James IV,* Edinburgh, 1989.

McGladdery, C., *James II.* East Linton, 1990.

Macleod, John, *Dynasty: The Stuarts,* London, 1999.

McLynn, Frank, *Charles Edward Stuart,* London, 1988

Mason, Gordon, *Castles of Glasgow and the Clyde,* Musselburgh, 2000

Metcalf, W., *A History of Paisley,* Paisley, 1909.

Murray, W.H., *Rob Roy MacGregor,* Edinburgh, 1982.

Nicholson, R.G., *Scotland in the Later Middle Ages,* Edinburgh, 1974.

Oram, Richard D., *Scotland in the Reign of Alexander II,* Leiden, 2005.

Oram, Richard D., *David I: the king who made Scotland,* Stroud, 2005.

Paul, J. Balfour, ed., *The Scots Peerage,* Edinburgh, 1914-14.

Penman, Michael, *David II,* Edinburgh, 2004.

Petrie, Charles, *The Marshal Duke of Berwick,* London, 1953.

Prebble, John, *Culloden,* London, 1961.

Quicherat, Jules, ed., *Procès de condamnation et de réhabilitation de Jeanne d'Arc,* Paris, 1841–9.

Rees, Peter, *Flodden,* Edinburgh 2003

Ross, Stuart, *Stuart Dynasty,* London, 1993.

Schweizer, K.W., ed., *Lord Bute,* Leicester, 1988

Sellar, W.D.H., *The Early Stewarts,* S.H.R., 1973.

Smout, T.C, *A History of the Scottish people 1560–1830,* London, 1969.

Stewart, David, *Sketches of the Character, Manners and Present State of the Highlanders of Scotland,* Edinburgh, 1822.

Stewart, Dugald, *Outlines of Moral Philosophy,* Edinburgh, 1793

Thomas, E.M., *The Bold Dragoon: the life of J.E.B. Stuart,* New York, 1986.

Thomson, Oliver, *The Bloody Heart,* Stroud, 2003

Thomson Oliver, *The Great Feud, Campbells and McDonalds,* Stroud, 2005

Traquair, Peter, *Freedom's Sword; Scottish Wars of Independence,* London, 1998.

Weir, Alison, *Mary Queen of Scots and the Murder of Darnley,* London, 2003.

White, J.M., *Marshal of France,* London, 1962.

Williams, Ethel C. *Anne of Denmark,* London, 1970.

Williams, Janet, ed., *Stewart Style, Essays on the Court of James V,* Edinburgh, 1996.

Wormald, Jenny, *Lords and Men in Scotland, Bonds of Manrent, 1442–1603,* Edinburgh, 1985

Index

Index of Places